C: An Advanced Introduction
(ANSI C Edition)

PRINCIPLES OF COMPUTER SCIENCE SERIES

Series Editors

ALFRED V. AHO, *Bell Telephone Laboratories, Murray Hill, New Jersey*
JEFFREY D. ULLMAN, *Stanford University, Stanford, California*

Narain Gehani
C: An Advanced Introduction

Narain Gehani
C: An Advanced Introduction, ANSI C Edition

David Maier
The Theory of Relational Databases

Leonard R. Marino
Principles of Computer Design

Christos H. Papadimitriou
The Theory of Concurrency Control

Theo Pavlidis
Algorithms for Graphics and Image Processing

Arto Salomaa
Jewels of Formal Language Theory

Stuart C. Shapiro
LISP: An Interactive Approach

Jeffrey D. Ullman
Computational Aspects of VLSI

ANOTHER BOOK OF INTEREST

Jeffrey D. Ullman
Principles of Database Systems, Second Edition

C: AN ADVANCED INTRODUCTION
(ANSI C Edition)

Narain Gehani

AT&T Bell Laboratories
Murray Hill, NJ 07974

Computer Science Press

Library of Congress Cataloging-in-Publication Data

Gehani, Narain, 1947–
    C: an advanced introduction.

    (Principles of computer science series)
    Bibliography: p.
    Includes index.
    1. C (Computer program language) I. Title.
    II. Series.
    QA76.73.C15G44   1988   005.13'3   88-24531
    ISBN 0-7167-8196-4

Printed in the United States of America

Computer Science Press, Inc.
1803 Research Boulevard
Rockville, MD 20850
An imprint of W. H. Freeman and Company
41 Madison Avenue, New York, NY 10010
20 Beaumont Street, Oxford OX1 2NQ, England

1 2 3 4 5 6 7 8 9 0   RRD   6 5 4 3 2 1 0 8 9 8

To
my friends and colleagues
at
AT&T Bell Labs

Contents

Preface xi

Acknowledgments xv

Chapter 1   Introduction and Basics 1
              1. A Sample C Program   1
              2. Basics   8
              3. Constant Identifiers   14
              4. Exercises   15

Chapter 2   Types and Objects 17
              1. Simple Types   18
              2. Derived Types   24
              3. Type Definitions   41
              4. Scope of Tags and Type Definitions   43
              5. Object Definitions and Declarations   43
              6. Type Conversions   57
              7. Exercises   60

Chapter 3   Operators and Expressions 63
              1. Operators   63
              2. Operator Precedence & Associativity Summary   75
              3. Expressions   75
              4. Exercises   76

Chapter 4   Control Flow 77
              1. The *Null* Statement   77
              2. The *Expression* Statement   77
              3. The *Compound* Statement or *Block*   78
              4. The `if` Statement   79
              5. The `switch` Statement   80
              6. Loops   82
              7. Statement Labels   83

8. Jump Statements   84
9. Exercises   86

Chapter 5   Functions and Complete Programs 89
1. Function Declarations (Prototypes)   89
2. Function Definitions   91
3. Calling Functions   94
4. Functions With Var. Number of Parameters   97
5. Controlling Function Visibility   98
6. Scope & Lifetime of Identifiers: An Example   99
7. Input/Output   100
8. Main Programs   105
9. Examples   106
10. Exercises   129

Chapter 6   Independent Compilation and Data Abstraction 133
1. Independent Compilation   133
2. Abstract Data Types and Information Hiding   134
3. Examples   135
4. Exercises   142

Chapter 7   Exceptions 145
1. Signals   146
2. Setting Up Signal/Exception Handlers   146
3. Generating/Sending Signals   148
4. Examples   148
5. Exercises   155

Chapter 8   The C Preprocessor 157
1. Macro Definition and Invocation   157
2. File Inclusion   163
3. Conditional Compilation   164
4. An Example   167
5. Exercises   169

Chapter 9   One Final Example 171
1. Exercises   177

Appendix A   C++ 179
1. Class Declarations   179
2. Other C++ Facilities   181
3. Examples   182
4. Exercises   188

Appendix B   Concurrent C   189
                  1. Overview of the Concurrent C Model   189
                  2. Concurrent C Facilities: A Summary   190
                  3. Examples   191
                  4. Exercises   199

Appendix C   Library Routines   201
                  1. Diagnostic Routines   202
                  2. Character Handling Routines   203
                  3. Mathematical Routines   205
                  4. Nonlocal Jump Routines   208
                  5. Signal Handling Routines   209
                  6. Macros to Handle Var. Number of Arguments   210
                  7. Input/Output Routines   211
                  8. General Utility Routines   224
                  9. String Handling Routines   230
                  10. Date and Time Functions   234

Appendix D   Differences between ANSI C and K&R C   237
                  1. General   237
                  2. Preprocessor   238
                  3. Constants   239
                  4. Types   239
                  5. Variable Declarations and Definitions   240
                  6. Initialization   240
                  7. Operators and Expressions   240
                  8. Statements   241
                  9. Functions   241
                  10. Libraries   242

Bibliography   245

Index   255

Preface

C was designed and first implemented by Dennis Ritchie in 1972 at AT&T Bell Laboratories. Despite a late start, C is now an immensely popular programming language. C compilers are now available for a large number of machines and the list of machines continues to grow. Two important reasons for the popularity of C are

1. *Flexibility*: C can be used for a wide variety of application domains with relative ease.

2. *Size*: C is a relatively small language which makes it easy to learn and allows building of efficient compilers.

The C language owes much of its initial popularity to the fact that most of the UNIX* system, a very popular operating system, is written in C and C is the primary language supported by the UNIX system.

Until very recently, the de facto C standard implemented by most compilers was the C language as described in *The C Programming Language* [Kernighan & Ritchie 1978]. This version of C is informally called K&R C. However, because K&R C is not a formal standard and because the K&R C implemented by most compilers differs in subtle ways, efforts have been underway to standardize C. The American National Standards Institute (ANSI) has recently proposed a draft formal standard for C [ANSI 1988a-b]. The ANSI standard version of C, referred to as ANSI C, is likely to be formally adopted as a standard by late 1988 or early 1989. As part of this standardization process, C is being modified to address issues such as better type checking and program portability. Most of the changes are minor but there are some important differences between ANSI C and K&R C. These differences are summarized in Appendix D.

In this book, I will discuss ANSI C, as described in the *Draft Proposed American National Standard for Information Systems — Programming Language C* [ANSI 1988a]. The final version of ANSI C is likely to be very similar, if not identical, to the draft standard. I have taken into account the few changes that were made to the ANSI C draft standard in April 1988

---

* UNIX is a trademark of AT&T Bell Laboratories.

[ANSI 1988a]. For example, the `noalias` type qualifier has been dropped. With these changes incorporated, the ANSI C draft standard is expected to be adopted as a formal standard without any further (significant) changes.

In addition to discussing ANSI C, I will also discuss two derivatives of C: C++ [Stroustrup 1986] and Concurrent C [Gehani & Roome 1986]. C++ is a superset of C that provides data abstraction facilities. Concurrent C is a superset of C that provides parallel programming facilities (and it also works in conjunction with C++).

1. About This Book

I have written this book especially for readers with a good knowledge of at least one procedural programming language, such as Pascal, FORTRAN or Ada. I will emphasize the advanced aspects of C, e.g., type declarations, data abstraction, exceptions and the C preprocessor.

C is a flexible programming language that gives a great deal of freedom to the programmer. This freedom is the source of much of its expressive power and one of the main strengths of C, making it powerful, versatile and easy to use in a variety of application areas. However, undisciplined use of this freedom can lead to errors.

There are many examples in this book. These examples have been drawn from a wide spectrum of application areas including interactive programming, systems programming, database applications, text processing and concurrent programming. Many have been taken from real programs and all of the examples have been tested. Each chapter includes exercises that complement the material presented in the chapter.

The book also contains

- an overview of C++,

- an overview of Concurrent C,

- a description of the ANSI standard C library functions,

- a summary of the differences between K&R C and ANSI C,

- an annotated bibliography of articles and books on C, and on related topics.

1.1 Notation

I use the constant-width (typewriter) font for displayed C programs or program fragments (e.g., `return;`) and the italic font for emphasis, abstract instructions and syntactic terms (e.g., *divide and conquer* strategy, *print error message* and *declarations*). Use of the constant-width font for C programs conforms with the accepted "C style" [Kernighan & Ritchie 1978]. For ease of reference, program line numbers are listed outside the left-hand sides of the boxes enclosing C programs.

2. Preparation of the Book

This book was prepared using the extensive document preparation tools including `pic` (preprocessor for drawing figures), `tbl` (preprocessor for making tables), `eqn` (preprocessor for formatting equations), `mm` (collection of `troff` macros for page layout) and `troff` (formatter), that are available on the UNIX system.

Murray Hill, NJ   Narain Gehani
August 1988

Acknowledgments

I wish to thank J. P. Linderman, W. D. Roome and R. F. Cmelik for their helpful suggestions and criticisms on drafts of this edition. I appreciate the efforts of M. E. Quinn and D. F. Prosser in providing me with the latest versions of the ANSI C documents. M. E. Quinn also helped me get access to the AT&T ANSI C compiler with which I tested the programs given in the book. I am also grateful to E. T. Dickinson and the AT&T ANSI C compiler development team.

Many friends and colleagues gave comments on drafts of the first edition of this book. They are A. V. Aho, R. B. Allen, M. Bianchi, R. L. Drechsler, J. Farrell, J. P. Fishburn, D. Gay, B. W. Kernighan, J. P. Linderman, C. D. McLaughlin, D. A. Nowitz, W. D. Roome, L. Rosler, B. Smith-Thomas, B. Stroustrup, T. G. Szymanski and C. S. Wetherell.

Chapter 1

Introduction and Basics

The C programming language was designed by Dennis Ritchie in 1972 as a systems programming language to replace assembly language programming at AT&T Bell Labs. The phenomenal success of C is shown by the enormous popularity of C for a wide variety of applications on all types of computers: from personal computers to large mainframes. For many years, K&R C [Kernighan & Ritchie 1978] was used as the informal C standard. But now an ANSI standard version of C has been drafted and it is expected that this draft will soon be adopted as the official standard [ANSI C 1988a]. This book is based on ANSI C.

1. A Sample C Program

I will now illustrate the flavor of C by showing you a small program that simulates a simple calculator that can add, subtract, multiply and divide. The data appear as a list of operations in the format

$$a \, \theta \, b$$

where operator θ is one of the symbols +, -, * or /, and the operands a and b are real values. For simplicity, no embedded blanks are allowed between the operands and the operator. It is also assumed that the only mistake made by the calculator user is to type an operator symbol that is not one of the four allowed symbols.

The reader familiar with high-level languages will be able to understand the calculator program without much difficulty. The program is followed by an explanation of the concepts and facilities used in it. I will discuss each briefly in this section, reserving detailed discussions for later sections and chapters.

```
   /*Two dollar calculator*/

   #include <stdio.h>
   #include <stdlib.h>
 5 #define PR putchar(':')

   main(void)
   {
       float a, b;
10     char opr;
       float result;

       while(PR,scanf("%f%c%f",&a,&opr,&b)!=EOF) {
           switch (opr) {
15             case '+': result = a + b; break;
               case '-': result = a - b; break;
               case '*': result = a * b; break;
               case '/': result = a / b; break;
               default:
20                 printf("ERROR, bad operator\n");
                   exit(EXIT_FAILURE);
           }
           printf("result is %g\n", result);
       }
25     exit(EXIT_SUCCESS);
   }
```

The name of the source file containing the above C program is printed on the right corner of the top side of the box enclosing the C program; in this case, the file name is `calc.c`. For ease of reference, line numbers corresponding to the lines in the program text are given just outside the left side of the box.

The first line in this C program is a comment. The character pair `/*` begins a comment while the pair `*/` ends a comment. The second line is a blank line which is simply ignored by the C compiler. Blank lines are used to enhance program readability by using them to separate logical program segments.

Lines 3–5 are C preprocessor instructions (all C preprocessor instructions begin with the character # which must be the first "nonwhite-space" character in the line). Each C program is processed by the C preprocessor before it is compiled. The first preprocessor instruction (line 3)

```
#include <stdio.h>
```

tells the C preprocessor to include the contents of the header file `stdio.h`. By convention, files containing declarations are called *header* files. Typically, header files are given the suffix `.h`. Files containing other C statements are called *source* files. Typically, source files are given the suffix `.c`. Header file `stdio.h` contains appropriate declarations for the standard input and output library functions that are provided by the C compiler. The angle brackets `<>` indicate that the file `stdio.h` will be found in one of the "standard places" on the computer system.

The second instruction (line 4) instructs the C preprocessor to include the file `stdlib.h`. In addition to other items, `stdlib.h` contains the definitions of the constants `EXIT_SUCCESS` and `EXIT_FAILURE`, which are used later (lines 21 and 25).

The third preprocessor instruction (line 5)

```
#define PR putchar(':')
```

instructs the C preprocessor to associate the symbolic name `PR` with the character sequence (actually, a function call) `putchar(':')` that prints the colon character; this character is printed to prompt the user for data. The C preprocessor will replace all future occurrences of `PR` by the character sequence `putchar(':')`.

The calculator program consists of one function (lines 7–26) of the form

```
main(void)
{
    ...
}
```

The name of this function is `main`, by default its result type is integer (`int`), the type `void`, which is given within the parentheses `( )`, indicates it is a parameterless function.[1] The curly braces, `{` and `}`, enclose the body of the function. C programs start by executing the function named `main`;

---

1. In K&R C, empty parentheses are used in a function definition to specify a parameterless function. For example, parameterless `main` function definitions have the form

```
main()
{
    ...
}
```

The above form is also accepted by ANSI C. However, the above form of function definitions may not be allowed in future versions of ANSI C [1988a].

consequently, every complete C program must have a function named `main`. The variable definitions in lines 9–11

```
float a, b;
char opr;
float result;
```

specify that a, b and `result` are floating-point variables and that `opr` is a character variable. Semicolons are used to terminate variable declarations and definitions, and statements (with the exception of statements ending in a curly brace, i.e., compound statements).

The next statement is the `while` loop (lines 13–24) which, in this case, has the form

```
while (exp) {
    statements
}
```

The list of statements inside the `while` loop is executed repeatedly as long as expression *exp* does not evaluate to 0 (which is interpreted as false). *exp* is a compound expression formed from the two expressions

```
putchar(':')
```

after **PR** has been replaced by the string associated with it, and

```
scanf("%f%c%f",&a,&opr,&b)!=EOF
```

by using the comma operator. **EOF** is a constant identifier which is defined as −1 in the header file `stdio.h`. The value of an expression formed by using the comma operator is the value of its second operand; the value returned by the first operand, which is evaluated first, is ignored. For example, the value of the expression

```
PR,scanf("%f%c%f",&a,&opr,&b)!=EOF
```

is the result of comparing the value returned by function `scanf` and EOF; the value returned by `putchar` is ignored.

Both functions `putchar` and `scanf` are standard library functions that must be provided by every C compiler. Function `scanf` corresponds to the formatted read statement found in languages like FORTRAN and PL/I. It takes as arguments a list of formats (e.g., %f, %c and %d) corresponding to the list of variables for which values are to be read and a list of addresses of these variables. Function `scanf` returns EOF on encountering the end of input or an error; otherwise it returns the number of input items that were successfully matched and assigned to the corresponding variables.

All arguments in C are passed by value. Consequently, addresses of variables (e.g., &a and &opr; note that operator & yields the address of its operand) must be passed if the variables themselves are to be changed. C has functions but no subroutines; the counterpart of a subroutine in C is a function with the void result type.

It was not necessary to call the function putchar from within the while loop expression. For example, the above loop could also have been written as

```
PR;
while(scanf("%f%c%f",&a,&opr,&b) != EOF) {
    statements
    PR;
}
```

but this would have required two instances of

```
PR;
```

i.e., it requires two calls to function putchar.

The body of the while statement consists of a switch statement (lines 14–22) that is used to select among several alternatives. Execution of the switch statement does not automatically terminate after the selected alternative has been executed. Instead, by default, statements after the alternative, up to the end of the switch statement, are executed. Consequently, the switch statement must be explicitly terminated after one of its alternatives has been executed. One way of doing this is by making the break statement be the last statement of each alternative.

There are five alternatives in the switch statement used in the calculator program:

```
switch (opr) {
    case '+': result = a + b; break;
    case '-': result = a - b; break;
    case '*': result = a * b; break;
    case '/': result = a / b; break;
    default:
        printf("ERROR, bad operator\n");
        exit(EXIT_FAILURE);
}
```

The first four alternatives deal with the cases when the value of opr is one of the characters +, -, * or /, respectively. The last alternative, the default alternative, deals with all other values of opr. In this case, the library function printf is called to print an error message. The character pair \n denotes the new-line character. The backslash character \ is called an *escape* character because it indicates that the character(s) following it mean something special. The `exit` function call

```
exit(EXIT_FAILURE);
```

causes the program to terminate with the status value `EXIT_FAILURE` (a constant defined in the header file `stdlib.h`). Many operating systems, e.g., the UNIX system, allow checking of the program status (exit) value to determine whether or not a program executed successfully.

The calculator program as written is not "user-friendly"; instead of helping the user correct mistakes, the program simply terminates after printing an error message. It can be made more user-friendly by replacing the `exit` function call

```
exit(EXIT_FAILURE);
```

with the statements

```
printf("Legal operators are +, -, * and /;");
printf(" Try again\n");
continue;
```

The `continue` statement causes program execution to resume (continue) from the beginning of the `while` loop where the program prompts the user for more data.

Following the `switch` statement is the call to the function `printf`:

```
printf("result is %g\n", result);
```

The effect of this function call is to print the string

`result is` *answer*

where *answer* is the current value of the variable `result`; this quantity is printed using the g format (specified by the characters %g) in which trailing zeros are elided and a decimal point is printed only if the value is not a whole number.

Finally, after determining that the end of input has been reached, the program terminates by calling function `exit` with the value `EXIT_SUCCESS` (defined in the header file `stdlib.h`) to signal that all is well:

```
exit(EXIT_SUCCESS);
```

It is not necessary to use the `exit` function to terminate a program; a program can also terminate by executing all the statements in the main function or by executing the `return` statement in the main function. However, use of the `exit` function to terminate a program allows other programs to determine success or failure of the program.

1.1 Compiling and Executing the Calculator Program

Once the program has been written, the programmer will want to compile and execute it. Suppose that the calculator program is stored in the file `calc.c`. On the UNIX system, the calculator program can be compiled by invoking the C compiler `cc` as follows:

```
cc calc.c
```

An error-free compilation produces the executable file `a.out` (default name) that can be executed directly as

```
a.out
```

The name `a.out` is not a very meaningful name for a program; the programmer can supply an appropriate name for the executable version of the program by using the `-o` option when invoking the compiler. Thus, the command

```
cc -o calc calc.c
```

causes the executable file to be named `calc`.[2]

Here is a sample execution of the calculator program:

```
$ calc
:59.0/4.0
result is 14.75
:39.0+44.0
result is 83
:^D$
```

The dollar character `$` is the UNIX system prompt character which indicates that the UNIX system is ready to execute the next user command. The program terminated because end of input was indicated by typing the control-D (`^D`) character in the last line (UNIX systems typically do not display the control-D character). By convention, the control-D character is used to indicate the end-of-input or the end-of-file on UNIX systems. On MS-DOS

---

2. Note that compilers on other systems may have different user interfaces. For example, on the MS*-DOS system used on personal computers, some C compilers require the user to first compile the program and then use a separate command to explicitly link the compiled program with appropriate libraries to produce an executable version of the program which is given the suffix `.EXE`. The program is executed by typing the prefix of the executable program's name. Other C compilers on the MS-DOS system provide the user with a visual interface for compiling and running programs.

* MS is a trademark of the Microsoft Corporation.

systems, end of input is indicated by typing the control-Z character followed by a carriage return.

Here is another sample execution of the program; this execution is eventually terminated because of an illegal operator:

```
$ calc
:2.0+37.5
result is 39.5
:5.0*4.5
result is 22.5
:5.0%4.5
ERROR, bad operator
$
```

2. Basics

2.1 Character Set

C specifies two character sets: the *source* character set and the *execution* character set. Programs are written using the source character set; characters interpreted by the execution environment belong to the execution character set. Each C compiler must support the basic source and the basic execution character sets that contain the following characters:

1. Upper-case characters.
2. Lower-case characters.
3. Decimal digits.
4. The following 29 graphic characters:

    ```
    !  "  #  %  &  '  (  )  *  +  ,  -  .  /  :
    ;  <  =  >  ?  [  \  ]  ^  _  {  |  }  ~
    ```

5. Space, horizontal-tab and form-feed characters.

In the source files, there shall be a way of indicating an end of line. ANSI C treats this indicator as a single new-line character.

The execution character set shall also include

1. the null character (a byte with all bits set to 0) for indicating the end of a string, and
2. control characters representing alert (which is used to attract the terminal user's attention), backspace, carriage return and new line.

Blank, tab and new-line characters, along with comments, are collectively called *white space*.

In the source character set, the following "trigraph" sequences[3] are supported:

trigraph sequence	character denoted
? ? =	#
? ? (	[
? ? /	\
? ?)	]
? ? '	^
? ? <	{
? ? !	¦
? ? >	}
? ? -	~

2.2 Identifiers

Identifiers are names given to program entities such as variables and functions. These names start with a letter or the underscore character "_" and may be followed by any number of letters, underscore characters or digits. However, only the first 31 characters of internal identifiers and only the first 6 characters of external identifiers are required to be considered to be significant.

As an example, consider the two external identifiers

```
movement_detector
movement_sensor
```

These may be considered identical by some compilers because they are required to treat only the first 6 characters as significant:

```
movem
```

C is *case sensitive*; i.e., it distinguishes between upper- and lower-case letters. However, in case of external names, compilers may ignore the distinction between upper- and lower-case letters.

2.3 Keywords and Reserved Identifiers

Some identifiers, called *keywords*, are treated specially by the C compiler and they can be used only as specified. They are

---

3. The C character set is based on the ISO 646-1983 Invariant Code Set which is a subset of the seven-bit ASCII code set. However, the C character set contains characters which are not in the above ISO character set but which are in the ASCII character set. Trigraph sequences, which are three character sequences that denote single characters, allow the input of the characters not in the ISO set by using characters from the ISO set to denote them [ANSI 1988a–b].

```
auto       double   int       struct
break      else     long      switch
case       enum     register  typedef
char       extern   return    union
const      float    short     unsigned
continue   for      signed    void
default    goto     sizeof    volatile
do         if       static    while
```

C compilers reserve the following sets of identifiers for their own use; these reserved identifiers (words) should not be used by the programmer to name program entities:

1. All external identifiers defined in the standard header files (see Appendix C) and identifiers beginning with an underscore. Programmers should not use these identifiers as names of user-defined external identifiers even if the header files containing the definitions of these identifiers are not included in the program.

2. All identifiers that begin with an underscore and are followed by an upper-case character or another underscore.

2.4 Constants

A *constant* is an explicit denotation of a value. Constants of type integer, character, enumeration, floating point and string can be specified.

2.4.1 Integer Constants: Integer constants can be written using decimal, octal or hexadecimal notation. Octal constants are preceded by the digit 0, while hexadecimal constants must be preceded by the digit 0 and the character x (or X). Letters A through F (or a through f) may be used for the hexadecimal digits 10 through 15, respectively. Long integer constants are specified as integer constants with an L (1) suffix. Unsigned integer constants are specified as integer constants with a U (u) suffix.

Some examples of integer constants are

integer constant	explanation
12	decimal notation
0 14	decimal 12 in octal notation
0 x c	decimal 12 in hexadecimal notation
0 X C	same as above
12 L	long constant in decimal notation

2.4.2 Character Constants: A character constant is formed by enclosing one or more characters within single quotes. A character constant can be used as an integer whose value is the integer interpretation of the bit representation of the character constant.

The single quote ´, the double quote ", the question mark ?, the backslash \, some nongraphic characters and arbitrary characters can be specified using escape sequences:

character	denotation
single quote	\ ´
double quote	\ "
question mark	\ ?
backslash	\ \
alert	\a
backspace	\b
form-feed	\f
new-line	\n
carriage-return	\r
horizontal-tab	\t
vertical-tab	\v
arbitrary character	\octal-digits
arbitrary character	\xhexadecimal-digits

The interpretation of characters specified with the last two escape sequences, the octal and hexadecimal escape sequences, are implementation dependent (note that the C character set is not tied to ASCII). The octal escape sequence can consist of up to three octal digits while the hexadecimal escape sequence can have as many hexadecimal digits as appropriate (it is terminated by the first character that is not a hexadecimal digit).

Examples of character constants are

character constant	explanation
´a´	character a
´\0´	null character
´\n´	new-line character
´\\´	backslash character
´\´´	single-quote character
´\107´	character G (in ASCII encoding)

2.4.3 Enumeration Constants: Enumeration constants are identifiers that are values of user-defined types called enumeration types. Each enumeration constant is an integer of type `int`. For details about enumeration types, see Section 1.4 of Chapter 2.

2.4.4 Floating-Point Constants: The usual notation is used for floating-point constants. By default, these constants are assumed to be double precision values (of type `double`). Single precision floating-point values (of type `float`) must have the suffix `f` (`F`) and extra large precision values (of type `long double`) must have the suffix `l` (`L`).

Some examples of floating-point constants are

```
24.0          2.4E1          2.4e1          240.0E-1
24.0F         24.0f          2.4e1f
24.0L         24.0l          2.4e1l
```

where the number following the letter `E` (or `e`) represents the exponent (base 10).

2.4.5 String Constants: String constants[4] are formed by enclosing a sequence of zero or more characters in double quotes. Here are some examples of string constants:

```
"  "        " "        "A"


"error"        "a longer string"
```

The double quote character can be included in a string constant by prefixing it with the escape character, that is, by using

```
"\""
```

A long string constant can be continued over a line boundary by splitting it into smaller string constants or by using the escape character at the end of the line. For example, consider the following long string constant:

```
"a very very very very very very very very"
"long string"
```

Adjacent string constants that are separated only by white space are pasted together to form one long string constant. Alternatively, the above string constant could have been written as

---

4. According to Dave Prosser of AT&T Bell Labs, string constants are called string literals in ANSI C for historical reasons. K&R C, but not ANSI C, allows modification of string literals. (In K&R C, the value of a string literal can be changed by updating the storage allocated for the literal; note that a string literal is of type pointer to a character array, i.e., it is a character pointer.) However, ANSI C compilers are not required to flag the modification of a string literal as an error. Consequently, it is likely that many ANSI C compilers with a large K&R C user base will allow modification of string literals. It is for this reason that ANSI C uses the term "string literal" instead of "string constant". However, I shall use the term "string constant" because, like ANSI C, I do not recommend user modification of string constants.

```
"a very very very very very very very very\
long string"
```

Note that the blanks preceding the word `long` on the second line (one in this example) will be part of the string constant.

Non-graphic characters such as the new-line and backspace characters can be included in string constants: For example, here is a string constant containing the new-line character \n:

```
"first line\nsecond line"
```

Assuming that the printer or display is positioned at the beginning of a new line, this string will be printed as

```
first line
second line
```

Strings are actually character arrays (see arrays and strings in Sections 2.1 and 2.4.8 of Chapter 2). For example, the string

```
"AT&T Bell Labs"
```

is equivalent to the character array

A	T	&	T		B	e	l	l		L	a	b	s
0	1	2	3	4	5	6	7	8	9	10	11	12	13

By convention, all strings in C are terminated with the null character \0. String processing in C is based on this convention. In case of string constants, the C compiler automatically appends a null character at the end of the string. However, a null character must be explicitly appended to the end of all strings constructed explicitly in the program, e.g., by storing characters in a character array.

2.5 Comments

Comments start with the character pair /* and are terminated by the character pair */. A comment may begin on one line and end on another line; however, comments cannot be nested.

2.6 Semicolon: The Statement Terminator

Semicolons are used to terminate declarations, definitions and statements. But there is one exception. A semicolon is not given after the right curly brace } at the end of a *compound* statement that has the form { ... }. Note that C, like Ada and PL/I, uses the semicolon as a terminator but Pascal uses it as a separator. Using the semicolon as a separator may be an elegant concept [Gries 1979], but it easily leads to errors [Gannon 1975].

3. Constant Identifiers

Constant identifiers (symbolic names for constants) are defined using the C
preprocessor macro definition instruction #define which has the form

>   #define *identifier replacement-string*

After this definition has been processed, all future occurrences of *identifier* (in
the file containing the definition) will be textually replaced by *replacement-
string* (provided the definition has not been removed with the #undef
instruction).

By convention, the following two special cases of the #define instruction are
used for defining constants:

>   #define *constant-name constant-or-constant-name*
>   #define *constant-name (constant-expression)*

It is not necessary to enclose the constant expression in parentheses as shown in
the second form of a constant definition. However, enclosing the constant
expression in parentheses will avoid unexpected interpretations (see Chapter 8
for more details).

Here are some examples of constant definitions that use the first form of the
#define instruction:

```
#define LN 20   /*length of name+1*/
#define LR 8    /*length of room+1*/

#define MAX_DB 100 /*max size of data base*/
```

Two examples of constant definitions that use the second form of the
#define instruction are

```
#define EOF (-1)
#define TOTAL_ELEM    (M*N)
         /*M and N are constant identifiers*/
```

Constant identifiers can be used in constant expressions, i.e., expressions that
can be evaluated at compile time. Constant expressions, not general
expressions, must be used with several C constructs, e.g., in the preprocessor
#if instructions and in array definitions. The scope of constant identifiers
ranges from the line following its definition to the end of the file.

Note that an expression associated with a constant identifier will be evaluated
once for each use of the identifier (note that each use of the identifier is
replaced by the expression associated with it). This may lead to problems if
evaluating the expression causes side effects such as modifying the values of
objects, accessing volatile objects (discussed later) or updating files.

4. Exercises

1. Write the calculator program in the language you are most familiar with (assuming it is not C) and compare it with the C version. How are nongraphic characters denoted? How are constants written? How are statements terminated?

2. What is the convention used in languages like Pascal and Ada for determining the end of a string? What are the pros and cons of terminating strings explicitly with the *null* character?

3. Why is using a semicolon as a statement separator more error prone than using it as a statement terminator?

Chapter 2

Types and Objects

A *type* is a set of values plus a set of operations that can be performed upon these values [Morris, Jr. 1973]. An *object* is a region of storage (contiguous sequence of bytes). A *variable* is an identifier (or an expression) with which is associated a type and an object for storing values of this type. Conforming with conventional use, I shall typically use the word "variable" to refer to a "variable identifier".

A variable is used to refer to the object associated with it, for example, to store in the object a value of the type associated with the variable. Storing a new value in the variable (to be precise, in the object associated with the variable) destroys the old value, if any, stored in the variable. If the type of the variable is qualified with the `const` type qualifier, then the variable is a "read-only" variable that is initialized in its definition and whose value cannot be subsequently changed.

Types in C are classified into three categories: object types, function types and incomplete types (types which describe objects but that are missing information about array size, or the content of a structure or a union). C has the following types: the empty or void type, several varieties of character, integer and floating-point types; it also provides facilities for constructing enumeration, array, structure, union, pointer and function types. Groups of types are often referenced collectively:

type group name	types in the group
basic	character, signed and unsigned integer and floating point
integral	character, integer and enumeration
arithmetic	integral and floating point
scalar	arithmetic and pointers
aggregate	array and structure
incomplete	void type, arrays with undetermined size, and a structure or an union of unknown content
derived	array, structure, union, function and pointer

discrete ⟶

composite ⟶

Before I delve into the details of the types in C, here is some additional terminology:

An object or function *declaration* is used to specify only the properties of the object or function; no storage is allocated.

An object or function *definition* is used to specify the properties of the object or function and to allocate storage for the it.[1]

Declarations allow references to entities that are defined later in the file or defined in other files.

While discussing types, it will sometimes be necessary to talk about declarations and definitions, because these are intimately related to types. Only simple forms of declarations and definitions will be used when discussing types; the general form of declarations and definitions will be discussed later.

1. Simple Types

Simple types are the predefined types plus the enumeration types.

---

1. The difference between an object declaration and an object definition is important not only because I shall use it often in the rest of the book, but also because many people confuse a declaration for a definition and vice versa. Note that the terms "type definition" and "tag definition" are usually used when defining new types and tags even though their definitions do not cause storage allocation.

1.1 Void Types $\left(\mathcal{P}oul\ \ 39\right)$

The `void` type is an empty type, i.e., no values are associated with this type. It is used

- to specify the result type of functions that do not return a value, i.e., functions used as subroutines,

- to specify parameterless functions, e.g.,

    ```
    int rand(void);
    ```

    If the `void` type is not specified then, as in K&R C, the declaration

    ```
    int rand();
    ```

    says nothing about the function parameters,

- to indicate that the value of an expression will not be used and that the expression is to be evaluated only for its side effects, and

- to specify pointers that can point to objects of any type.

The `void` type is classified as an incomplete type that cannot be completed, i.e., a type for which additional information cannot be supplied.

1.2 Character Types

There are three character types in C: `char`, `signed char` and `unsigned char`. `char` is used for character manipulation while `signed char` and `unsigned char` are meant to be used primarily as small integer types; `unsigned char` may also be used in bit manipulation.

An example illustrating the use of type `char` is the definition

```
    char c, ch;
```

which defines `c` and `ch` to be character variables.

Character values are stored as integers that correspond to the internal representation of the character. Consequently, characters can be treated as integers and vice versa.[2] This duality is exploited in programming; for example, functions that return characters may be declared as integer functions instead of character functions to allow them to return arbitrary integer values such as −1, which does not correspond to the internal representation of any character, to indicate failure or the end-of-file.

---

2. Because characters are treated as integers and vice versa, a compiler cannot detect potential errors such as the inadvertent addition of character and integer variables.

Programmers must be careful when defining variables of type `char` because of this programming convention. For example, variables that store characters returned by a function of type `int` should be `int` defined variables so that they can store integer values that do not correspond to the internal representation of any character. As mentioned above, such values may be returned by a function in unusual or limiting cases. For example, the library function `getc`, which reads the next character from standard input, returns `EOF` upon encountering the end-of-file. `getc` returns values of type `int` and not `char`. Variables assigned values returned by `getc` should therefore be defined to be `int` variables.

The character type is often used as a small integer type (occupying one byte of storage) or for bit manipulation. However, interpretation of `char` values as integers is implementation dependent, e.g., an implementation may treat the `char` value as a signed or unsigned integer, i.e., `char` may be implemented as `signed char` or `unsigned char`. This uncertainty can be removed by using either the type `signed char` or the type `unsigned char`.

1.3 Integer Types

There are four signed integer types. In nondecreasing order of size, they are

integer type	alternative designation
`signed char`	
`short int`	`short, signed short, signed short int`
`int`	`signed, signed int,` or omitted
`long int`	`long, signed long, signed long int`

Examples of integer variable definitions are

```
signed char small;
short int low, high;
int i, n;
long int max;
```

These definitions define

- `small` to be a `signed char` variable,
- `low` and `high` to be `short int` variables,
- `i` and `n` to be `int` variables and
- `max` to be a `long int` variable.

An ordinary integer variable (i.e., a variable of type `int`) is stored in the "natural" storage unit of the underlying machine. The storage allocated for `signed char`, `short int` and `long int` variables depends upon the implementation. Note that $S(\text{unsigned char}) \leqslant S(\text{short int}) \leqslant S(\text{int}) \leqslant S(\text{long int})$ where $S(x)$ is the amount of storage allocated for a variable of type x.

Depending upon the implementation, using a small integer type for example, `short int` instead of `int`, may or may not save storage. However, using the smaller integer types may in some cases increase program execution time because arithmetic operators convert values of these types to `int` values before using them. Consequently, the smaller integer types should be used only when it is necessary to economize on storage.

1.3.1 Unsigned Integers: If the sign bit is not needed as such, then one of the following four unsigned integer types (corresponding to the four signed integer types) can be used:

integer type	alternative designation
`unsigned char`	
`unsigned short`	`unsigned short int`
`unsigned`	`unsigned int`
`unsigned long`	`unsigned long int`

Unsigned integers are typically used to access bits or to "squeeze an extra bit" out of a machine word whenever the sign bit is not needed [Ritchie, Johnson, Lesk and Kernighan 1978]. No overflow occurs in unsigned integer arithmetic because an unrepresentable value is reduced modulo $n+1$, where n is the largest representable unsigned value (of the appropriate type).

1.3.2 Integer Limits: File `limits.h` contains constant definitions specifying information such as the largest and smallest values of integers of various sizes. For details, see the *ANSI C Reference Manual* [ANSI C 1988a].

1.4 Enumeration Types

Enumeration types allow identifiers to be used as values. The use of enumeration types may improve program clarity because meaningful names may be assigned to nondescript values. For example, it is more meaningful to use the identifiers `jan`, `feb`, `mar`, to represent the months of a year instead of the integers 1, 2, 3.

The set of values associated with an enumeration type must be declared by explicitly listing the values. Enumeration type definitions[3] have the form

```
typedef enum {a_0, a_1, ..., a_n} e;
```

---

3. The type definition mechanism `typedef` is discussed in detail later in Section 3.

where e is the enumeration type being declared and a_i are the enumerators (enumeration values) which are constants of type int. The value of the constant a_i is i. Values of some or all of the enumerators can be explicitly specified by using the form

a_i = *enumerator-value*

An enumerator whose value is not explicitly specified is assigned a value equal to that of the preceding enumerator plus one. For example, in the type definition

```
typedef enum {a₀=v,    a₁, ..., aₙ} e;
```

the value of enumerator a_i is $v+i$.

Two examples of enumeration type definitions are

```
typedef enum {
    sun, mon, tue, wed, thu, fri, sat
} day;
typedef enum {red, yellow, green} traffic_light;
```

An enumerator cannot belong to more than one type. For example, in the presence of the definition of traffic_light, the type definition

```
typedef enum {yellow, blue, red} color;
```

is illegal because enumerators yellow and red also belong to the type traffic_light.

Variables of the enumeration types day and traffic_light may be defined as

```
day d;
traffic_light signal;
```

An example illustrating the use of an enumeration type is[4]

---

4. As mentioned in the preface, I shall use italics to indicate "abstract" statements that I will use when explaining or developing programs. Before a program is compiled, the abstract statements must be replaced by C statements that have the same effect.

```
switch (signal) {
case red: brake; wait for traffic light to turn green; break;
case yellow: stop if possible; otherwise keep going; break;
case green: go; break;
default: error;
}
```

Instead of declaring enumeration types, *enumeration tags*[5] can also be declared and used to define variables. For example, `day` and `traffic_light` may be declared as enumeration tags using the following declarations:

```
enum day {mon, tue, wed, thu, fri, sat, sun};
enum traffic_light {red, yellow, green};
```

Enumeration tags are similar to enumeration types. For example, using the above enumeration tags, enumeration variables `d` and `signal` can be defined as

```
enum day d;
enum traffic_light signal;
```

Like enumerators, enumeration variables are also of type `int`. Consequently, the erroneous use of enumeration values as integers will not be detected by C compilers. For example, the meaningless expression

```
tue + sat
```

that adds two days will not be detected as an error.

C does not provide a special mechanism for iterating over the values of an enumeration type. However, this iteration can be easily performed[6] by using one of the C loop statements. For example, the `for` loop

```
enum day d;
...
for (d=sun; d <= sat; d++) {
    ...
}
```

iterates over all the values of type `day` with the loop variable `d` being assigned

---

5. The enumeration tag mechanism is redundant in the presence of the more general `typedef` definition. Note that both enumeration tags and the `typedef` facility were added to C during its evolution.

6. Assuming that noncontiguous values have not been assigned to the enumerators (when defining the corresponding enumeration type).

each of the enumerators in order of their appearance in the definition of type `day`.

1.5 Boolean or Logical Type

C does not have Boolean values; instead integers are used as substitutes for Boolean values. A nonzero value is interpreted as *true* and zero is interpreted as *false*. By convention, the predefined operators and functions return one for *true* and zero for *false*.

For clarity, the constants `TRUE` and `FALSE` are often used to denote Boolean values. They are defined as

```
#define TRUE 1
#define FALSE 0
```

1.6 Floating-Point Types

There are three floating-point types: `float` (single precision), `double` (double precision) and `long double` (extra precision). Examples of definitions of variables using these types are

```
float x, y;
double eps;
long double extra;
```

Variables `x` and `y` are defined to be of type `float`, variable `eps` is defined to be of type `double` and `extra` is defined to be of type `long double`.

1.6.1 Floating-Point Limits: File `float.h` contains constant definitions specifying information such as the largest and smallest values of floating-point types of various sizes and the number of decimal digits of precision. For details, see the *ANSI C Reference Manual* [ANSI C 1988a].

2. Derived Types

Derived types are constructed from simple types and/or other derived types.

2.1 Array Types

An array is a composite object consisting of components (called elements), all of which have the same type. Simple array definitions have the form

$$data\text{-}type \ \ x[n_1] \ \ [n_2] \ \ ... \ \ [n_k]$$

where x is an identifier that is the name of the array being defined and n_i is a constant integral expression specifying the size of the ith dimension of the array. Array x is said to be a *k-dimensional* array with elements of type *data-type*. The elements of the ith dimension of x are indexed from 0 to n_i-1.

An array element type can be any type except the `void` type or a function type; however, the element type can be a pointer to a function type. (Pointers are discussed in Section 2.4).

Some examples of array definitions are

```
int page[10]; /*1-dimensional array with 10*/
              /*elements numbered 0 to 9   */
char line[81];
float big[9][9], sales[REGION][MONTHS][ITEMS];
```

The last definition defines two arrays. `big` is defined as a 2-dimensional array and `sales` is defined as a 3-dimensional array (`REGION`, `MONTHS` and `ITEMS` are constant identifiers).

Elements of a k-dimensional array x are referenced using the notation

$x[i_1] \ [i_2] \ ... \ [i_k]$

where the subscripts i_j are integer expressions and $0 \leqslant i_j \leqslant n_j-1$, n_j being the size of the jth dimension of x. Some examples are

```
page[5]
line[i+j-1]
big[i][j]
```

A p-dimensional subarray of a k-dimensional array ($p \leqslant k$) can be referenced by giving only the first $k-p$ subscripts, e.g.,

element	refers to
`sales[i]`	2-dimensional subarray of `sales`
`sales[i][j]`	1-dimensional subarray of `sales`

2.1.1 Incomplete Array Types: An incomplete array type is one in which the array size is not specified, For example, the "external" integer array declaration

$Schan. 104$

```
extern float data[];
```

declares `data` to be an array of an unspecified size (incomplete type). The size of the array must be specified elsewhere in an array definition. (See Section 5.1 for more on external declarations.)

2.2 Structure Types

A *structure* (record in Pascal and Ada terminology) is a composite object that consists of members (elements) of any object type except the `void`, function or incomplete types.[7] Unlike array elements, structure elements can, and usually do, have different types.

Structure types have the form

```
struct {
    component-declarations
}
```

Simple definitions of structure objects have the form

structure-type declarators;

where *declarators* contains identifiers representing the names of the objects being defined as structures. In its simplest form, *declarators* is a list of ordinary variable names, array names, pointer names and function names. (Definitions and declarators will be discussed in detail in Section 5; for the moment, I will continue to illustrate them with examples.)

As an example, consider the following definition

```
struct {
    double x, y;
} a, b, c[9];
```

which defines a and b to be structures, each with two components x and y; c is defined as an array of 9 such structures.

Here is another example of a structure definition

```
struct {
    int year;
    short int month, day;
} date1, date2;
```

which defines two variables date1 and date2, each with three components: year, month and day.

Structure types can be given names by using a type definition of the form

```
typedef struct {
    component-declarations
} structure-type-name;
```

---

7. The type of a structure component cannot be the structure type itself, because the definition of a structure type is not complete until the closing curly brace is encountered. And structure component types cannot be incomplete types. However, the component type can be a pointer to the structure type, because pointer types are not incomplete types.

These names can then be used to define structures (i.e., objects of type structure). The general form of the `typedef` definition is discussed in detail later in Section 3.

An example of a structure type is `employee`, which is declared as

```
typedef struct {
    char name[30];
    int id;
    dept d;
    family f;
} employee;
```

where `dept` and `family` are types that were previously declared. Structure type `employee` can now be used to define variables; e.g., the definition

```
employee chairperson, president;
```

defines variables `chairperson` and `president` to be structures of type `employee`.

Structure types can also be referenced by using *structure tags*. Structure tags are similar to enumeration tags. They are defined as

```
struct tag {
    list-of-declarations
};
```

where *tag* is an identifier. For example, the definition

```
struct student {
    char name[25];
    int id, age;
    char sex;
};
```

declares `student` to be a structure tag. Structure definitions that use structure tags have the form

```
struct tag identifier-list;
```

Here is a definition that uses structure tags:

```
struct student s1, s2;
```

Structure tags are necessary for declaring recursive structures because they cannot be declared by using just the `typedef` mechanism. Structures cannot be directly recursive. As mentioned before, a structure of type *s* cannot contain a component of type *s*. However, it can contain a component which points to a structure of type *s*.

An example of a recursive structure tag definition is

```
struct node {
  int data;
  struct node *next;
};
```

The definition of the structure tag `node` is recursive because the tag is used in its own definition, i.e., in declaring `next`. (The character `*` in the declaration of `next` specifies it to be a pointer.)

2.2.1 Accessing Structure Components: Structure components are accessed using the *selected component* notation. The general form of this notation is

    s . c

where *s* is a structure with component *c* (note that *s* can be an expression, including a function call that returns a structure). Components of the structure variable `date 1` defined above can be accessed as

```
date1.year
date1.month
date1.day
```

2.2.2 Bit-Fields: Structures can be used to access bits of a word. Components of a structure may be packed into storage units (words or bytes) by specifying the position and the number of bits occupied by each component. The types allowed for these components, which are called *bit-fields*, are `int`, `unsigned int` and `signed int`. (Note that the *address-of* operator cannot be applied to bit-fields.)

Bit-fields are necessary only in a few cases, such as programs in which it is important to economize on storage and in programs that access the hardware directly. For example, when writing device drivers, it may be necessary to access specific bits of the device register.[8]

In general, a *bit-field* structure (a structure whose components are bit-fields) type has the form

---

8. On computers with memory-mapped I/O, a device register is a location in memory; I/O is controlled via memory locations.

```
struct {
```
  type-and-identifier-1$_{opt}$: *field-width$_1$* ;
  type-and-identifier-2$_{opt}$: *field-width$_2$* ;
          ...
  type-and-identifier-n$_{opt}$: *field-width$_n$* ;
```
}
```

where *field-width$_i$* is a constant integer expression specifying the number of bits to be allocated to the bit-field *identifier$_i$*. Subscript *opt* indicates an optional item. A field width of zero specifies that no more fields are to be allocated in the current storage unit; it specifies alignment with the next storage unit boundary.

Bit-fields are allocated contiguously; they are allocated right-to-left (from the least significant bit to the most significant bit) on some machines (e.g., the PDP-11 and the VAX-11) and left-to-right on others. Unnamed bit-fields (bit-fields for which only the width is specified) are used to specify bits that will not be accessed. Bit-fields cannot be wider than the storage unit. A bit-field that is wider than the number of bits left in the current storage unit is allocated in the next storage unit.

Structures with bit-fields can also contain ordinary components (e.g., a `char` component). Such components are allocated automatically at appropriate storage unit boundaries as a result of which some bits may be left unused.

As an example, consider the bit-field structure `save_211` specified according to the format for the command and status register (two bytes long) of the RX211 disk used on the VAX-11 computer:

```
   struct {
       unsigned int go          :1; /*bit 00     */
       unsigned int function    :3; /*bits 01-03*/
       unsigned int unit_select:1; /*bit 04     */
 5     unsigned int done         :1; /*bit 05     */
       unsigned int int_enable  :1; /*bit 06     */
       unsigned int trans_req    :1; /*bit 07     */
       unsigned int density     :1; /*bit 08     */
       unsigned int             :2;
10                   /*unnamed bit-field because bits*/
                     /*09-10 are not used           */
       unsigned int rx02         :1; /*bit 11     */
       unsigned int unibus_addr:2; /*bits 12-13*/
       unsigned int initialize :1; /*bit 14     */
15     unsigned int error        :1; /*bit 15     */
   } save_211;    /*RX211 Disk command and status*/
                   /*register format*/
```

Bit-fields are referenced the same way as components of ordinary structures are referenced.

2.2.3 Incomplete Structure Types: Incomplete structure types are structure types whose components have not been specified. The complete definition of such a type must eventually be given (in the scope containing the incomplete definition). An incomplete structure type is used for "registering" the type name in the current scope so as to avoid referencing another type in the outer scope but with the same name. Incomplete structure types are typically used to define mutually recursive structures, and they can be used only in situations in which the structure size information is not needed. For example, the size information is not needed when defining a structure pointer, but it is needed when defining a structure variable.

As an illustration of the use of incomplete structure type, consider the following mutually recursive structure tag definitions:

```
   struct person { struct address *a; };
   struct address { struct person *p; };
```

These recursive definitions will work as expected provided there is no type `address` in the surrounding scope, e.g., as in

```
       ...
struct address { ... int p; ...};
main(void)
{
       ...
       struct person { ... struct address *a; ...};
       struct address { ... struct person *p; ...};
       ...
}
```

In this case, the structure tag `address` in the definition of `person` will refer to the structure tag defined in the scope enclosing `main` (i.e., it will refer to the `address` tag defined on line 2). For the tag `address` in line 6 to refer to the second `address` structure tag declaration (line 7), an incomplete definition of `address` must be given inside `main` before the definition of `person`:

```
       ...
struct address { ... int p; ...};
main(void)
{
       ...
       struct address;
       struct person { ... struct address *a; ...};
       struct address { ... struct person *p; ...};
       ...
}
```

2.3 Union Types

A *union* is like a structure except that only one of its components is active at any given time. The active component is the component that was most recently assigned a value.

Union types have the form

```
union {
       declaration-of-component₁ ;
       declaration-of-component₂ ;
       ...
       declaration-of-componentₙ ;
}
```

All components of a union are allocated the same storage in memory, i.e., they are overlaid. This memory, i.e., the union, should be accessed only via the active union component. If a union object is accessed via inactive components, then the result of this access will be implementation dependent with one exception: if a union contains several structures each having a set of initial elements with identical corresponding types, and if one of these structures is the active union component, then the common initial elements of any of these structures can be used to examine the contents of the union.

Union components are accessed like structure components. Union tags can be declared and used just like structure tags.

Unions are used to

- share storage when it is known that only one of several objects will be active at any given time and

- interpret the underlying representation of an object of one type as if it were of another type.

Unions play a role in C similar to that played by the *equivalence* facility in FORTRAN. Components a and b of a union object have the same relationship to each other as two objects *equivalenced* to each other in FORTRAN.

Consider the following example of the definition of a union object:

```
union {
    float radius;      /*circle*/
    float a[2];        /*rectangle*/
    int b[3];          /*triangle*/
    position p;        /*point; position is a*/
                       /*user-declared type*/
} geom_fig;
```

In this example, it is meaningful to access only the active component of the union geom_fig. For example, after assigning a value to the component radius, it may not make sense to access b[0].

2.3.1 Incomplete Union Types: Incomplete union types are similar to incomplete structure types.

2.3.2 Variant Structures: Programs often contain objects that differ from each other only in minor details. For example, consider the representation of geometric figures. Each geometric figure has common features such as area and perimeter but their dimension specifications may be different depending upon their shape.

Languages like Ada and Pascal provide a type called the *variant record* whose objects contain a set of common components plus some components that vary from object to object. In C, a similar type, which I will call a *variant structure*, can be implemented by nesting a union within a structure. As an example, consider the structure `figure`:

```
typedef struct {
    float area, perimeter;/*common components*/
    int type;      /*active component tag keeps*/
                   /*track of the figure      */
    union {        /*variant component */
        float radius; /*circle   */
        float a[2];   /*rectangle*/
        float b[3];   /*triangle */
        position p;   /*point    */
    } geom_fig;
} figure;
```

Each object of type `figure` has three common components: `area`, `perimeter` and `type`. Component `type` is called the *active component tag* because it indicates which of the components of the union `geom_fig` (i.e., `radius`, `a`, `b` or `p`) is currently active. Such a structure is called a variant structure because its components change with the value of the active component tag.

Now assume that the following constant definitions

```
#define CIRCLE 0
#define RECT 1
#define TRIANGLE 2
#define POINT 3
```

have been given and that variable `fig` has been defined as

```
figure fig;
```

Then, by convention, before assigning a value to the union components, an appropriate value must be assigned to (or be present in) the active component tag `fig.type` to indicate the active component, e.g.,

```
fig.type = CIRCLE;
fig.geom_fig.radius = 5.0;
```

Processing a union object or accessing its components should be based on the value of the active component tag:

```
switch (fig.type) {
case CIRCLE: process a circle; break;
case RECT: process a rectangle; break;
case TRIANGLE: process a triangle; break;
case POINT: process a point; break;
default: error;
}
```

Variant structures will in general consist of three parts: a set of common components, the active component tag and the variant component part. The general form of a variant structure is

```
struct {
        declaration-of-common-components_opt ;
        active-component-tag;
        union {
                declaration-of-component_1 ;
                declaration-of-component_2 ;
                ...
                declaration-of-component_n ;
        } identifier;
}
```

Another example of a variant structure is `health_record`, defined as

```
struct {
        /*common information*/
                char name[25], sex;
                int age;
        /*active component tag*/
                marital_status ms;
        /*variant part*/
                union {
                        /*single*/
                                /*no components*/
                        /*married*/
                                struct {
                                        char marriage_date[8];
                                        char spouse_name[25];
                                        int no_children;
                                } marriage_info;
                        /*divorced*/
                                char date_divorced[8];
                } marital_info;
} health_record;
```

where `marital_status`, the type of the active component tag `ms`, is declared as

```
typedef enum {
    SINGLE, MARRIED, DIVORCED
} marital_status;
```

Some examples of references to components of the above variant structure are

```
health_record.name
health_record.ms
health_record.marriage_info.marriage_date
```

2.4 Pointer Types

A *pointer* refers to some region of storage; typically, the value of a pointer is the address of some object. Simple pointer definitions have the form

$$data\text{-}type \ *id_1, \ *id_2, \ ..., \ *id_n;$$

Variables id_1, id_2, ..., id_n are defined as pointers to objects of type *data-type*, i.e., they are objects of type *data-type* *.

Some examples of pointer definitions are

```
int *pi, *qi; /*pointers to integer objects*/

struct { int x, y; } *p;
            /*pointer to a structure with*/
            /*components x and y*/

complex *x;   /*pointer to an object of a */
              /*user-declared type complex*/
void *p;      /*void pointer*/
```

`void` pointers are "generic pointers", i.e., a `void` pointer value can be used wherever a pointer value is expected and vice versa. No explicit type conversions are required because the necessary conversions are automatically performed. A `void` pointer cannot be used directly to reference an object. The `void` pointer must first be converted to a pointer of an appropriate type (say by assigning it to a variable that points to objects of this type) and this pointer then used to reference the object.

2.4.1 Dynamic Objects: Dynamic objects are created and manipulated by using pointers. Defined objects are created by means of object definitions.[9]

Dynamic objects, on the other hand, are created dynamically and explicitly during program execution by calling the storage allocators `malloc` and `calloc`. The number of dynamic objects, unlike the number of defined objects, is not fixed by the program text. Dynamic objects can be created or destroyed as desired during program execution. Unlike defined objects, dynamic objects do not have explicit names, and must be referenced by using pointers.

The null pointer constant `NULL` (defined in the header file `stddef.h`) is associated with all pointer types. The null pointer constant is used to indicate that a pointer is not pointing to any object. Using the null pointer to reference an object, i.e., "dereferencing" a null pointer, results in an error.

2.4.2 Creating Dynamic Objects: The storage allocators `malloc` and `calloc` have the prototypes (declarations with parameter types specified)

```
void *malloc(size_t size);
   /*size: amount of storage to be allocated*/

void *calloc(size_t nelem, size_t size);
   /*nelem: number of elements for which   */
   /*       storage is to be allocated      */
   /*size: amount of storage to be allocated*/
   /*       for each element                 */
```

Both `malloc` and `calloc` return `void` pointers that point to the allocated storage. `size_t` is a synonym for `unsigned int` and is defined in the header file `stddef.h`.

The `sizeof` operator may be used to determine the amount of storage that needs to be allocated:

form	meaning
`sizeof` *expression*	storage required for storing *expression*
`sizeof(`*T*`)`	storage required for storing values of type *T*

The storage allocators `malloc` and `calloc` return a pointer to the dynamic object created. Actually, the storage allocators return `void` pointers that must be converted, either explicitly by casting (see Section 6.2) or implicitly by assignment to an appropriate pointer variable, before they can be used to access the dynamically created object.

---

9. *Defined* objects are also called *static* objects. However, I will not use the adjective *static* so as to avoid any ambiguity with the C storage class `static`.

As an example of dynamic object creation, consider the statement

```
pi = malloc(sizeof(int));
```

which creates one integer object. The address of this object is the `void` pointer returned by `malloc` which is assigned to variable `pi` (which is of type `int *`, i.e., pointer to integer). Pictorially, the dynamic object pointed to by `pi` may be depicted as

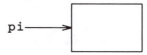

where the empty box is a placeholder for an integer value.

2.4.3 Accessing Dynamic Objects: A value is assigned to the object pointed to by `pi` by using its name `*pi`, e.g.,

```
*pi = 55;
```

Pictorially, the effect of this assignment may be depicted as

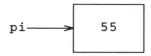

The same pointer value may be assigned to more than one pointer variable. Thus, a dynamic object may be referenced by one or more pointers. An object that can be referenced by two or more pointer objects is said to have *aliases*. For example, as a result of the assignment

```
qi = pi;
```

both variables `qi` and `pi` point to the same object, i.e., they are aliases of each other. Pictorially, the effect of this assignment may be depicted as

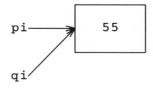

Uncontrolled use of aliases can be detrimental to program readability because the same object can be accessed and modified using the various aliases; this access and modification may not be obvious from a local analysis of the program.

2.4.4 Lifetime of a Dynamic Object: Dynamic objects must be deallocated explicitly if the space occupied by them is to be returned to "free store", i.e., the storage allocation pool, for reuse. Explicit deallocation is performed by calling function `free`, which has the following prototype:

```
void free(void *ptr);
    /*ptr: points to the storage to */
    /*be freed; no value is returned*/
```

Care must be taken to avoid errors resulting from the *dangling reference* problem [Horowitz 1983]; that is, errors caused by referencing deallocated objects.

Storage occupied by inaccessible objects can be reclaimed automatically if the implementation provides a *garbage collector*. However, unlike Lisp and Snobol, C does not provide a garbage collector.

2.4.5 Pointing to Defined Objects: Pointers can be made to point to defined objects. The address of a defined object can be determined by using the *address-of* operator &. For example, consider the variables `i` and `pi` defined as

```
int i, *pi;
```

The assignment

```
pi = &i;
```

makes `pi` point to `i` (to be precise, the object associated with `i`); as a result, `i` can also be referenced as `*pi`. The above assignment makes `*pi` to be an alias of `i`. The *address-of* operator is often used to pass addresses of objects to functions (so that the objects can be modified by the functions or to avoid copying objects; see Chapter 5). Note that, unless care is taken, use of the *address-of* operator can also lead to the dangling reference problem.

2.4.6 Pointing to Arbitrary Locations in Memory: Pointers can be made to point to arbitrary memory locations. For example, suppose `pt` is a pointer of type `T *`; it can be made to point to location 0777000 in memory as follows:

```
pt = (T *) 0777000;
```

Referencing specific memory locations is often necessary in programs that interact with the hardware. For example, in device driver programs specific memory locations, such as those associated with the device's buffer and status registers, must be accessed to control the device. Although accessing arbitrary memory locations is useful and even necessary for some applications, it must be used with care. Otherwise, it may cause errors and lead to system crashes. Consequently, although users can write programs that access arbitrary locations, many operating systems will prevent general users from referencing some absolute memory addresses to preserve the integrity of the system facilities and to protect other users.

2.4.7 Pointers and Arrays: Arrays and pointers are intimately related in C; in fact, arrays may be considered to be syntactic sugar for pointers. Except in a handful of cases, e.g., when used as the operand of the $sizeof$ operator, an array name is converted to a pointer to the first element of the array. For example, the array element $a[i]$ is the element pointed to by $a+(i)$, i.e., it is the element $*(a+(i))$, where the value of a is the address of the $a[0]$. Expression $a+(i)$ is an example of pointer arithmetic: integer expression i is being added to a pointer, the address of the first element of the array a. The value of this expression is a plus the amount of storage occupied by i elements of a. See Section 1.5 of Chapter 3 for more details about pointer arithmetic.

As another example, suppose that x is a 2-dimensional array. Then a reference to the subarray $x[i]$ is a reference to row i of array x; $x[i]$ yields the address of the first element of this row, i.e., $*(x+(i))$. Elements of each row are stored contiguously because arrays are stored in *row-major* order; i.e., the last subscript varies the fastest when laying out the elements in storage.

Similarly, $y[i]$, where y is an n-dimensional $(n > 1)$ array, refers to the $(n-1)$-dimensional subarray of y whose elements are $y[i, j_2, j_3, \ldots j_n]$ where j_k have values consistent with the definition of y; $y[i]$ yields the address of the first element of this subarray, i.e., $*(y+(i))$. All elements of this $(n-1)$-dimensional subarray are stored contiguously.

2.4.8 Strings, Pointers and Arrays: Strings are arrays of characters. By convention, the last character of a string must be the null character \0. Because an array name is really a pointer to the first element of an array, string variables can also be considered to be variables of type $char$ $*$. For example, the second variable $string\_array$ in the following definition

```
char *string_pointer, string_array[81];
```

can also be treated as a read-only character pointer. Storage must be allocated explicitly for the string represented by the first variable $string\_pointer$; storage is automatically allocated for the array $string\_array$ and the variable $string\_array$ points to it. Note that storage must also be allocated or reserved for the string terminator \0.

Not only is the interpretation of string variables as character pointers quite common, but strings are often treated in a dual fashion: both as arrays and as pointers—in the same program! This is especially important when strings are passed as arguments to a function. The calling program may treat the string as a character array while the called function may treat it as a character pointer.

Using character pointers (and dynamically allocated storage) to store strings can be advantageous, especially in case of variable-length strings. Although arrays can also be used, this can waste storage and imposes an upper bound on the string length. For example, an array of character pointers can be made to "hold" strings of different lengths. On the other hand, using a 2-dimensional character array to do this will in general waste storage because there must be enough columns in the array to hold the largest possible string.

2.4.9 Pointers and Structures: Consider the structure tag `student` which was declared earlier as

```
struct student {
    char name[25];
    int id, age;
    char sex;
};
```

and the pointer `new_student` defined as

```
struct student *new_student;
```

Suppose that storage has been allocated to make `new_student` point to a `student` object. Then components of this object are referenced as

```
(*new_student).name
(*new_student).id
(*new_student).age
(*new_student).sex
```

Because pointers are commonly used to point to structures, C provides the *right-arrow* selection operator especially for referencing components of such structures. For example, the above components can also be referenced using the *right-arrow* operator -> as

```
new_student->name
new_student->id
new_student->age
new_student->sex
```

As another example illustrating the interaction between structures and pointers, consider the type `stat_reg` declared as

```
    typedef struct {
        unsigned int go          :1; /*bit 00    */
        unsigned int function    :3; /*bits 01-03*/
        unsigned int unit_select:1; /*bit 04    */
5       unsigned int done        :1; /*bit 05    */
        unsigned int int_enable  :1; /*bit 06    */
        unsigned int trans_req   :1; /*bit 07    */
        unsigned int density     :1; /*bit 08    */
        unsigned int            :2;
10                   /*unnamed bit-field because bits*/
                     /*09-10 are not used          */
        unsigned int rx02       :1; /*bit 11    */
        unsigned int unibus_addr:2; /*bits 12-13*/
        unsigned int initialize :1; /*bit 14    */
15      unsigned int error       :1; /*bit 15    */
    } stat_reg;    /*RX211 disk command and status*/
                   /*register format*/
```

Variable `ptr_rx_sr` is defined as a pointer to objects of type `ptr_rx_sr`

```
    stat_reg *ptr_rx_sr;
```

and is made to point to the RX211 disk command and status register located at address 0777170 by the assignment

```
    ptr_rx_sr = (stat_reg *) 0777170;
```

Components of the RX211 register can now be accessed as

```
    ptr_rx_sr->error
    ptr_rx_sr->density
    ptr_rx_sr->int_enable
```

and so on.

2.5 Function Types

A function type describes a function: the number and types of the function parameters and its result type. For details about functions, see Chapter 5.

3. Type Definitions

Type definitions are used to give names to enumeration and derived types, or to give new names to predefined or previously defined types. These type names can then be used in subsequent declarations and definitions. Type definitions have the form

```
typedef type-specifier declarator-list;
```

where *type-specifier* is a simple or derived type, or a previously defined type. The new type names are represented by the identifiers in the declarators (one identifier per declarator; see Section 5.4).

In the preceding two sections, I have already shown you several examples of type definitions. Here are some more examples:

```
typedef float miles, speed;
            /*defines "miles" and "speed" as*/
            /*synonyms for "float"           */

typedef float a[5], *pf;
    /*defines type "a" as an array of 5   */
    /*floating-point components; type "pf"*/
    /*is declared as a pointer to "float" */
    /*objects                             */

typedef struct { float x, y; } point;

typedef struct {
    char name[LN];
    char room[LR];
    char ext[LE];     /*extension*/
    char desig[LD];   /*designation*/
    char compid[LC];  /*company id*/
    char sig[LS];     /*electronic signature*/
    char logid[LL];   /*login id*/
    char maild[LM];   /*directory where mail*/
                      /*is received*/
} emp;
    /*type "emp" specifies the layout of */
    /*database records; the constants    */
    /*used here were defined previously   */
```

These types can now be used to define objects, just as types float and int are used to define objects. For example, the definition

```
point s1, s2, *p;
```

defines s1 and s2 as structures of type point and p as a pointer to a structure of type point.

Type definitions do not introduce new types; instead, they are used to define synonyms for existing types or to give names to enumeration or derived types. For example, types miles and speed, which were defined above, are synonyms of each other and the predefined type `float`; they are all equivalent.

4. Scope of Tags and Type Definitions

The scope of structure, union and enumeration tags begins just after the appearance of the tag in the type specifier. The scope of a type name begins after the completion of its declarator (i.e., its definition). Tags and type identifiers have file scope if their definitions are given outside a function body (see Chapter 5) and they have block scope if their definitions are given within a block (see Chapter 4).

5. Object Definitions and Declarations

Identifiers are defined and declared as variables and declared as functions by using definitions and declarations of the form

storage-class-specifier$_{opt}$ *type-specifier*$_{opt}$ *type-qualifiers*$_{opt}$ *init-declarator-list*;

where the *storage-class-specifier* and the *type-specifier* apply to each *init-declarator* and the *type-qualifiers* qualify the specified type. Each *init-declarator* is a declarator that may be followed by an initial value and the declarator itself contains the identifier that is being defined or declared. Note that the *storage-class-specifier*, the *type-specifier* and the *type-qualifiers* can appear in any order in a declaration or definition.

Note that a variable can be an identifier or an expression that refers to the object. For example, the expression

    *p

is the name of the object referred to by the pointer p.

5.1 Storage-Class Specifiers

The *scope* of an identifier is the region of the program where it is visible. The *lifetime* (or *storage duration*) of an identifier is the duration for which it exists; during this period the identifier is accessible provided it is not hidden by a local variable.

The lifetime and the scope of an identifier are determined by the *storage class* associated with it. There are four storage classes:[10]

---

10. Note that the type definition specifier `typedef` is called a storage class in the *ANSI C Reference Manual* [ANSI C 1988a] only for syntactic convenience.

storage class	use and implication
auto	Default storage class for local variable identifiers; storage for these variables is allocated at block (i.e., compound statement) entry and deallocated at block exit.
static	Used for defining local variable identifiers that are to exist across block executions and defining external variables and functions whose visibility is to restricted to the file containing them (i.e., specifying "file static" variables and functions). External variables (identifiers) are variables declared or defined outside a function body. Storage for static variables is allocated only once—at the beginning of program execution and it exists for the duration of the program.
extern	Used for defining and declaring external variables that will be used for communicating between functions, including functions in other files. An external variable is visible in the file containing its definition and in files containing corresponding external declarations (which must match the definition). This is also the default storage class for identifiers denoting functions. The keyword extern is not in external variable definitions (this is assumed to be the default storage class); its presence indicates an external variable is being declared (and not defined). As in the case of static variables, storage for extern variables is allocated only once: at the beginning of program execution and it exists for the duration of the program.
register	Used for suggesting to the compiler that, if possible, variables should be allocated registers (instead of memory) for fast access. In almost all other respects, register variables are like auto variables.

Because most computers have a limited number of registers, only the first few register variables will be stored in registers. Register declarations can speed up program execution especially in case of nonoptimizing compilers. However, in some cases, if not used properly, register declarations may actually slow program execution. For instance, allocating a register for a variable that is only lightly used can slow program execution if it prevents better use of the register by the compiler. Some C compilers do not heed register declarations. The address of a register variable cannot be computed, e.g., by using the *address-of* operator &. The types of objects that can be stored in registers is implementation dependent.

The only storage class that can be explicitly specified for a function identifier declared within a block is `extern`.

When declaring `extern` arrays, the size of the first dimension need not be specified; it will be determined from the corresponding definition.

If the storage class of an identifier is not specified explicitly, then its storage class is determined by the textual location of its definition or declaration. If a variable identifier is defined inside a function, then the default storage class is `auto`; otherwise, it is `extern`. The default storage class for function identifiers is `extern`.

5.1.1 More on `extern` Identifiers: Consider a C program whose source text is distributed over many files. Functions in these files use `extern` identifiers to share data (to communicate with each other). If a function references an `extern` identifier, then the file containing it must contain a declaration or a definition for this identifier. Although there may be many files containing a declaration of an `extern` identifier, only one file must contain its definition. In the absence of an initial value in the definition, the definition is considered to be tentative. Suppose a program has no "firm" definition of an `extern` object but it has one or more tentative definitions. Then these definitions will be treated as if they were declarations and a firm definition with the default initial value zero is supplied automatically.

5.1.2 Storage Classes: An Example: As an example, consider the definitions and declaration of the external variables x and i given in two files named a.c and b.c. File a.c contains the definitions

File: a.c
```
int x = 0;
static int i;
    ...
```

and file b.c contains the declaration and definition

File: b.c
```
extern int x;
static int i;
    ...
```

Variable x is shared between the two files; storage for it is allocated by the definition in file a.c and it may be used for communication between functions in the two files. On the other hand, each file has its own variable i because each file contains a definition of i; storage is allocated for the i variable in each file. Each instance of variable i is file static, i.e., it can be accessed only by functions in the file containing its definition.

5.2 Type Qualifiers

Type qualifiers modify the type specified in a declaration or a definition. There are two type qualifiers: const and volatile. Note that qualifiers following the dereferencing operator * apply to the pointer.

5.2.1 Read-only Objects: Type qualifier const is used for specifying read-only variables. const objects must be initialized in their definitions; their values cannot subsequently be changed.

Here are some examples of read-only variables:

```
const float m = 4.0, n = 5.0;
const int diag[2][2] =  {{1, 0}, {0, 1}};
const struct coord {float x, y;} origin={0,0};
const int *pci;   /*pointer to "const int"; */
                  /*type qualified is int    */
```

m and n are defined as float read-only variables, diag as a read-only 2-dimensional array, origin as a read-only coord structure and pci as pointer to a read-only int object. The value of pci can be changed but not that of the object pointed to by it.

Note that structure tag coord is not qualified as a const type. It can be used to define ordinary variables whose values can be changed, e.g.,

```
struct coord a;
...
a.x = 0;
```

5.2.2 Volatile Objects: Type qualifier volatile is used for specifying objects whose values may be changed by the hardware and to which assigning values may cause side effects such as printing output. C compilers are required to not optimize uses of volatile objects and to accurately reflect accesses to such objects in the translated code.

As an example illustrating the use of a volatile variable, consider a personal computer with memory-mapped I/O in which output is written to the display by writing characters to address 500. Here is a code fragment that writes to the display using a volatile variable:

```
                                            File: vol.c
    #define N 81
        ...
    main(void)
    {
5       char a[N];
        int i;
        volatile char *out = (volatile char *) 500;
        ...
        for (i = 0; i < N; i++)
10          *out = a[i];
        ...
    }
```

out is defined as a volatile char pointer. Had *out not been a volatile object, an optimizing compiler could have optimized the above for loop (lines 9–10) to just the statement:

```
    *out = a[N-1];
```

5.2.3 Read-only Volatile Object Example: Here is an example in which both the type qualifiers, const and volatile are used together [ANSI 1988a]:

```
    extern volatile const int clock;
```

clock is a read-only variable whose value is the number of "clock ticks" that have elapsed since the beginning of program execution. Its value is updated automatically by the hardware.

5.3 Type Specifiers

The data type in a declaration or a definition must be one of the object types discussed earlier. Here is a summary of the type specifiers that can be used to specify the object types:

type specifier	alternative names
`void`	
`char`	
`signed char`	
`unsigned char`	
`short`	`signed short`, `short int` and `signed short int`
`unsigned short`	`unsigned short int`
`int`	`signed`, `signed int` and default
`unsigned`	`unsigned int`
`long`	`signed long`, `long int` and `signed long int`
`unsigned long`	`unsigned long int`
`float`	
`double`	
`long double`	
`struct` *tag*	
`struct` *tag*$_{opt}$ {*component-decls*}	
`union` *tag*	
`union` *tag*$_{opt}$ {*component-decls*}	
`enum` *tag*	
`enum` *tag*$_{opt}$ {*enumerator-list*}	
typedef-name	

If the data type is not specified explicitly, then it is assumed to be `int` by default. Note that when one of the type specifiers

```
struct tag
union tag
enum tag
```
typedef-name

is used, then the tag or type name specified in these specifiers must in general have been previously defined.

5.4 The Declarators

Each declarator contains exactly one identifier that is the name of the object being declared or defined. The *init-declarator-list* in a definition or a declaration is a list of *init-declarators* separated by commas:

init-declarator , *init-declarator* , ... , *init-declarator*

Each *init-declarator* is a declarator that may be followed by an initial value:

> *declarator*

or

> *declarator* = *initializer*

I will discuss declarators in this section and initializers in the next section.

The form and semantics of declarators are explained in the table given below; assume that T is the data type specified in the object definition or declaration containing the declarator:

declarator	meaning
identifier	*identifier* of type T is being defined or declared.
(*declarator*)	Same as *declarator*.
∗ type-qualifiers$_{opt}$ declarator	Same as *declarator* in a definition or a declaration with the data type "pointer to T"; if type qualifiers are present, then the data type is "qualified pointer to T".
declarator (*param-type-list$_{opt}$*)	same as *declarator* in a definition or a declaration with the data type "function returning a value of type T and, if specified, no parameters or parameters of the specified types".
declarator [n_{opt}]	Same as *declarator* in a definition or a declaration with the data type "array with n, if specified, elements of type T". n must be a constant expression. Note that the elements will be numbered from 0 to $n-1$ (the upper bound applies only if n is given; it can be omitted in declarations but it must be supplied in a matching definition).

There are some restrictions on the declarators allowed in C. Functions cannot return arrays or functions as values (they can return pointers to arrays or pointers to functions). Also, arrays of functions cannot be declared or defined nor can functions be components of a structure or a union.

The dereferencing (indirection) operator ∗ has a lower precedence than the operators [ ] (which specifies arrays) and ( ) (which specifies functions).

5.4.1 Examples of Declarators: The definition[11]

```
int i, *ip, f( ), *fip( ), (*pfi)( );
```

which contains the declarators i, *ip, f( ), *fip( ) and (*pfi)( ).
Identifiers in these declarators are defined or declared as[12] as follows:

identifier	defined as
i	an integer variable
ip	a pointer to an integer variable
f	a function returning an integer
fip	a function returning a pointer to an integer
pfi	a pointer to a function that returns an integer

All the variables in the above definition have, by default, the storage class
auto.

The following definition, given outside a function body,

```
emp *db[MAX_DB];
```

defines db as be an extern array of pointers to elements of type emp.

The definition

```
static int size, cur = 1;
```

defines size and cur to be static variables of type int; cur is
explicitly initialized to 1.

Finally, here is an example of a declarator with a qualified pointer:

```
int *const cpi;   /*constant pointer to int;  */
                  /*type qualified is "int *" */
```

cpi is declared as a read-only pointer to an int object. The value of cpi
cannot be changed but the value of the object pointed to it can be changed.

---

11. The semantics of definitions and declarations depend upon whether they have been given inside
or outside a function. In this book, I will use the convention that definitions and declarations
are given inside functions unless it is clear from the context or it has been explicitly specified
that they have been given outside functions.

12. Definitions and declarations can be intermingled as illustrated by the hybrid definition-
declaration

```
int i, *ip, f( ), *fip( ), (*pfi)( );
```

I shall generally call such a hybrid a definition. In this definition, identifiers i, ip and pfi
are defined while identifiers f and fip are declared. Identifiers f and fip refer to functions
defined elsewhere and for which no storage is allocated here.

5.5 Syntactic Difference Between Declarations and Definitions

A declaration can be syntactically distinguished from a definition by observing the following points:

1. The keyword `extern` specifies that the objects are being declared and not defined.

2. The absence of a function body indicates that a function is being declared and not defined.

Here are some more examples of declarations and definitions:

```
/*declarations*/
    char *strcpy(char *s1, const char *s2);
    char *strcat(char *s1, const char *s2);
    extern int max(int[]), no_of_processes;
    extern float a[];

/*definitions*/
    struct node *head; /*structure definition*/
                        /*using tag "node"*/

    point x, y;        /*structure definitions*/
                        /*using type "point"   */
    static union {
        automobile a;
        bus b;
        truck t;
    } vehicle;

    day d;
    emp list_of_emp[100];
```

5.6 Initializers

Initializers are used for specifying initial values of variables in their definitions. Initializers can have one the following four forms:

value

{ *list-of-values* }

{ *list-of-values*, }

"*sequence-of-characters*"

where each value is a constant expression and the elements in the *list-of-values* are separated by commas. Initial values for `static` and `extern` variables must be constant expressions. Note that a value can be an *aggregate value*, i.e., a list of values enclosed in curly braces.

By default, `static` and `extern` arithmetic variables are initialized to zero and pointer variables are initialized to the null pointer. This rule also applies to array, structure and union elements. Automatic variables are not initialized by default.[13]

Some examples of variable initialization are

```
    static float eps = 0.0001;
    int i = 0, j = 0;

    int year[12] = {31, 28, 31, 30, 31, 30, 31,
5                                31, 30, 31, 30, 31};

    float x[4] = {1, };

    char thanks[25] = "Thank you for using AT&T";
10  char error[] = "Buffer length exceeded";
    char *msg = "Be Careful";

    float matrix[5][3] = { {1.0, 1.0, 1.0},
                           {2.0, 2.0, 2.0},
15                         {3.0, 3.0, 3.0},
                           {4.0, 4.0, 4.0},
                           {5.0, 5.0, 5.0}
                         };

20  point p = {0.0, 0.0};
    point q = p;
```

Now for some comments:

1. Array `year` is initialized to the number of the days in each month (lines 4–5).

2. The first element of array `x` is initialized to 1 (line 7); the remaining elements are not explicitly initialized.

---

13. I shall always explicitly initialize variables before using them because explicit variable initialization tends to clearly state programmer intent.

3. The size of array `thanks`, which is initialized to a string constant (line 9), must be at least equal to the length of the initial string value plus one (for the terminating null character).

4. The size of array `error` is not specified (line 10). The size of an explicitly initialized array need not be specified explicitly because the C compiler can determine it from the initial value.

5. Character pointer `msg` is initialized to point to a string constant (line 11). `msg` should not be used to change the value of the constant; this is, in fact, prohibited by ANSI C.

6. Initialization of the 2-dimensional array `matrix` (lines 13–18) relies on the fact that arrays in C are stored in row-major order. Elements of row *i* are assigned the value *i*.

7. p is defined as structure type `point`, which was defined earlier as

   ```
   typedef struct { float x, y; } point;
   ```

   Components of p are initialized to 0.

8. q is defined as a structure of type `point` and is initialized to the value of structure p (line 21). Note that this definition must be given inside a function because the initial value of q is not a constant expression.

5.7 Comments on Declaration/Definition Syntax

The syntax of object declarations and definitions is similar to the syntax used for referencing these objects. On the other hand, the syntax of object declarations in languages like ALGOL 68, Pascal and Ada reflects the structure of the object type. Declarations and definitions in C are sometimes hard to read and understand, particularly if they involve type expressions that contain the dereferencing operator *. The primary reason for this difficulty is that * has a lower precedence than the operators [ ] and ( ). The reader not familiar with C may at first find it hard to understand definitions and declarations such as

```
int *(*(*x)[6])();
char (*(*y())[])();
```

where x is defined as a pointer to an array of 6 elements, each of which is a pointer to a function returning a pointer to an integer object; and y is declared as a function that returns a pointer to an array of pointers to functions that return character values.

Declarations and definitions in C become easier to understand if one remembers that object declarations and definitions resemble references to the objects.

Anderson [1980] suggests that programmers use the following approximate equivalences with ALGOL-like or Pascal-like declarations and definitions to help understand and write C declarations and definitions (intermediate forms of declarations and definitions are used to help determine the equivalences):

C syntax	intermediate form	Pascal-like syntax
`int x`		`x:`int
`int *x`	`*x:`int	`x:`*pointer to* `int`
`int x[ ]`	`x[ ]:`int	`x:`*array*`[ ]` *of* `int`
`int x( )`	`x( ):`int	`x:`*function returning* `int`

The colon character : should be interpreted as "is of type". Type `int` is used only for illustration. Similar equivalences apply to other types as well.

When converting a Pascal-like declaration or definition to a C declaration or definition, or vice versa, remember that the pointer dereferencing operator * has a lower precedence than the operators `[ ]` and `( )` used to declare or define arrays and functions, respectively. For example, the declaration

```
extern char *a[];
```

parses as

```
extern char *(a[]);
```

which declares `a` as an array of pointers to characters and not as

```
extern char (*a)[];
```

which declares `a` as a pointer to an array of characters. Parentheses may be used freely to override the precedence rules or for clarity.

5.7.1 Examples Illustrating the Use of Equivalences: I will now use the equivalences suggested by Anderson to illustrate how to understand and construct complicated C declarations and definitions.

As an example, consider the definition

```
int *(*(*x)[6])();
```

given earlier. An equivalent Pascal-like definition is constructed as follows:

```
  *(*(*x)[6])():int;
≡ (*(*x)[6])():pointer to int;
≡ (*(*x)[6]):function returning pointer to int;
≡ *(*x)[6]:function returning pointer to int;
≡ (*x)[6]:pointer to function returning pointer to int;
≡ (*x):array[0..5] of pointer to function returning pointer to int;
≡ *x:array[0..5] of pointer to function returning pointer to int;
≡ x:pointer to array[0..5] of pointer to function returning pointer to int;
```

As another example, we want to declare y as a function that returns a pointer to an array of pointers to functions that return character values, i.e., we want to construct the declaration

```
char (*(*y())[])();
```

using the equivalences suggested by Anderson:

```
  y:function returning pointer to
                array of pointer to function returning char;
≡ y():pointer to array of pointer to function returning char;
≡ *y():array of pointer to function returning char;
≡ (*y()):array of pointer to function returning char;
≡ (*y())[]:pointer to function returning char;
≡ *(*y())[]:function returning char;
≡ (*(*y())[]):function returning char;
≡ (*(*y())[])():char;
≡ char (*(*y())[])();
```

5.8 Using typedef to Understand Declarations and Definitions

Zahn [1979] suggests that a series of type definitions can be used to simplify the writing of complex definitions and declarations. For example, variable x, which is to be defined as

x:*pointer to array*[0..5] *of pointer to function returning pointer to* int;

can be defined to be of the type PA6PFPI, which can be constructed gradually by using the following series of type definitions:

```
typedef int *PI;       /*PI pointer to int*/

typedef PI FPI();
        /*FPI: function returning pointer to int*/

typedef FPI *PFPI;
        /*PFPI: pointer to function*/
        /*returning pointer to int */

typedef PFPI A6PFPI[6];
        /*A6PFPI: array of pointer to*/
        /*function returning pointer to int*/

typedef A6PFPI *PA6PFPI;
        /*PA6PFPI: pointer to array of pointer*/
        /*to function returning pointer to int*/
```

Variable x can now be defined as

```
PA6PFPI x;
```

5.9 Concluding Comments on C Definitions and Declarations

Fortunately, complicated definitions and declarations do not turn up often in real C programs. Most programmers will rarely encounter definitions and declarations as complicated as those given in the preceding examples.

I will discuss one more difference between C and Pascal-like definitions and declarations. All objects in a Pascal-like definition or declaration have exactly the same type; for example, in the definition

```
a, b:array[0..5] of integer;
```

both a and b are defined as integer arrays; the common type information is factored out. On the other hand, in C definitions and declarations, only a limited amount of common type information can be factored out. For example, in the definition

```
int a[6], b[6];
```

only the element type int is factored out. It is not possible to factor out the array size without defining a new type name even though a and b are arrays of the same size.

In contrast to Pascal, C allows variables of different types to be defined or declared together; e.g., in the definition

```
int a[6], *c;
```

a is defined as an int array, while c is defined as a pointer to an int object.

It is just not possible to write such definitions in Pascal-like languages.

5.10 Type Compatibility (Type Equivalence)

Two common schemes for determining type compatibility (type equivalence) are *structural type compatibility* and *name type compatibility*. According to structural type compatibility, two types are compatible only if they are the same or if they have the same number of components, matching component names and compatible component types. According to name type compatibility, two types are compatible only if their names are the same. Structural type compatibility is used in C.

6. Type Conversions

Values may be converted from one type to another, either implicitly or explicitly.

6.1 Implicit Type Conversions

The following implicit type conversions are automatically performed by operators.

6.1.1 Integral Promotions: Values of type char, short int and int bit-fields, or their signed or unsigned counterparts can be used wherever an int value is expected. Conversions of these values to int values are called the *integral* promotions.

6.1.2 Signed and Unsigned Integers: Conversions are performed between signed and unsigned integers with obvious semantics, provided the original value fits into the new type.

6.1.3 Floating-Point Types: Conversions are performed between the floating-point types with obvious semantics provided the original value fits into the new type. If the original value cannot be represented exactly by the new type, then the nearest higher or lower floating-point value is chosen.

6.1.4 Floating-Point and Integral Types: A floating-point value is converted to an integral value by using truncation. The behavior is undefined if the resulting value cannot be represented with the target integral type. If an integral value is converted to a floating-point type that cannot be represented exactly, then the nearest higher or lower floating-point value is chosen.

6.1.5 Usual Arithmetic Conversions: Many binary arithmetic operators automatically convert their operands to a common type. These conversions are called the *usual arithmetic conversions* and are described as follows [ANSI 1988a]:

1. If either operand type is long double, then the other operand is converted, if necessary, to long double.

2. Otherwise, if either operand type is `double` then the other operand is converted, if necessary, to `double`.

3. Otherwise, if either operand type is `float` then the other operand is converted, if necessary, to `float`.

4. Otherwise, the integral promotions are performed first and then the following conversions performed:

    a. If either operand type is `unsigned long int`, then the other operand is converted, if necessary, to `unsigned long int`.

    b. Otherwise, if one operand type is `long int` and the other operand type is `unsigned int`, then the `unsigned int` operand is converted to `long int` provided it is large enough. Otherwise, both operands are converted to the type `unsigned long int`.

    c. Otherwise, if either operand type is `long int`, then the other operand is converted, if necessary, to `long int`.

    d. Otherwise, if either operand type is `unsigned int` then the other operand is converted, if necessary, to `unsigned int`.

    e. Finally, if cases 2 through 4 do not apply, then both operands must be of type `int`.

6.1.6 Pointer Types: Any pointer value can be converted to the generic pointer type `void *` and vice versa.

6.1.7 Function Designator: Except in case of the `sizeof` and *address-of* operators, a function designator with the type "function returning type *x*" is converted to "pointer to function returning type *x*"

6.2 Casting (Explicit Type Conversion)

C allows expressions of one type to be cast (explicitly converted) to another type. Casts are allowed only for scalar (arithmetic and pointer) types. There is, however, one exception to this rule: an expression of any type can be cast to the `void` type; note that a `void` expression cannot be cast to any other type.

An expression *exp* is cast to a type *type-name* by writing it as

  (*type-name*) *exp*

where *type-name* is of the form

  type-specifier abstract-declarator

An abstract declarator is similar to a declarator except that it does not contain an identifier that is to be defined or declared. The meaning of a *type-name* of the form

T abstract-declarator

where *T* is a type specifier, can be determined from the following table:

abstract declarator	meaning of "*T abstract declarator*"
empty	type *T*
(*abstract-declarator*)	type *T abstract-declarator*
type-qualifiers$_{opt}$ abstract-declarator	optionally qualified pointer to type *T*
declarator(param-type-list$_{opt}$)	function returning a value of type *T* and, if specified, no parameters or parameters of the specified types.
declarator[n$_{opt}$]	array with *n*, if specified, elements of type *T*; *n* must be a constant expression.

Some examples of type names are

```
char
char[8]
char *
char()
char *()
char (*)()
```

Suppose the following definitions and declaration have been given:

```
int i;
char *pc, *name;
emp *pe;
char *strcpy(char *s1, const char *s2);
```

Then some examples of casts are

```
(char) i /*convert an int to a char*/

pc = (char *) 0777;
          /*converts octal constant 0777 to*/
          /*a character pointer            */

(void) strcpy(name, "gehani");
          /*discard the value returned by*/
          /*strcpy;                      */
```

Note that the values of expressions that are converted to statements (by appending a semicolon) are automatically discarded; there is no need for the `void` cast in the last example.

It is not necessary to cast a `void` * pointer to a pointer of another type or vice versa; this is done automatically, e.g.,

```
pe = calloc( 1, sizeof( emp ) );
```

There is no loss of information when converting a pointer to a `void` pointer and then back to the original pointer type, i.e., the final value is the same as the original value.

7. Exercises

1. Why does C not allow an enumerator to be an element of two different enumeration types?

2. Write a variant structure type that allows structures to hold data about different kinds of vehicles such as trucks, buses, cars and motorcycles. All vehicles have some common information, e.g., owner, make and model. Vehicles of different types have specialized information that may not be appropriate for other types of vehicles, e.g.,

trucks	number of axles, weight
buses	seating capacity
cars	number of doors (2 or 4)
motorcycle	engine type (2-stroke or 4-stroke)

3. Explain how the *address-of* operator & can lead to the dangling reference problem.

4. Consider the program

```
#include <stdio.h>
main(void)
{
    char *test[5];
    int i;

    for (i=0; i<=4; i++)
        test[i] = "0123456789";
    test[1][3]='*';
    for (i=0; i<=4; i++)
        printf("%s\n", test[i]);
}
```

What will be the output of this program?[14] Is the assignment

```
test[1][3]='*';
```

legal? If yes, then does it affect just the string pointed to by `test[1]`, or all the elements of `test`? Run the program on your C compiler to see the result.

How can elements of `test` be made to point to different strings with the same value?

5. What is the type of `k` in the following declaration?

```
int *(*k())()[]
```

6. Why is the following function declaration illegal?

```
int ((*F())())[];
```

7. Define a variable `x` as an array of pointers to functions that return pointers to an array of pointers to integers. Use equivalences to Pascal-like notation in arriving at the definition.

8. Use a series of `typedef`s to define the variable `x` in Exercise 7.

---

14. The `for` loop statement

```
for (i=0; i<=4; i++)
    S
```

causes statement S to be executed five times. Variable i has the value 0 for the first execution of S; this value is increased by 1 for each successive execution of S.

Chapter 3

Operators and Expressions

An expression is a sequence of operators and operands, possibly containing balanced pairs of parentheses, that denotes a value. Operands can be constants, variables (including array, structure and union components) and function calls. The value of an expression depends upon the values of its operands, the semantics of its operators and the grouping specified by using parentheses to explicitly identify subexpressions.

1. Operators

C has a rich variety of operators. Associated with each operator are two properties: *precedence level* and *associativity.* If an expression contains only operators with the same precedence level, then the expression is evaluated left-to-right or right-to-left as specified by operator associativity (all operators of the same precedence level have the same associativity). If an expression has operators with different precedence levels, then operators with the highest precedence are evaluated first, followed by operators with the next highest precedence, and so on. As before, operators with the same precedence are evaluated in the order specified by their associativity.

The order in which an expression is evaluated can be changed by using parentheses, for example, the expression a+b+c is evaluated from left-to-right but in the expression a+(b+c) the second addition operator is evaluated first. When evaluating an expression, if an operator with an operand that is a parenthesized expression is encountered, then this expression must be evaluated before the operator can be applied to its operands.

I will now present groups of operators in order of decreasing precedence; operators with the same precedence are grouped together. The precedences of the operators are summarized later in Section 1.17.

1.1 Postfix Operators

C treats as operators the parentheses used for a function call, the square brackets used for specifying an array element subscript, and the dot and the right arrow used for selecting structure and union components as operators.

63

Postfix Operators
Precedence level 1; associativity left-to-right

operator	name	operand types	result type	examples/comments
[ ]	array subscript	Array expression type should be a pointer to some object type T; subscript expression type should be integral.	T	`sales[i]`, `sales[i][j]`
( )	function call	Function expression type should be a function pointer and argument types, if specified, must match parameter types.	function result type	`sqrt(x)`, `puts(s)`, `strcpy(s, t)`
.	structure component selector	structure type and identifier	component type	`fig.type`, `(*ps).name`
->	structure component selector	pointer to structure and identifier	component type	`ps->name`
++	increment	scalar type	operand type	Operand is incremented by one; the result is the original operand value. See compound assignment and additive operators for more details.
--	decrement	scalar type	operand type	Similar to ++ but the operand is decremented.

As mentioned in the previous chapter, except in a handful of cases, an array name is converted to a pointer to the first element of the array and function names (designators) are converted to pointers to functions.

1.2 Unary Operators

The operators classified as unary operators are all prefix operators. The
`sizeof` operator has two syntactic forms: prefix operator and unary function.

Unary Operators

Precedence level 2; associativity right-to-left

operator	name	operand type	result type	comments
*	indirection/ dereferencing	pointer to any type *T*	*T*	Cannot be used to dereference `void` pointers.
&	address of	function type or a variable of type *T*	pointer to function or pointer to *T*	Cannot be used to determine addresses of bit-fields or `register` variables.
+	plus	arithmetic	operand type after integral promotion	
–	minus	arithmetic	same as above	
!	logical negation	scalar	`int`	If the operand value is 0, then the result is 1; otherwise, it will be 0.
~	bitwise complement	integral type	operand type after integral promotion	
++	increment	scalar	operand type	Adds one to operand; result is the final operand value. See discussion of compound assignment and additive operators for details.
– –	decrement	scalar	operand type	Similar to ++ but operand value is decremented.
`sizeof`	size in bytes	name or expression of any type	integer constant	Two forms: `sizeof(`*type-name*`)` and `sizeof` *expression*.

The `sizeof` operator can be used to determine the number of elements in an array. For example, the number of elements in `a` is given by the expression:

```
sizeof(a) / sizeof(a[0])
```

The `sizeof` operator cannot be applied to function or incomplete types, or bit-fields.

1.3 Cast Operator

Cast Operator
Precedence level 3; associativity right-to-left

operator	name	operand types	result type	example
( )	cast	a scalar type T and a scalar expression	T	`(char *) 100` returns a character pointer that refers to memory location 100.

1.4 Multiplicative Operators

Multiplicative Operators
Precedence level 4; associativity left-to-right

operator	name	operand types	result type	comments
*	multiplication	arithmetic	arithmetic	The result type is the same as the operand types after the usual arithmetic conversions have been performed.
/	division	arithmetic	arithmetic	See above comments for the result type.
%	remainder	integral	integral	See comments in the multiplication operator for the result type.

Integer division and the remainder operations are related by the following equivalence:

$$(a/b)*b + a\%b \equiv a \ (b \neq 0)$$

If both operands of the division operator are positive integers, then the quotient is the largest integer less than the real (floating-point) quotient. Otherwise, if the operands are integers and one operand is negative, then the quotient may be the largest integer less than the real quotient or the smallest integer greater than the real quotient, depending upon the implementation.

If both operands of the remainder operator are positive integers, then the result is positive. Otherwise, if the operands are integers and one operand is negative, the result may be positive or negative, depending upon the implementation.

1.5 Additive Operators

Additive Operators
Precedence level 5; associativity left-to-right

operator	name	operand types	result type
+	plus	arithmetic and pointer	arithmetic or pointer
–	minus	arithmetic and pointer	arithmetic or pointer

Both operands of the plus and minus operators can have arithmetic types. Alternatively, for the plus operator, one operand one can have an object pointer type and the other an integral type. Both operands of the minus operator can be pointers to objects of compatible types (excluding the type qualifiers), or the left operand can be a pointer and the right operand an integral expression.

If both operands have arithmetic types, then the result type is the same as the operand types after the usual arithmetic conversions have been performed on the operands. Otherwise, the result has the same type as the pointer operand.

Pointer arithmetic is performed if one of the operands is a pointer. Let us first consider the plus operator. Assuming that the pointer points to element i of an array of type T, then $j*sizeof(T)$, where j is the right operand, will be added to the pointer. This means that the result will point to element $i+j$ of the array in question. The behavior is undefined unless both the pointer and the result point to elements of the same array.

Now let us consider the minus operator. If both operands are pointers, then the result type is the signed integral type $ptrdiff\_t$ defined in the standard header file $stddef.h$; otherwise, if only the left operand is a pointer then the result type is the same as the pointer type.

Suppose that the two operands, say p and q, point to elements i and j of the same array, then $p-q$ will be equal to $i-j$. The result is undefined if the two operands do not point to elements of the same array. There is one exception to this rule: if p points to the last element of the array, and q points to an element of the same array, then $p+1$ will be greater than q.

Suppose the left operand p of the minus operator is a pointer that points to element i of an array of type T and the right operand j is of an integral type. Then $j*\texttt{sizeof}(T)$ is subtracted from the pointer which means that the result will point to element $i-j$. The behavior is undefined unless both the pointer and the result point to elements of the same array.

1.6 Shift Operators

Bitwise Shift Operators
Precedence level 6; associativity left-to-right

operator	name	operand types	result type	comments
<<	left shift	integral	left operand type after integral promotion	Right operand must not be negative or greater than the size (in bits) of the promoted left operand. The left operand is left shifted by the right operand value; vacated bits are 0-filled.
>>	right shift	integral	left operand type after integral promotion	Right operand must not be negative or greater than the size (in bits) of the promoted left operand. The left operand is right shifted by the right operand value. If the left operand has an unsigned type or it is positive, then a logical shift (0-fill) is performed; otherwise, the result is implementation dependent.

1.7 Relational Operators

Relational Operators

Precedence level 7; associativity left-to-right

operator	name	operand types	result type	comments
<	less than	arithmetic types or compatible pointer types	int	The value returned is 1 or 0 depending upon whether or not the condition indicated by the operator name is satisfied.
>	greater than	same as above	int	same as above
<=	less than or equal to	same as above	int	same as above
>=	greater than or equal to	same as above	int	same as above

If both operands of the relational operators have arithmetic types, then the usual arithmetic conversions are performed. In case of pointer operands, they must both point to elements of the same aggregate or union. There is one exception to this rule: if one operand, say p, points to the last array element and the other operand, say q, points to an element of the same array, then $p+1$ will be greater than q even though $p+1$ does not point to an element of the array.

1.8 Equality/Inequality Operators

Equality/Inequality Operators
Precedence level 8; associativity left-to-right

operator	name	operand types	result type	comments
==	equality	Both operands must be arithmetic or compatible pointers, or one can be a pointer and the other either a `void` pointer or the null pointer.	`int`	The value returned is 1 or 0 depending upon whether or not the condition indicated by the operator name is satisfied.
!=	inequality	same as above	`int`	same as above

1.9 Bitwise *and* operator

Bitwise *and* operator
Precedence level 9; associativity left-to-right

operator	name	operand types	result type
&	bitwise *and*	integral	The result type is the same as the operand types after the usual arithmetic conversions have been performed.

1.10 Bitwise *exclusive or* Operator

Bitwise *exclusive or* Operator
Precedence level 10; associativity left-to-right

operator	name	operand types	result type
^	bitwise *exclusive or*	integral	The result type is the same as the operand types after the usual arithmetic conversions have been performed.

1.11 Bitwise *inclusive or* Operator

Bitwise *inclusive or* Operator
Precedence level 11; associativity left-to-right

operator	name	operand types	result type
		bitwise *inclusive or*	integral	The result type is the same as the operand types after the usual arithmetic conversions have been performed.

1.12 Logical (Conditional) *and* Operator

Logical (Conditional) *and* Operator
Precedence level 12; associativity left-to-right

operator	name	operand types	result type	comments
&&	logical *and*	scalar	`int`	Result will be 0 if either operand is 0; otherwise the result will be 1. Note that the second operand is not evaluated if the first one is 0.

1.13 Logical (Conditional) *or* Operator

Logical (Conditional) *or* Operator
Precedence level 13; associativity left-to-right

operator	name	operand types	result type	comments
¦ ¦	logical *or*	scalar	int	The result is 1 if either operand is nonzero; otherwise the result will be 0. The second operand is not evaluated if the first is nonzero.

1.14 Conditional Operator

Conditional Operator
Precedence level 14; associativity right-to-left

operator	name	operand types	result type	comments
? :	conditional operator	see below	see below	Takes three operands; see discussion below for explanation of semantics.

The conditional operator is the only operator that requires three operands; it has the form

a ? *b* : *c*

where *a*, *b* and *c* are expressions. If *a* is nonzero, then the above expression evaluates to *b*; otherwise, it evaluates to *c*. Only one of the second or third operands is evaluated. Here is an example of a conditional expression:

```
max = (x>y) ? x : y
```

The result of this expression is the maximum of x and y. In most languages, the above computation would have to be written as (using Pascal syntax)

if x > y **then** max := x **else** max := y

which requires the programmer to make an explicit assignment to a variable (possibly a temporary variable).

The first operand must be a scalar, and the second and third operands must both have arithmetic types, compatible structure or union types, void types or compatible pointer types, or one operand must be a pointer and the other must be the null pointer constant or a `void` pointer.

If the second and third operands have arithmetic types, then the usual arithmetic conversions are performed to determine a common type for the operands, which is then also the result type. If these operands have structure, union or void types, then the result is this type. If these operands are pointers or one is a pointer and the other a null pointer constant, then the result type is the pointer type.

1.15 Assignment Operators

Assignment Operators
Precedence level 15; associativity right-to-left

operator	name	operand types	result type	comments
=	simple assignment	see below	left operand type (without any qualifiers)	If necessary, the right operand is converted to the left operand type before the assignment; also, see below.
*=, /=, %=, +=, -=, <<=, >>=, &=, ^=, !=	compound assignment	see below	left operand type (without any qualifiers)	see below

Both operands of the simple assignment operator must have either arithmetic types, compatible structure or union types, or compatible pointer types. Alternatively, one operand can be a pointer of any type and the other a `void` pointer or the left operand can be a pointer and the right operand the null pointer constant.

The assignment expression

   v = *e*

where *v* is a variable and *e* is an expression, results in the value of *e* becoming the new value of *v*.

In case of the compound operators, the operand types must be arithmetic types as allowed by the corresponding binary operators. There is one exception: for the operators += and -=, the left operand can be a pointer to an object and the right operand an integral expression.

The assignment expression

$$v \; \theta = \; e$$

where $\theta =$ is one of the operators $*=$, $/=$, $\%=$, $+=$, $-=$, $<<=$, $>>=$, $\&=$, $\char`\^=$ and $|=$ is roughly equivalent to the assignment expression

$$v \; = \; v \; \theta \; e$$

The operand and result types of the compound assignment operator can be determined by using this equivalence.

The above equivalence is not quite correct: operand v is evaluated only once in the expression

$$v \; \theta = \; e$$

but it is evaluated twice in the expression

$$v \; = \; v \; \theta \; e$$

This makes a difference only when evaluating v causes a side effect. For example, evaluating the left operand in the assignment expression

```
a[i++] *= n
```

a[i++] has the side effect of incrementing i. Consequently, this assignment is not equivalent to the (ill-defined) assignment

```
a[i++] = a[i++] * n
```

which causes i to be incremented twice.

1.16 Comma Operator

Comma Operator
Precedence level 16; associativity left-to-right

operator	name	result type	comments
,	comma	right operand type	The result of the expression a, b is the value of b; a is evaluated but its value is discarded; a is evaluated only for side effects.

Expressions with the comma operator must be enclosed in parentheses in contexts where the comma has other uses such as separating arguments.

2. Operator Precedence and Associativity Summary

The operators are listed vertically in order of decreasing precedence:

Operator precedence and associativity summary

precedence	operators	symbols	associativity
1	postfix	( ) [ ] . -> ++ --	left-to-right
2	unary	& * + - ~ ! ++ -- sizeof	right-to-left
3	cast	( )	right-to-left
4	multiplicative	* / %	left-to-right
5	additive	+ -	left-to-right
6	bitwise shift	<< >>	left-to-right
7	relational	< > <= >=	left-to-right
8	equality/inequality	== !=	left-to-right
9	bitwise *and*	&	left-to-right
10	bitwise *exclusive or*	^	left-to-right
11	bitwise *inclusive or*	|	left-to-right
12	logical *and*	&&	left-to-right
13	logical *or*	||	left-to-right
14	conditional	? :	right-to-left
15	assignment	= *= /= %= += -= <<= >>= &= ^= !=	right-to-left
16	comma	,	left-to-right

3. Expressions

Expressions are evaluated in an order that is consistent with operator semantics and with operator precedence and associativity rules. As explained earlier, parentheses can be used to change the order of evaluation imposed by the precedence of the operators.

3.1 Constant Expressions

Constant expressions are expressions that can be evaluated at compile time and can be used in places where a constant is expected. Operands allowed in constant expressions are integer, character and floating-point constants, and enumerators. Constant expressions cannot contain assignment, increment, decrement or comma operators, or function calls. Operands of the `sizeof` operator can be arbitrary expressions, because the size of an expression can be determined from its type at compile time without actually evaluating the expression.

Constant expressions are used in several places, e.g., in the `switch` statement (after the `case`), for specifying array bounds and initializing external and static variables, and in the preprocessor `#if` statement (see Chapter 8). Constant expressions used in `#if` statements cannot contain the `sizeof` and cast operators, or enumerators.

4. Exercises

1. The logical *or* and *and* operators (`||` and `&&`) are conditional logical operators, i.e., their second operands are evaluated only if necessary. Logical operators in other languages such as Pascal and FORTRAN are unconditional operators in that they always evaluate both operands even if the result can be determined by evaluating just one operand. What are the pros and cons of conditional and unconditional logical operators?

2. Unlike FORTRAN, C does not provide an exponentiation operator; it does, however, provide the library function `exp` for performing exponentiation. Give one reason for not providing an exponentiation operator. Suppose you have to write an exponentiation function (only for positive integer exponents). The obvious, but inefficient, way of implementing exponentiation to an integer value is to use repeated multiplications. A better algorithm is

```
a = x;  b = y;  z = 1;   /*zaᵇ≡xʸ initially*/
                         /*at the end of the*/
                         /*algorithm z≡xʸ */
while (b != 0) {
    if (odd(b)) {
        z *= a;
        b--;
    } else {
        a *= a;
        b /= 2;
    }
}
/*value of "z" is the result */
```

Operation *odd*(x) returns 1 if x is an odd number and 0 if x is an even number. How will you implement operation *odd*?

Are you convinced that this algorithm works? An argument to show that it does can be based on the fact that the program tries to preserve the equivalence relationship $za^b \equiv x^y$ while moving b towards 0. At the end of the algorithm, b will be 0, at which point the equivalence relationship becomes $z \equiv x^y$.

Chapter 4

Control Flow

Control flow statements in C are similar to those found in languages like Pascal and Ada. In the spirit of the structured programming philosophy advocated by Dijkstra [Dahl, Dijkstra & Hoare 1972], these statements are primarily *one-entrance, one-exit* constructs. Although C provides the `goto` statement which has been considered detrimental to program readability and understandability [Dijkstra 1968], it also provides the `break` and `continue` statements for controlled jumps. In contrast, languages like FORTRAN and Pascal do not provide mechanisms for controlled jumps.

1. The *Null* Statement

The *null* statement is denoted by a semicolon:

```
;
```

It is used in situations in which the C syntax requires a statement, but where no statement is logically needed. For example, a *null* statement is used as the body of the following `while` loop

```
while ((c = getchar()) == BLANK)
    ;
```

which skips to the first nonblank character (where `BLANK` is a user-defined constant).

2. The *Expression* Statement

Any expression can be converted to a statement by appending a semicolon to it:

expression;

expression is evaluated and its value is discarded. An expression statement is executed for its side effects.

The assignment statement is a special case of the expression statement. For pedagogical reasons, because it is used quite frequently, I will discuss the assignment statement separately.

77

2.1 Assignment Statement

The assignment statement has the form

   variable = *expression*;

where *variable* is an identifier or an expression that refers to an object, and *variable* and *expression* have appropriate types (see Section 1.15 of Chapter 3). The value of *expression* is the value assigned to the object referred to by *variable*.

Consider two examples:

```
i = j + 3;
*pc = 'c';
```

The first statement assigns the value of j+3 to i (to the object associated with i to be precise), and the second assignment assigns the character constant 'c' to the object pointed to by pc.

Because assignment is an operator in C, multiple variables can be assigned values by using multiple assignment operators in one statement, for example, the multiple assignment

```
i = j = k = 0;
```

assigns 0 to the variables i, j and k. Remember that the value of an assignment expression is the value assigned to the left operand.

An assignment statement can also be constructed from compound-assignment operators. Such an assignment statement has the form

   variable θ= *expression*;

where θ is one of the operators *, /, %, +, -, <<, >>, &, ^, ! (see Section 1.15 of Chapter 3 for more details).

3. The *Compound* Statement or *Block*

A *compound* statement or a *block* is used

- to group many statements into one logical statement,
- as the body of a function and
- to restrict (localize) the visibility of identifiers.

The *compound* statement has the form

```
{
        definitions-and-declarations_opt
        statement-list
}
```

Variables defined inside a *compound* statement override (hide) definitions of variables with the same name for the scope of the *compound* statement. These variables will be visible (accessible) only inside the *compound* statement. Global variables are visible inside a *compound* statement provided their definitions are not overridden by local definitions.

4. The `if` Statement

The `if` statement has two forms:

```
if (expression) statement₁
```

and

```
if (expression)
    statement₁
else
    statement₂
```

If *expression*, which must have a scalar type, evaluates to true (nonzero), then *statement*$_1$ is executed in both cases. If it evaluates to false (zero), then this completes execution of the first form of the `if` statement, while in case of the second form, *statement*$_2$ is executed.[1]

Intermixing the two forms of the `if` statement results in an ambiguity called the "dangling else" problem. For example, the nested `if` statement

```
if (e₁) if (e₂) sₐ else s_b
```

could be interpreted as

```
if (e₁)
    if (e₂)
        sₐ
    else
        s_b
```

or as

---

1. Syntactically, *statement*$_1$ and *statement*$_2$ must be single statements. Consequently, if more than one statement needs to be executed in their place, then these statements must be combined into one logical statement by enclosing them in curly braces (i.e., by using a *compound* statement).

```
if (e₁)
      if (e₂) sₐ
else
      s_b
```

Note that the two interpretations are shown by indenting them appropriately. Unlike human readers, the C compiler is not influenced by indentation.

This ambiguity is resolved by using the rule that an else part is always associated with the syntactically rightmost (innermost) if statement without an else part. Consequently, the first interpretation is the interpretation used in C.

A simple way of avoiding this ambiguity is to avoid mixing the two forms of if statements. A *null* statement may be used when necessary. For example, the second interpretation given above may be written as

```
if (e₁)
      if (e₂)
            sₐ
      else
            ;      /*a semicolon by itself denotes*/
                   /*the null statement*/
else
      s_b
```

Alternatively, compound statements may be used to resolve the ambiguity. For example, the above two interpretations may be written explicitly as

```
if (e₁) {
      if (e₂)
            sₐ
      else
            s_b
}
```

and

```
if (e₁) {
      if (e₂) sₐ
}
else
      s_b
```

5. The switch Statement

The switch statement is used for multiway branching. It has the form

```
switch (e) {
case ce₁:    statement-list₁
case ce₂:    statement-list₂
...
case ceₖ:    statement-listₖ
default:    statement-listₖ₊₁
}
```

The switch expression e is an integral expression, case labels ce_i are integral constant expressions and $statement\text{-}list_i$ represents the ith alternative of the switch statement. The case labels identify the alternatives; no two labels can have the same value. Only one alternative can have the default label.

Execution of the switch statement causes the selection of an alternative whose case label is equal to the value of the switch expression e. If there is no such case label, then the default alternative ($statement\text{-}list_{k+1}$) is executed. After an alternative has been executed, execution continues with the next alternative unless the switch statement is explicitly terminated by a jump statement such as the break statement. If no case label matches the switch expression and there is no default alternative, then this completes execution of the switch statement.

If the actions of two or more alternatives are identical, then these alternatives can be combined by using multiple case labels for an alternative:

```
switch (e) {
case ce₁₁:  case ce₁₂:  ...  :  case ce₁ₙ₁:  statement-list₁
case ce₂₁:  case ce₂₂:  ...  :  case ce₂ₙ₂:  statement-list₂
    ...
case ceₖ₁:  case ceₖ₂:  ...  :  case ceₖₙₖ:  statement-listₖ
default:  statement-listₖ₊₁
}
```

An example of a switch statement is a program segment from a simple Polish notation interpreter:

```
switch (c) {
case '+':  add;   break;
case '-':  subtract;  break;
case '*':  multiply;  break;
case '/':  divide;  break;
default:  put on stack;
}
```

As illustrated in the above example, a jump statement, usually the break statement, is often used to make the switch statement alternatives mutually exclusive. Also, the `default` alternative is not required by C. In the interest of program readability, reliability and modifiability the `switch` statement alternatives should be made mutually exclusive.

6. Loops

There are three kinds of loops: the `while`, the `do` and the `for` loops.

6.1 The `while` Statement

The `while` statement has the form

> `while` (*expression*) *statement*

where the type of *expression* must be a scalar. The loop body, i.e., *statement*, is repeatedly executed as long as *expression* is nonzero. The loop test *expression* is evaluated prior to each execution of *statement*.

6.2 The `do` Statement

The `do` statement has the form

> `do` *statement* `while` (*expression*);

where the type of *expression* must be a scalar. The loop body, i.e., *statement*, is executed as long as *expression* is nonzero. Unlike the `while` statement, the `do` statement evaluates the loop test *expression* after each execution of *statement*. Consequently, *statement* will be executed at least once, even if *expression* is false to start with. The `do` loop is the counterpart of the *repeat* loop in Pascal, with one difference. The *repeat* loop is executed until some terminating condition becomes true while the `do` loop, as mentioned earlier, is executed as long as some condition is true.

6.3 The `for` Statement

The `for` statement has the form

> `for` (*expression-1*$_{opt}$; *expression-2*$_{opt}$; *expression-3*$_{opt}$) *statement*

`for` loop expressions must be scalar expressions. *expression-1* is the loop initialization, *expression-2* is the loop test and *expression-3* is the loop reinitialization. If *expression-2* is omitted, it is replaced by a nonzero constant (i.e., the loop test always evaluates to true).

The `for` loop is a convenient way of expressing the following paradigm written using the `while` loop:

$$expression-1_{opt};$$
```
while (expression-2) {
    statement
    expression-3_opt;
}
```

The `for` loop with expressions *expression-1* and *expression-3* missing

```
for (; expression-2; ) statement
```

is equivalent to the `while` loop

```
while (expression-2) statement
```

The `for` loop with all the expressions missing

```
for (;;) statement
```

is equivalent to the `while` loop

```
while (1) statement
```

This loop is an infinite loop and it can be terminated only by explicitly exiting from it by executing a `break`, `goto` or `return` statement (given in the body of the loop).

Although it looks similar, the `for` loop of C is not the semantic counterpart of the iterative *for* loops of Pascal and Ada, or the iterative `do` loops of FORTRAN and PL/I. The C `for` loop is more general than the *for* and *do* loops of the other languages; however, unlike these other loops, the number of iterations of C's `for` loop cannot, in general, be determined prior to the execution of the loop.

The `for` loop and its alternative `while` loop form have almost equivalent semantics; however, their semantics are not identical, as indicated in the *C Reference Manual* [Ritchie 1980]. For example, consider the case when statement *s* is the `continue` statement or a *compound* statement containing the `continue` statement. The effect of the `continue` statement is to skip to the end of the loop. This has different effects in the `for` loop and its equivalent `while` loop form. In the case of the `for` loop, the reinitialization expression *expression-3* is executed prior to evaluating *expression-2*, while in the case of the equivalent `while` loop, the reinitialization expression *expression-3* is skipped.

7. Statement Labels

Any statement in a C program can be prefixed by a label:

label: *statement*

where *label* is an identifier. Statements are labeled so that they can be targets of goto statements (see next section).

The scope of a label is the body of the function containing it and its lifetime is the lifetime of the function.

8. Jump Statements

The goto, break, continue and return statements cause program execution to jump from one part of a program to another.

8.1 The goto Statement

A goto statement is used to jump to a statement with the specified label. The goto statement has the form

        goto *label*;

Unrestricted and frequent use of gotos in a program will make the program difficult to read and comprehend [Dijkstra 1968]. break and continue statements, which are restricted forms of the goto statement, should be used in preference to goto statements whenever possible.

8.2 The break Statement

The break statement has the form

        break;

The break statement is used to exit from the immediately enclosing while, do, for or switch statements. For example, the effect of the break statement in the bodies of following loops is equivalent to a goto to the label next.[2]

```
while (...) {
    ...
    break;
    ...
}
next:;
```

---

2. Assuming that the break statement is not inside a nested loop or switch statement.

```
do {
    ...
    break;
    ...
} while (...);
next:;


for (...) {
    ...
    break;
    ...
}
next:;
```

8.3 The `continue` Statement

The `continue` statement is used to skip the remaining portion of the current iteration of the immediately enclosing loop. The next iteration is then initiated provided it is allowed by the loop conditions; otherwise, the loop is terminated. The `continue` statement has the form

```
continue;
```

The effect of the `continue` statement in the bodies of following loops is equivalent to a `goto` to the label `next`.[3]

```
while (...) {
    ...
    continue;
    ...
    next:;
}
```

---

3. Assuming that the `continue` statement is not inside a nested loop.

```
do {
    ...
    continue;
    ...
    next:;
} while (...);
```

```
for (...) {
    ...
    continue;
    ...
    next:;
}
```

8.4 The return Statement

A return statement is used inside a function body ==to terminate the function== executing it, return a function result, if appropriate, and return control to the calling function. The return statement has the form

> return *expression*$_{opt}$;

expression is omitted when used in a function whose result type is void. A function can have zero or more return statements. The return statement is discussed in more detail in Chapter 5.

9. Exercises

1. What is the result of executing the following program segment:

    ```
    int i, test[2];

    i = 0;
    test[i] = i = i + 1;
        /*multiple assignment with side effects*/
    ```

    Confirm your result experimentally by running a test program on your C compiler.

2. Write a nested if statement equivalent to the general form of the switch statement shown in the text. Is the nested if statement more powerful than the switch statement?

3. The switch statement does not require the use of the break statement at the end of each alternative. If some or all of these break statements were omitted, then can this version of the switch statement be simulated easily using if statements?

4. Suggest an alternative syntax for the `if` statement that will avoid the ambiguity problem arising from nesting the two forms of `if` statements.

5. Why are constant integer expressions required in `case` labels of the `switch` statement? What would be the impact of allowing general integer expressions instead of constant integer expressions? Examine both user convenience and implementation aspects.

6. The *for* loops in FORTRAN, Pascal and Ada always terminate; the `for` loop in C is more general and it may or may not terminate. What restrictions can be imposed upon the form of the `for` loop in C so that it will always terminate?

Chapter 5

Functions and Complete Programs

Control abstraction is provided in C by means of functions. Functions can be recursive. C does not have a syntactic construct specially for specifying subroutines (procedures); but, functions with the `void` return (result) type are equivalent to subroutines.

1. Function Declarations (Prototypes)

A function must be declared or defined before it can be referenced. Function declarations must also be given if independently compiled functions (functions defined in other files) are referenced.

Function declarations have the form

$static_{opt}$ *result-type function-name* (*parameter-type-or-decl-list$_{opt}$*) ;

A function is given the `extern` storage class, by default; specifying its storage class to be `static` restricts its visibility to the file containing its definition.

If the function parameter types are specified in a function declaration, i.e., if the first form of the declaration is used, then the declaration is called a *function prototype*. In the first form of the declaration, the parameter type or declaration list is a list of the function parameter types or their declarations. The list can be terminated by a trailing ellipsis "`...`" indicating that information about the remaining parameters is not available. The ellipsis notation specifies that the function accepts a variable number of arguments (e.g., the library function `fprintf`). A parameter type list that consists only of the type `void` specifies a parameterless function.

The second form of the function declaration ensures upward compatibility with K&R C. It says nothing about the function parameters.

Because function prototypes contain information about parameters, they allow function calls to be checked for syntactic correctness (this is done at compile time). I shall therefore, in this book, use function prototypes instead of the ordinary function declarations.

Here are some examples of function declarations:

```
void free(void *ptr);
double root();
int rand(void);
int isalnum(int c);
int fprintf(FILE *stream, const char *format, ...);
char *strcpy(char *s1, const char *s2);
```

The effect of these function declarations is as follows:

1. `free` is declared a function with a parameter of type `void *` and which does not return a value.

2. `root` is declared as a function for whose parameters no information is available and which returns a `double` value (K&R C style function declaration),

3. `rand` is declared as a parameterless function that returns an `int` value.

4. `isalnum` is declared as a function with an `int` parameter and which returns an `int` value.

5. `fprintf` is declared as a function with a variable number of parameters and which returns an `int` value. Its first parameter is of type `FILE *` and its second parameter is of type `const char *`. Information about the remaining parameters is not known.

6. `strcpy` is declared as a function with two parameters, one of type `char *` and the other of type `const char *`, and which returns a `char *` value.

Except for the declaration of `root`, all the other function declarations are function prototypes.

1.1 Function Specifications

The user interface of a function, called the "syntactic specification" of a function, by convention, consists of two parts:

1. A list of `#include` statements specifying the header files to be included. These files usually contain the function declaration and other related declarations.

2. The function prototype, or the K&R C function declaration along with parameter declarations.

Typically, the function declaration is contained in the specified header files.

A function specification provides the user with sufficient information to

1. include all files necessary for using the function,
2. declare variables that will be used as arguments,

3. declare variables that will be used to store the function result,
4. use a function in an expression in a manner consistent with its type and
5. write syntactically correct function calls.

A function specification does not supply any semantic information about what the function does other than what is implied by the function name and type, and the parameter names and types.

Here is an example of a function specification:

```
#include <stdio.h>
int putc(char c, FILE *stream);
```

2. Function Definitions

Function definitions can have one of two forms:[1]

$static_{opt}$ *result-type function-name* (*parameter-type-or-decl-list*)
{
    definitions-and-declarations$_{opt}$
    statement-list
}

or

$static_{opt}$ *result-type function-name* (*parameter-list$_{opt}$*)
    parameter-declarations$_{opt}$
{
    definitions-and-declarations$_{opt}$
    statement-list
}

Functions cannot return arrays or functions, but they can return pointers to arrays and functions. As mentioned earlier, the default storage class of a function is `extern`; specifying its storage class to be `static` restricts its visibility to the file containing its definition.

The first form of the function definition is called the function prototype definition (it corresponds to the function prototype declaration). As with declarations, the parameter type or declaration list is a list of parameter types or parameter declarations that can be terminated by a trailing ellipsis to indicate that the function accepts a variable number of arguments. The second

---

1. Specification of the *result-type* of a function is optional in C. If the result type is not specified, then it is assumed to be `int`.

form of the function definition is a carry over from K&R C to ensure upward compatibility with existing C programs.

There is one important difference in using these two forms of function definitions. Use of the first form forces arguments in a function call to be converted so that they correspond to the parameter types. In case of the K&R C form of a function definition, default argument conversions are performed (discussed later).

Functions terminate by completing execution of their bodies or by executing a `return` statement which has the form

```
return result_opt ;
```

Functions that return a result (i.e., functions with a result type that is not `void`) should only terminate by executing a `return` statement that returns a result.

As a simple example of a function definition, consider the following function `max` that computes the maximum of its two parameters:

File: `max.c`
```
int max(int a, int b)
{
    return a > b ? a : b;
}
```

This function definition is a prototype definition. Using the alternative K&R C form of function definitions, the above function would be defined as

```
int max(a, b)
    int a, b;
{
    return a > b ? a : b;
}
```

2.1 Function Parameters

Function parameters behave just like automatic local variables in the function body. Parameter declarations are similar to variable definitions. The only storage class that can be explicitly associated with parameters is `register`. Parameters declared as arrays and functions are "adjusted" to make them pointers to the corresponding array element type and function type, respectively.

When declaring array parameters, the size of the first dimension may be omitted, e.g.,

```
int a[], int b[4], int d[][4], int e[2][4]
      /*legal array parameter declarations*/
```

The parameter declaration

```
int c[][] /*invalid array parameter declaration*/
```

is illegal because the size of the second dimension of c has not been specified.

2.2 Referencing Functions Before Their Definitions: An Example

As was mentioned before, functions can be referenced before their definitions are encountered; functions defined in other files can also be referenced, provided they have the storage class extern. In both cases, the references should be preceded by function declarations. The following is an example:

```
   void add(char *x, item_type it);
   int in_table(char *x);
      ...
   main(void)
5  {
      char *a; item_type it;
      ...
      if (!in_table(a))
          add(a, it);
10    ...
   }

   void add(char *x, item_type it)
              /*add item x which has the token*/
15            /*type it to the symbol table   */
   {
     ...
   }

20 int in_table(char *x)
   {
     ...
   }
     ...
```

Note that the declarations of functions add and in_table (lines 1–2) precede references to these functions (lines 8 and 9). Had the definitions of functions add and in_table (lines 13–18 and lines 20–23) been given before the definition of main, then it would not have been necessary to give their declarations.

3. Calling Functions

Function calls have two forms:[2]

> *function-name* (*argument-list$_{opt}$*)

or

> *ptr-to-function* (*argument-list$_{opt}$*)

function-name is an identifier, *ptr-to-function* is an expression and the argument[3] list consists of expressions specifying values to be passed to the function; these values are assigned to the corresponding parameters.

Here are some examples of calls to functions that return values:

```
a = max(a, 5);
max(max(a, 5), e)
while ((c = getchar()) != EOF) { ... }
fs = fopen(argv[1], "r");
```

Now here are examples of calls to functions that do not return a value:

```
delay(0.5);
least_square(x, y, n, &a, &b);
partition(a, 1, u, &i, &j);
quicksort(a, 1, j);
```

3.1 Automatic Conversion of Arguments

Arguments that are array expressions and function designators are converted to pointers to the first array elements and pointers to functions, respectively. If the K&R C form has been used to define or declare a function (note that either a function declaration or a definition must have been encountered before the function call), then integral promotions are performed on each argument and all `float` arguments are converted to `double`. These conversions are called the *default argument promotions*. If the number and type of arguments does not match the number and type of parameters, then the behavior is undefined.

---

2. To be precise, functions calls have only one form: the one in which the function is specified by a pointer to the function. The first function call form automatically gets converted to the second form; the function name is converted to a pointer to the function. I have listed the first form separately because it is the form that is used most often.

3. Identifiers specified in a function header are called "parameters". The expressions specified in a function call are called "arguments". Parameters and arguments are also called "formal parameters" and "actual parameters", respectively.

If the function prototype form has been used to define or declare the function, then the arguments are implicitly converted to the types of the parameters. The default argument promotions are used for the arguments that correspond to the trailing ellipsis in the function prototype. If the number and type of arguments do not match those in the corresponding function prototype, the C compiler will flag an error.

3.2 Passing Arguments

Arguments are "passed by value" in C, i.e., argument values are copied to the parameters before the function is executed. Thus argument values become the initial values of the parameters.

Passing arguments by value means that argument values cannot be changed by calling a function, because the final parameter values are not copied back to the arguments. To change object values by calling functions, pointers to objects, rather than the objects themselves, are passed as arguments. Although the argument values (the pointers) themselves cannot be changed, the objects pointed to by the arguments can be changed. Pointers to objects are also passed to avoid copying objects, especially large objects. Note that in case of an array argument, the array is not passed to the function; instead, C automatically passes a pointer to the array.

3.3 An Example of Argument Passing

Consider the function `swap` that is supposed to exchange the values of its parameters:

```
      /*initial version of "swap"*/
void swap(int a, int b)
{
      int temp;

      temp = a;
      a = b;
      b = temp;
}
```

Calling this function has no effect on the arguments; e.g., the call

```
    swap(x, y);
```

has no effect on the values of `x` and `y` (which are `int` variables). This is because the values of the arguments `x` and `y` are copied to the parameters `a` and `b`, respectively, and only the parameter values are exchanged. Values of `x` and `y` are left unchanged.

Function `swap` must be modified if it is to exchange the values of its arguments. This version of `swap` will expect to receive the addresses, rather than the values, of the variables whose values are to be exchanged:

File: `swap.c`

```
void swap (int *a, int *b)
{
    int t;
    t = *a;
    *a = *b;
    *b = t;
}
```

To swap the values of **x** and **y**, their addresses must now be passed to function `swap`. The *address-of* operator & is used to determine addresses as illustrated in the following function call:

```
swap(&x, &y);
```

Note the difference in the two versions of `swap`: when addresses of objects are passed as arguments, the dereferencing operator * must be used to reference the objects.

3.4 Passing Functions as Arguments

A function can be passed as an argument by giving the function name as the argument. The value that is actually passed is the address of the function. As an example, consider a function `compare` that compares two elements of structure type `employee` and returns 1 if the value of its first operand precedes the value of its second operand according to some ordering rule; otherwise it returns 0:

```
int compare(employee e1, employee e2);
```

`compare` is passed as an argument to a function `sort` that sorts arrays with elements of type `employee`:

```
sort(emp, n, compare);
```

`emp` is the array to be sorted, `n` is the size of the array and `compare` is the ordering function discussed above.

The definition of `sort` may look like

```
void sort(employee a[], int n, int (*fp)())
        /*fp points to the comparison function*/
{
    ...
    if (fp(a[i], a[j])) ...
    ...
}
```

The ability to pass functions as arguments is very useful. For example, suppose that the call

```
    sort(emp, n, greater);
```

where greater is a comparison function, sorts array emp in increasing order. greater(x, y) returns 1 if x is greater than y according to some ordering rule; otherwise, it returns 0.

Now consider the function smaller that does the opposite. smaller(x, y) returns 1 if x is smaller than y; otherwise it returns 0. To sort an array in decreasing order, sort is called with smaller as an argument, e.g., the call

```
    sort(emp, n, smaller);
```

will sort the array emp in decreasing order.

By parameterizing sort with a comparison function, an array can be sorted according to any ordering rule. This allows us to write a *generic* sort function, i.e., a sort function that represents a family of sort functions.

4. Functions With Variable Number of Parameters

ANSI C provides facilities for writing, in a portable manner, functions that accept a variable number of arguments. These facilities consist of the type va_list, and the macros va_start and va_arg, and the function va_end.

As an example, consider the function print_strings that takes a variable number of strings (of type char *) as arguments and prints each string on a new line:

```
                                                    File: var.c
    #include <stdarg.h>
    #include <stdio.h>

    void print_strings(int n, ...)
5   {
        va_list ap;
        int i;

        va_start(ap, n);
10              /*n is the last parameter before*/
                /*the ... in the function header*/
        for (i = 0; i < n; i++)
            printf("%s\n", va_arg(ap, char *));
        va_end(ap);
    }
```

Header file stdarg.h (line 1) contains definitions of the variable argument macros. First a variable of type va_list is defined (line 6), then accessing of the arguments is initiated by calling macro va_start (line 9); each new argument is accessed by calling macro va_arg (line 11) and, finally, accessing of the variables is terminated by calling macro va_end. Note that the parameter preceding the variable parameters specified by the ellipsis, i.e., n, has a special significance; it is the one given as the second argument in the va_start macro invocation (line 8).

5. Controlling Function Visibility

Functions cannot be nested in C. Consequently, it is not possible to define functions that are local to another function; that is, it is not possible to define functions that are not visible outside the function containing them. This restriction is not a problem in most practical situations, because function visibility can be controlled by using the static attribute. For example, suppose that function a is to be called only from within function b. This restriction on the visibility of a can be implemented by defining just the functions a and b in a separate file, and specifying the storage class of a to be static:

```
static int a(...)
{
    ...
}

int b(...)
{
    ...
}
```

6. Scope and Lifetime of Identifiers: An Example

As an example of the scope and lifetime of identifiers, consider the following
program skeleton:

File: scope.c

```
   #include <math.h>
   extern float lower, upper;
   static float accuracy;
   float f(float a);
5
   float integrate(float (*fp)(float), float a,
                                  float b, float eps)
   {
       float sum;
10
       ... fabs(...) ...
   }

   main(void)
15 {
       ... integrate(f, lower, upper, accuracy); ...
   }

   float f(float a)
20 {
       float accuracy;

       ...
   }
```

The scope of the identifiers fabs (line 1; declaration is contained in the
header file math.h), lower and upper (line 2), f (line 4) and
integrate (line 6) ranges from their declarations and definitions to the end

of the file `scope.c` and to other files containing matching declarations and definitions. The scope of identifier `accuracy` (line 3) is restricted to file `scope.c` and it also does not include the body of function `f` (lines 20–24) which contains a local variable with the same name. The lifetime of these `extern` and `static` identifiers is the lifetime of the program. The scope of the local identifier `accuracy` ranges from its definition (line 21) to the end of the function `f` (line 24) and its lifetime is the same as the lifetime of `f`.

The scope of the parameters of the functions ranges from their declarations to the end of the body of the function containing them.

7. Input/Output

C programs read input from and write output to logical files called "streams" which are associated with files.[4] Streams hide details associated with files such as the block size and the type of device on which they are located. There are two kinds of streams: text and binary. Text streams are sequences of lines, each of which is a sequence of characters terminated with the newline character. Binary streams are sequences of characters which correspond to the internal representation of data.

Streams are associated with files by opening the files and they are referenced using stream pointers which point to objects of the predefined type `FILE` (defined in the header file `stdio.h`). A stream pointer refers to a structure that contains information about the corresponding file, e.g., its location, file buffers and a file position indicator.

Normally three streams, called the *standard streams*, are opened automatically for every program. These streams are the standard input, the standard output and the standard error streams. The standard error stream is used for writing error and diagnostic messages. By default, the standard input stream is associated with the keyboard and the standard output and error streams are associated with the display. Using separate output streams for normal output, and for error and diagnostic output allows the separation of these two outputs written to them (by means of output redirection; see Section 8).

The standard streams are referenced using predefined constant pointers whose definitions are stored in the header file `stdio.h`:

---

4. A *file* is an entity supported by the operating system controlling the computer; files are used to hold text or data permanently.

stream pointer	associated file
stdin	standard input file
stdout	standard output file
stderr	standard error file

Each of the standard stream pointers is an expression of type FILE *. By default, the standard input and output streams are buffered but the standard error stream is not.[5]

C has many functions and macros for reading from and writing to streams, and for stream manipulation. I will briefly some of describe them in this section; for details, see Appendix C.

First, here are some of the input functions and macros:

input functions and macros	explanation
getc	Get the next character from the specified stream (macro).
getchar	Get the next character from stdin.
fgetc	Same as getc, but fgetc is a function.
getw	Get the next word from the specified stream.
scanf	Read different types of variables from stdin as specified in the format string.
fscanf	Read different types of variables from the specified stream as specified in the format string.
gets	Get a string from stdin.
fgets	Get a string from the specified stream.

Now, here are some of the output functions and macros:

---

5. Input from and output to a file is most efficiently performed in blocks of *pbs* characters, where *pbs* is the physical block size associated with the device on which the file is located. Prior to the first program input request, a block of *pbs* characters is read from the file into an internal buffer. The program reads its input from this array, instead of from the file. The next block of characters is read only when necessary. Similarly, program output is collected in another internal buffer; the contents of this array are written to the file only when the array is filled or upon program completion. The standard error stream is not buffered so that output written to it is made available to the programmer at the earliest possible moment.

output functions and macros	explanation
putc	Write a character to the specified stream (macro).
putchar	Write a character to stdout.
fputc	Same as putc, but fputc is a function.
putw	Write a word to the specified stream.
printf	Write the list of values specified on stdout as specified in the format string.
fprintf	Write a list of values specified on the specified stream as specified in the format string.
puts	Write a string to stdout.
fputs	Write a string to the specified stream.

Most of these functions and macros take a stream pointer as one of their arguments. However, some commonly used input and output functions and macros do not take a stream pointer as an argument; they implicitly write to the standard streams.

The following examples illustrate the use of the input and output functions and macros:

```
putchar(':');

printf("copy: cannot open file %s\n", src);

printf("%f\n", sine(x * 3.1416/180.0, eps));
                /*sine is a user-defined function*/

fprintf(stderr, "Error, No free storage0);

scanf("%f%c%f",&a,&opr,&b);

while ((c = fgetc(fs)) != EOF) ... ;
```

Several miscellaneous functions are used in manipulating data. Function ungetc is used to push a character back to the input stream; this character can be subsequently read (more precisely, it can be reread). Functions fseek and rewind are used to reposition the *file position indicator* associated with a stream. A file position indicator marks the position in the file from which input will be read or to which output will be written. Function sprintf is used to write output to a string; function sscanf is used to read input from a string. These two functions may be used for converting data items from one format to another.

7.1 Using Streams Other Than The Standard Streams

A stream is associated with a file by opening the file for reading or writing, for example, by calling function `fopen` with an appropriate argument; note that `fopen` returns a stream pointer. Data can be read from the file by using a function such as `fscanf` and data can be written to a file using a function such as `fprintf`. When the stream is no longer needed, it must be closed by calling function `fclose`. Note that all streams are closed automatically upon program termination.

The following program segment illustrates the use of a stream other than one of the standard streams:

```
     #include <stdio.h>
     #include "db.h"
     main(void)
     {
5        FILE *fp;
         char *dbfile; /*points to the database*/
                       /*file name             */
         int i;

10       ...

         if ((fp = fopen(dbfile, "r")) == NULL) {
           fprintf(stderr,"Cannot open %s\n",dbfile);
           exit(1);
15       }
         ...
         while(fscanf(fp,"%s%s%s%s%s%s%s%s",
             db[i]->name, db[i]->room, db[i]->ext,
             db[i]->desig, db[i]->compid, db[i]->sig,
20           db[i]->logid, db[i]->maild) == 8)
         {
             ...
         }
         ...
25       fclose(fp);
     }
```

7.2 Redirection of Input and Output

On many systems, including the UNIX and MS-DOS systems, standard streams can be associated with files instead of with the keyboard and the display. This is done by redirecting the standard streams.[6] In the following example, I will illustrate redirection of the standard input, output and error streams on the UNIX system.

Suppose a C program, which is stored in file `enhance.c`, reads its input from the standard input stream and writes it output to the standard output stream. This program is compiled and its executable version is stored in the file `enhance` by the following command:

```
cc -o enhance enhance.c
```

By default, program `enhance` expects to get its input directly from the keyboard[7] because it reads its input from the standard input stream; similarly, it sends the output to the display because it writes output to the standard output stream. This is the mode of operation when `enhance` is executed as the command

```
enhance
```

By default, all output written to the standard error stream is sent to the display.

Input for program `enhance` can be redirected so that it is read from a file instead of from the keyboard by using the UNIX command-level input redirection operator `<`. For example, in the command

```
enhance <data
```

`enhance` takes its input from the file `data`. (Program `enhance.c` has not been changed!) Output is still sent directly to the display.

The output produced by `enhance` can also be redirected so that it goes to a specified file instead of to the display. For example, the command

```
enhance >result
```

directs `enhance` to send its output to the file `result`. However, output written to the standard error stream is still sent to the display. Error output is redirected using the operator `2>`:

```
enhance >result 2>error
```

---

6. On the MS-DOS system, the standard error stream cannot be redirected.

7. End of input on UNIX systems is indicated by a typing a line with the control-D character ^D and on MS-DOS systems by typing a line with the control-Z character ^Z followed by a carriage return.

Input and output can be redirected simultaneously, e.g.,

```
enhance <data >result
```

8. Main Programs

A typical C program has the form

> *preprocessor statements (macro definitions, file inclusions)*
> *declarations and definitions*
> main (*parameter-type-or-decl-list*)
> {
>> *definitions-and-declarations$_{opt}$*
>> *statement-list*
>
> }
> *function-definitions*

where all of the above text is contained in one file. A C program can also be split across many files. In every C program, there must be a function named main; this is the function that is executed first.

The form given for C main programs is informal and it does not cover all cases. For example,

- C preprocessor statements can be given anywhere in the file (and this is often done) and are not restricted to the initial portion of a program.

- Function definitions can precede the definition of main.

To allow the writing of parameterized commands, i.e., commands that can be called with arguments, C allows command-line arguments to be passed to the main function. The declaration of the parameters of main are illustrated by the following program segment:

```
main(int argc, char *argv[])
        /*argc: number of arguments   */
        /*argv: array of pointers to  */
        /*      command-line arguments*/
{
   ...
}
```

Suppose a complete program cmd.c is compiled, named cmd and is executed as the command

cmd a_1 a_2 ... a_n

Inside the main program in `cmd.c`, `argc` has the value *n*+1, where *n* is the number of command line arguments (`argc` is *n*+1 because the command name is implicitly passed as the first argument). Elements of array `argv` point to the name of the program and to the arguments. Element `argv[0]` points to the name of the compiled program; elements `argv[1]`, `argv[2]`, ..., `argv[argc-1]` are pointers to the arguments given to command `cmd`. Each of these arguments is a string of characters terminated by the null character \0. Finally, `argv[argc]` is the null pointer constant.

As an example, consider the command `echo`, which just prints its command-line arguments:

File: echo.c

```
     #include <stdio.h>
     #include <stdlib.h>

     main(int argc, char *argv[])
5    {
         int i;

         for (i = 1; i < argc; i++)
             printf("%s ", argv[i]);
10       printf("\n");

         exit(EXIT_SUCCESS);
     }
```

9. Examples

I will now give several examples to illustrate the versatility of C for writing a variety of programs. The first example is a simple text processing application. The second example, taken from a prototype electronic form system, produces a 2-dimensional display from a tabular description. The third example underlines text that is be displayed on a Hewlett-Packard 2621 CRT terminal (HP2621). To produce an underlined display, control characters must be sent to the terminal to tell it when to start underlining and when to stop. The fourth and fifth examples, computation of the *sine* function and curve fitting, illustrate C's usefulness for scientific programming. The sixth example, the *quicksort* sorting algorithm, illustrates the use of recursion. The seventh example is a simple device driver. The eighth example, on integration, illustrates the passing of functions as arguments. The final example, that of linearly searching an array, illustrates simple pointer arithmetic and the use of both the `typedef` and the structure tag mechanisms in a single declaration.

9.1 Stripping Formatting Characters Sequences From Ada Program Text

When I was writing Ada programs for publication in a book [Gehani 1983b], I had to insert font control characters, macros and escape characters in the program text. To test the programs directly from their machine readable form, the font control characters, macros and escape characters had to be stripped off and replaced by appropriate equivalent characters where necessary.

The problem is to write a program that performs the following actions on the font control characters, macros and escape characters:

character sequence	explanation	action
\fI	change to italic font	remove
\fR	change to roman font	remove
\fP	change to previous font	remove
\fB	change to bold font	remove
\-	minus sign	replace by -
$-$	minus sign	replace by -
dd	macro	replace by --
$*$	macro	replace by *
$star$	macro	replace by *
app	macro	replace by '

The backslash and dollar characters are used in Ada program text only as described above and not for any other purpose.

As an example, consider the following Ada routine

```
procedure SWAP(X,Y:in out FLOAT) is
    T: FLOAT; --temporary variable
begin
    T := X;
    X := Y;
    Y := T;
end SWAP;
```

which was produced by the using the following text:

```
\fBprocedure\fR SWAP(X,Y:\fBin out\fR FLOAT) \fBis\fR
    T: FLOAT; $dd$temporary variable
\fBbegin\fR
    T := X;
    X := Y;
    Y := T;
\fBend\fR SWAP;
```

The above text must be stripped of the formatting characters before it can be compiled and executed as an Ada program:

```
procedure SWAP(X,Y:in out FLOAT) is
          T: FLOAT; --temporary variable
begin
          T := X;
          X := Y;
          Y := T;
end SWAP;
```

The program that removes the formatting character sequences is based on the following abstract algorithm, which is described using a mixture of C and English:

```
while ((c = getchar()) != EOF)
    if (c == '$')
        switch (c = getchar()) {
        case '-': replace $-$ by minus sign; break;
        case 'd': replace $dd$ by 2 minus signs; break;
        case 's': replace $star$ by *; break;
        case '*': replace $*$ by *; break;
        case 'a': replace $app$ by '; break;
        default: print error message;
    } else if (c == '\\')
        switch (c = getchar()) {
        case '-': replace \- by minus sign; break;
        case 'f': remove \fx where x is B, I, R or P;
                                          break;
        default: print error message;
    } else
        putchar(c);
```

The final program is

File: clean.c

```
   #include <stdio.h>
   #include <stdlib.h>

   void fatal(char *s);
 5 void replace(char in[], char out[]);
   main(void)
   {
       int c;
       while ((c = getchar()) != EOF)
10         if (c == '$')
               switch (c = getchar()) {
               case '-':
                   replace("$", "-"); break;
               case 'd':
15                 replace("d$", "--"); break;
               case 's':
                   replace("tar$", "*"); break;
               case '*':
                   replace("$", "*"); break;
20             case 'a':
                   replace("pp$", "'"); break;
               default:
                   fatal("misuse of $");
           } else if (c == '\\')
25             switch (c = getchar()) {
               case '-':
                   putchar('-'); break;
               case 'f':
                   if ((c = getchar()) != 'B' &&
30                     c != 'I' && c != 'R' &&
                       c != 'P')
                       fatal("B/I/R/P expected");
                   break;
               default:
35                 fatal("misuse of \\");
           } else
               putchar(c);
       exit(EXIT_SUCCESS);
   }
```

File: replace.c

```
#include <stdio.h>

void fatal(char *s);
void replace(char in[], char out[])
{
    int i;

    for (i = 0; in[i] != '\0'; i++)
        if (getchar() != in[i])
            fatal("bad string");
    printf("%s", out);
}
```

File: fatal.c

```
#include <stdio.h>
#include <stdlib.h>

void fatal(char *s)
{
    fprintf(stderr, "Error, %s\n", s);
    exit(EXIT_FAILURE);
}
```

9.2 Producing the Form Display From a Table

The problem is to write a program that takes tabular input describing the display part of a 2-dimensional electronic form and produces a 2-dimensional version of the form. The form uses a 2-dimensional display with 79 columns and 23 rows. It has border lines in columns 0 and 78 (using the character |), and in rows 0 and 22 (using the character –).

The tabular input describing the form gives the rectangular coordinates of the items to be displayed. The position of each item is described by a data line; each such line has the format

RowNumber ColumnNumber DisplayText

where $1 \leqslant RowNumber \leqslant 21$ and $1 \leqslant ColumnNumber \leqslant 77$. For example, the input

```
1 20 Tuition Reimbursement Application
1 60 Form#:
3 5 Last Name, Initials:
3 50 Company Id#:
4 5 Room#:
4 30 Extension:
6 5 School Name:
7 5 Address:
9 7 Course#
9 20 Title
9 35 Credits
9 50 Tuition
10 3 1.
11 3 2.
12 3 3.
13 40 Total Cost
15 5 Working for Diploma? Yes or No:
16 10 Diploma Title:
17 10 Credits Required:
17 35 Credits Finished:
19 5 Signature:
19 30 Date:
20 7 Supervisor Signature:
20 50 Date:
21 7 Department Head Signature:
21 50 Date:
```

should lead to the production of the following 2-dimensional image (shown in reduced size characters):

```
|------------------------------------------------------------------|
|              Tuition Reimbursement Application       Form#:       |
|                                                                   |
|    Last Name, Initials:                      Company Id#:         |
|    Room#:                    Extension:                           |
|                                                                   |
|    School Name:                                                   |
|    Address:                                                       |
|                                                                   |
|       Course#        Title          Credits          Tuition      |
| 1.                                                                |
| 2.                                                                |
| 3.                                                                |
|                                      Total Cost                   |
|                                                                   |
|    Working for Diploma? Yes or No:                                |
|         Diploma Title:                                            |
|         Credits Required:        Credits Finished:                |
|                                                                   |
|    Signature:              Date:                                  |
|       Supervisor Signature:                  Date:                |
|       Department Head Signature:             Date:                |
|------------------------------------------------------------------|
```

The following program converts the tabular input of a form into a 2-dimensional image:

```
     #include <stdio.h>
     #include <stdlib.h>
     #define ROWS 23
     #define COLS 79
 5
     main(void)
     {
         int i, j; /*i is the row and j is the col*/
         char c, display[ROWS][COLS];
10
         /*initialize display*/
             for(i = 0; i < ROWS; i++)
                 for (j = 0; j < COLS; j++)
                     if (j == 0 || j == COLS-1)
15                       display[i][j] = '|';
                     else if (i == 0 || i == ROWS-1)
                         display[i][j] = '-';
                     else
                         display[i][j] = ' ';
20
         /*read the tabular description and*/
         /*construct the form*/
             while(scanf("%d%d%c",&i,&j,&c) != EOF)
                     /*c is used to read the extra*/
25                   /*blank after col#--discard  */
                 while ((c = getchar()) != '\n')
                     display[i][j++] = c;

         /*put the display mask on standard output*/
30           for(i = 0; i < ROWS; i++) {
                 for(j = 0; j < COLS; j++)
                     putchar(display[i][j]);
                 putchar('\n');
             }
35       exit(EXIT_SUCCESS);
     }
```

9.3 Enhancing Form Display on an HP2621 Terminal

This example illustrates how a user program can control the display format of
a terminal. Although the example is specific to a HP2621 terminal, programs
that control the display format of other terminals will be similar.

When providing electronic versions of paper forms, it is important to distinguish the *display text* of a form from the information filled by the user. On terminals, such as bitmap terminals, where different fonts can be used for individual characters, one font can be used for the display text and another for the text filled in by the user. The HP2621 terminal, on which the form is to be displayed and filled out by the user, does not have different fonts. However, underlining can be used to distinguish between the two different texts.

The problem is to write a program that takes a text file and produces a new file with appropriate insertions of the HP2621 escape sequences to underline the letters and digits when the modified file is displayed on a HP2621 terminal.

The underline function of the HP2621 terminal is turned on and off by means of the following character sequences:

code	description
ESC & d A	Enable underline function; subsequent characters sent to the terminal will be underlined on the display screen.
ESC & d @	Disable underline function.

where ESC is the escape character that has the ASCII code 27.

The algorithm to generate a file with the above sequences can be described as the abstract program

```
while ((c = getchar() ) != EOF)
    if ( c is an alphanumeric character ) {
        enable the underline function
        putchar(c);
        print characters up to the first nonalphanumeric character
        disable the underline function
        if (c != EOF) putchar(c);
    }
    else putchar(c);
```

The corresponding C program for enhancing files is

File: hp2621.c

```
#include <stdio.h>
#include <stdlib.h>
#include <ctype.h>
#define START_UNDERLINE "\33&dA"
                /*33 is decimal 27; \33 represents*/
                /*the escape character ESC        */
#define STOP_UNDERLINE "\33&d@"

main(void)
{
    int c;

    while ((c = getchar()) != EOF)
        if (isalnum(c)) {
            fputs(START_UNDERLINE, stdout);
            /*print all characters up to first*/
            /*non-alphanumeric character*/
            do {
                putchar(c);
                c = getchar();
            } while (isalnum(c));
            fputs(STOP_UNDERLINE, stdout);
            if (c != EOF)
                putchar(c);
        }
        else
            putchar(c);
    exit(EXIT_SUCCESS);
}
```

Note that a program like this one that interacts with the hardware by means of escape sequences cannot be written in standard Pascal because control characters such as ESC are not legal elements of Pascal's predefined character type.

9.4 The Sine Function [Wirth 1973]

The following example illustrates the implementation of the *sine* function in which the accuracy of the result is specified by the user (within the bounds of the accuracy that can be achieved with double precision arithmetic). Of course, for normal use it will be more convenient to use the sine function sin provided by C (see Appendix C).

The *sine* of a value x (in radians) is given by the series

$$sine\,(x) = x - \frac{x^3}{3!} + \frac{x^5}{5!} - \cdots + (-1)^{i-1}*\frac{x^{2i-1}}{(2i-1)!} + \cdots$$

Computation of the sine should be terminated when the value of the last term is less than or equal to the sum of the earlier terms multiplied by *eps*, an arbitrary small value.

The above series consists of the recursive terms

$$k_j = k_{j-1}+2$$

$$t_j = -t_{j-1}*\frac{x^2}{k_j*(k_j-1)}$$

where $k_1 = 1$ and $t_1 = x$.

The sine is computed by the function `sine` defined as

File: `sine.c`

```
    #include <math.h>    /*contains decl. of fabs*/
    double sine(x, eps)
        double x, eps; /*computes sine of "x" with*/
                       /*an accuracy of "eps"      */
5   {
        double sum, term;
        int k;

        term = x; k = 1; sum = term;
10      while (fabs(term) > eps*fabs(sum)) {
            k += 2;
            term *= -(x*x) / (k*(k-1));
            sum += term;
        }
15      return sum;
    }
```

9.5 The Least-Squares Method of Curve Fitting [Hamming 1973]

Suppose we have n measured values that are Cartesian coordinates of the form (x_i, y_i) to which we would like to fit a straight line of the form

$$y\,(x) = a + b\,x$$

where coefficients a and b are parameters. The values of these parameters are to be determined by the *least-squares method* which minimizes the sum of the squares of the differences between computed and measured values; i.e., it minimizes the function

$$\sum_{i=1}^{n} [y\,(x_i) - y_i]^2$$

with respect to the coefficients a and b. Differentiating the above expression with respect to a and b, setting the result to and rearranging the resulting equations produces

$$an + b\sum_{i=1}^{n} x_i = \sum_{i=1}^{n} y_i$$

$$a\sum_{i=1}^{n} x_i + b\sum_{i=1}^{n} x_i^2 = \sum_{i=1}^{n} x_i y_i$$

From these equations the values of a and b are determined to be

$$b = \frac{\sum\limits_{i=1}^{n} x_i \sum\limits_{i=1}^{n} y_i - n\sum\limits_{i=1}^{n} x_i y_i}{(\sum\limits_{i=1}^{n} x_i)^2 - n\sum\limits_{i=1}^{n} x_i^2}$$

$$a = \frac{\sum\limits_{i=1}^{n} y_i - b\sum\limits_{i=1}^{n} x_i}{n}$$

where $n \geqslant 2$ (at least two points are needed to determine a straight line). An implicit assumption made here is that the line whose coefficients are being computed is not a vertical line; otherwise, the denominator of the expression for b will be 0.

The problem is to write a program that reads in the measured values and computes the coefficients a and b using the above equations. First, here is a function `lsq` that computes the coefficients a and b:

```
                                              File: lsq.c
void lsq(float x[], float y[], int n, float *pa,
                                       float *pb)
{
    int i;
    float sum_x=0, sum_y=0, sum_xy=0, sum_x2=0;
    for (i = 0; i < n; i++) {
        sum_x += x[i]; sum_y += y[i];
        sum_xy += x[i]*y[i]; sum_x2 += x[i]*x[i];
    }
    *pb = (sum_x*sum_y - n*sum_xy) /
                      (sum_x*sum_x - n*sum_x2);
    *pa = (sum_y - *pb * sum_x) / n;
}
```

The coefficients are returned in the objects pointed to by the parameters pa and pb.

Now, here is the main function that reads the data points, calls lsq and prints the coefficients.

```
                                              File: lsq_fit.c
    #include <stdio.h>
    #include <stdlib.h>
    #define MAX 500

 5  void lsq(float x[], float y[], int n, float *pa,
                                          float *pb);
    void fatal(char *s);

    main(void)
10  {
        float x[MAX], y[MAX];    /*measured values*/
        float a, b;      /*coefficients of the     */
                         /*equation "y(x) = a + bx"*/
                         /*which are to be computed*/
15      int n = 0;
        float p, q;

        while (scanf("%f%f", &p, &q) == 2)
            if (n >= MAX)
20              fatal("Too many sample values");
            else {x[n]=p; y[n]=q; n++;}

        if (n <= 1)
            fatal("Less than 2 input points\n");
25      lsq(x, y, n, &a, &b);
        printf("coefficients: a=%g & b=%g\n", a, b);
        exit(EXIT_SUCCESS);

    }
```

Note that this function calls function `fatal`, which was shown earlier, to print error messages.

9.6 Quicksort

The problem is to write a function to sort an array with elements of type float using the quicksort technique [Hoare 1962]. Quicksort uses the *divide and conquer* strategy to sort. First, the array is divided (i.e., partitioned) into two parts, a left part and a right part, such that all the elements of the left part are less than or equal to all the elements of the right part. Then quicksort recursively sorts the two parts to produce a sorted array.

The quicksort algorithm can be described in more detail as the following abstract algorithm:

```
void quicksort(float a[], int 1, int u)
                /*a: array to be sorted*/
                /*1, u: bounds of the array*/
{
```
> if (a *has 2 elements and they are not in order*)
>   *order (swap) them* ;
> **else if** (*there are more than 2 elements*) {
>   *divide* a *into two partitions such that*
>   *the left partition has elements* $\leqslant$ r ,
>   *and the right partition has elements* $\geqslant$ r
>   *(where* r *is an arbitrary element of the array* a*)*
>
>   `quicksort` *the left partition* ;
>   `quicksort` *the right partition* ;
> }
}

To ensure that the recursion terminates, each partition must have at least one fewer element than the original array. The process of dividing the array into two parts can be described abstractly as follows:[8]

Let r *be the middle element of* a
`i = 1;  j = u;`
> `/*left partition a[1..i-1] will always contain*/`
> `/*elements <= r; initially it is empty;        */`
> `/*similarly, the right partition a[j+1..u]     */`
> `/*contains elements >= r                       */`
`while (i <= j) {`
> *Extend left partition* `a[1..i-1]` *as far as possible by increasing* i
> *Extend right partition* `a[j+1..u]` *as far as possible by decreasing* j
> *Exchange elements* `a[i]` *and* `a[j]` *so that extending of*
>   *partitions can continue; update the values of* i *and* j
`}`

With this algorithm, it is possible that the two partitions overlap by one element whose value is equal to r.

---

8. Notation a[i..j] refers to the subarray of a with elements from a[i] to a[j] inclusive. If j is less than i, then the subarray a null array, that is, an array with no elements.

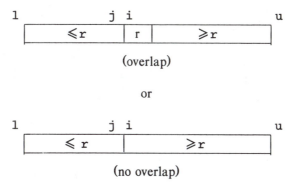

(overlap)

or

(no overlap)

The overlapping element need not be sorted because it is already in position— the elements to its left are less than or equal to r and the elements to its right are greater than or equal to r. Upon termination of the loop, there will be an overlap if i = j + 2 and no overlap if i = j + 1. Sorting of the overlapping element can be avoided by taking a[1..j] to be the left partition and a[i..u] to be the right partition.

Using the above algorithm, function partition is defined as

File: partition.c

```
     void partition(float a[], int lo, int hi,
                                int *ri, int *rj)
     {
          float r, temp;
 5        int i, j;

          r = a[(lo+hi)/2];        /* middle element */
          i = lo; j = hi;
          while (i <= j) {
10             while (a[i] < r)
                    i++;
               while (a[j] > r)
                    j--;
               if (i <= j) {
15                  temp=a[i]; a[i]=a[j]; a[j]=temp;
                    i++; j--;
               }
          }
          *ri = i; *rj = j; /*partition points*/
     }
```

Function quicksort can now be defined as

```
                                              File: quicksort.c
  void partition(float a[], int lo, int hi,
               int *ri, int *rj);

  void quicksort(float a[], int lo, int hi)
5 {
      int i, j;
      float temp;

      if (hi-lo == 1 && a[hi] < a[lo]) {
10        temp = a[lo];a[lo] = a[hi];a[hi] = temp;
      }
      else if (hi-lo > 1) {
          partition(a, lo, hi, &i, &j);
          quicksort(a, lo, j);
15        quicksort(a, i, hi);
      }
  }
```

9.7 Automobile Cruise Controller

This problem involves writing a program to monitor and maintain an automobile at a constant speed, i.e., an *automobile cruise controller*. The cruise controller program will be executed by a dedicated microprocessor. The cruise controller is activated when memory location 020 of the microprocessor becomes nonzero and deactivated when it becomes zero. The current speed of the automobile, an integer value, can be accessed from memory location 024. The speed of the automobile can be increased or decreased by writing the amount of change to memory location 026. The automobile takes about half a second to respond to the change in speed. The externally defined function delay may be used to suspend program execution until the automobile speed has changed as instructed.

The cruise controller should accept only speeds between 25 and 55 miles per hour as valid cruising speeds; if the driver attempts to set a cruising speed outside these limits, an alarm signal is sent by writing a nonzero value to memory location 022. An alarm signal is also sent if the controller is unable to maintain the automobile within 2 miles of the desired cruising speed. In both cases, the controlling mechanism should deactivate automatically.

The cruise controller program is

```
                                                    File: cruise.c
    #include <stdlib.h>
    #define ON_OFF    020
    #define ALARM     022
    #define SPEED     024
 5  #define CHNG_SPEED        026

    #define VAR       2
    #define RESPONSE_TIME    0.5
    #define LOW       25
10  #define HIGH      55

    void delay(int d);
    main(void)
    {
15    volatile int *on = (int *) ON_OFF;
      volatile int *alarm = (int *) ALARM;
      volatile int *speed = (int *) SPEED;
      volatile int *change_speed=(int *) CHNG_SPEED;
      int cur_speed, cruise_speed;
20
      for (;;) {    /*infinite loop*/
        while (*on == 0) ;  /*busy wait*/
        cruise_speed = *speed;
        if (cruise_speed<LOW || cruise_speed>HIGH) {
25        *alarm = 1; *on = 0;
        }
        else {
          while (*on != 0) {
            cur_speed = *speed;
30          if (abs(cruise_speed-cur_speed) > VAR) {
              *alarm = 1; *on = 0; break;
            }
            else
              *change_speed=cruise_speed-cur_speed;
35          delay(RESPONSE_TIME);
          }
        }
      }
    }
```

Note that this program must be loaded with the function delay.

The cruise controller program *busy waits* until the cruise mechanism is activated. A program is said to *poll* if it actively and repeatedly checks for the occurrence of an event that originates outside the program. A program *busy waits* if in between polling it does nothing useful (as in the case of checking for the activation of the cruise controller). Polling and busy waiting are acceptable only in some situations; e.g., in a program that executes on a dedicated processor. It is usually undesirable on computers that are shared by many different programs because it wastes system resources.

The cruise control microprocessor is likely to be very small and have only limited capabilities. High-level programs for such microprocessors are often compiled on a bigger computer[9] and the translated version is then transferred to the microprocessor. Typically such programs are first tested under simulated conditions on the computer where the program is compiled. The program given above was tested only under simulated conditions.

9.7.1 Implementation of the `delay` Function: Implementation of the `delay` function on the microprocessor will require access to a real-time clock to compute the delay interval. Alternatively, if such a facility is not available, a program can be delayed by making it execute a large number of instructions, such as the following nested loop:

```
for (i=0; i<=M; i++)
    for (j=0; j<=N; j++)
        ;
```

The time required to execute such a loop can be determined analytically by examining the code produced by a C compiler and using the execution times of these instructions on the microprocessor or experimentally by running the program on the microprocessor. Parameters M and N can be tuned to achieve the desired delay.

9.8 Integration: An Example of Passing Functions as Arguments

Write a function `integrate` that finds the definite integral of a function f

$$f : real \rightarrow real$$

between the limits a and b:

---

9. Compiling a program on one machine for use on another machine is called *cross compilation*.

$$I = \int\limits_{i=a}^{i=b} f(x) \ dx$$

using the trapezoidal rule. It should be possible to integrate different functions by passing them as arguments to `integrate`.

The trapezoidal rule approximates the integral of a function between the two limits a and b by the area of the trapezoid with base $b-a$ and heights $f(a)$ and $f(b)$.

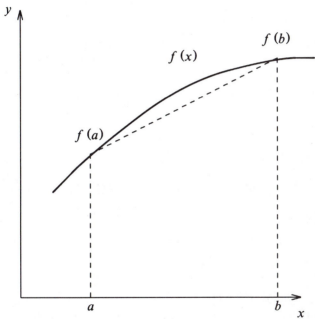

This approximation can be improved by dividing a and b into two equal subintervals, taking the area of the two resulting trapezoids and adding them up. Each of these subintervals can be further divided into two more equal subintervals and the process repeated.

The approximate integral I_n of a function f between the limits a and b using n subintervals

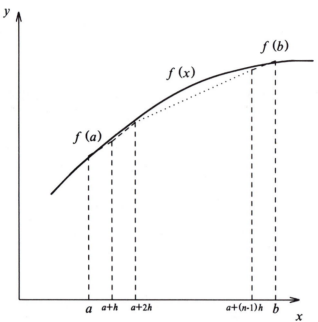

is given by the equation

$$I_n = h\left[\frac{f(a)}{2} + f(a+h) + f(a+2h) + \cdots + f(a+(n-1)h) + \frac{f(b)}{2}\right]$$

where h, the width of the interval, is given by

$$h = \frac{(b-a)}{n}$$

The subdividing process is repeated until two successive approximations of the integral of the function f as calculated by the trapezoidal rule differ in absolute value by less than eps (a small positive value), the desired stopping tolerance.

The trapezoidal integration algorithm can be described abstractly as

```
new_approx = 0;
do {
     previous_approx = new_approx;
     Calculate new_approx;
     Divide each subinterval into two equal subintervals;
} while (abs(new_approx-previous_approx)>=eps);
```

Based on this integration algorithm, function `integrate` is defined as

```
                                                    File: integ.c
     #include <math.h>   /*contains "fabs" prototype*/

     float integrate(float (*fp)(float), float a,
                                  float b, float eps)
 5          /*"fp": function to be integrated*/
            /*a, b: integration interval     */
            /*eps:  desired accuracy          */
     {
         float new = 0.0, previous;
10       int n = 1;      /*number of intervals*/
         double h;       /*interval size*/
         double sum;     /*temporary variable*/
         int i;          /*loop variable*/

15       h = (b - a);    /*initial interval size*/
         do {
             previous = new;
             /*calculate new approx*/
                 sum = fp(a) / 2.0;
20               for (i = 1; i < n; i++)
                     sum += fp(a+i*h);
                 sum += fp(b) / 2.0;
                 new = sum * h;
             n *= 2;      /*number of intervals for*/
25                        /*next approximation*/
             h /= 2.0;    /*size of interval for next*/
                          /*approximation*/
         } while (fabs(new-previous) >= eps);
         return new;
     }
```

As an alternative to using the math library function `fabs`, we could have defined a private absolute value function or macro like the macro `ABS` that was used earlier:

```
#define ABS(x) (((x)>0)?(x):-(x))
```

Function `integrate` does not work correctly if the first approximation of the integral of a function is within `eps` of 0.0, the initial value assigned to `new_approx`. This problem can be solved by forcing the computation of at least a few approximations, say 10.

Calling function `integrate` is straightforward. For example, if a function `cube`, which is declared as

```
float cube(float);
```

is to be integrated between two limits `l` and `u` with an accuracy of `small`, then `integrate` is called as

```
integrate(cube, l, u, small)
```

The definition of function `integrate` also illustrates the use of the various compound assignment operators.

9.9 Searching an Array

Process table `pt` is an array whose elements are structures of type `pcb`:

```
typedef struct pcb
   {
        long pid;
        proc_states state;
        long delay;
        int fp;
        struct pcb *parent;
   } pcb;
```

Notice the combination of a `typedef` and a structure tag. Identifier `pcb` is declared both as a type and a structure tag. It was necessary to declare `pcb` as a structure tag because the declaration of `pcb` is recursive. On the other hand, although it was not necessary to declare `pcb` as a type name by using `typedef`, such a declaration does allow `pcb` to be used like the predefined types (i.e., it is not necessary to use the keyword `struct` when declaring or defining structures of type `pcb`).

The enumeration type `proc_states` used in `pcb` is declared as

```
typedef enum
   {
        ready,
        service,
        select,
        transaction,
        completed
   } proc_states;      /*process states */
```

These type declarations and the following constant and variable declarations are contained in file `proc.h`:

```
#define NULL_PID (-1)

extern pcb pt[];        /*the process table*/
extern pcb *pt_last;    /*last element of  */
                        /*process table    */
```

The external variables are defined and initialized in another file. The address of the first element of pt is denoted by pt itself (or &pt[0]); the pointer variable pt_last is initialized to point to the last element of pt.

The problem is to write a function next_ready that returns the address (not the index) of an element of pt such that its component pid has a value that is not equal to NULL_PID and its component state has the value ready. If there is no such element, then next_ready returns NULL:

File: next.c

```
     #include <stddef.h>
     #include "proc.h"

     pcb *next_ready(void)
 5   {
         pcb *p;

         for (p = &pt[0]; p <= pt_last; p++) {
             if (p->pid!=NULL_PID && p->state==ready)
10               return p;
         }
         return NULL;
     }
```

Note that the pointer expression p++ increments p by the sizeof(pcb) rather than just one.

10. Exercises

1. Write a function sqrt that computes the square root of a floating-point value x using Newton's method. According to this method, the $k+1^{th}$ approximation of the square root of a value x is given by the formula

$$a_{k+1} = 0.5 (a_k + \frac{x}{a_k})$$

The iteration is stopped when the absolute difference between two successive approximations is less than the user-supplied stopping value eps.

2. The *least-squares curve fitting* program expects to read an even number of input values. The result is meaningless if the user supplies an odd number of input values; however, the program does not indicate an error in such a case. Modify the program so that it prints an error message if the user does not supply an even number of input values. (*Hint*: function scanf returns the number of items successfully matched except when the input ends before the first item is read, in which case it returns EOF.)

3. Write a function merge that merges two sorted arrays a and b to produce a third sorted array c:

   ```
   void merge(a, b, c)
   ```

4. Write a function mergesort that sorts an array using a divide-and-conquer strategy similar to the one used in quicksort. The basic idea is to divide the array into two parts, sort each part and then to merge the two sorted parts (using function merge of the previous exercise) to produce the sorted array. The mergesort algorithm may be described abstractly as (adapted from [McGettrick & Smith 1983])

   ```
   void mergesort(float a[], int l, int u)
                   /*a: array to be sorted*/
                   /*l, u: bounds of the array*/
   {
         if (a has 2 or more elements) {
               divide a into two nonempty partitions p and q;
               mergesort the partition p;
               mergesort the partition q;
               merge(p, q, a);
         }
   }
   ```

5. The series for computing the *sine* of a value x, given earlier, converges quickly only for small values of x satisfying

$$0 \leqslant abs(x) \leqslant \frac{\pi}{4}$$

For larger values of x, the following equivalences should be used [Wirth 1973]:

equivalence	condition
$sine\,(x) \equiv sine\,(x-2\pi n)$	$2\pi n \leqslant abs\,(x) < 2\pi(n+1)$
$sine\,(x) \equiv -sine\,(x-\pi)$	$\pi \leqslant abs\,(x) < 2\pi$
$sine\,(x) \equiv sine\,(\pi-x)$	$\dfrac{\pi}{2} \leqslant abs\,(x) < \pi$
$sine\,(x) \equiv cosine\,(\dfrac{\pi}{2}-x)$	$\dfrac{\pi}{4} < abs\,(x) < \dfrac{\pi}{2}$
$sine\,(x) \equiv -sine\,(-x)$	$x < 0$

where $cosine\,(x)$ is given by the series

$$cosine\,(x) = 1 - \frac{x^2}{2!} + \frac{x^4}{4!} - \cdots$$

Modify function `sine` to incorporate these equivalences.

6. What will happen to the least-squares function `lsq` if all the input data points have the same x coordinate? Modify `lsq` to take care of this problem.

7. On the UNIX system, characters `^H` (backspace) and `@` are often used as special characters that erase the last character typed and delete the current line, respectively. Write a program that reads text input containing these characters and produces, as output, a version of the input edited by these characters. For example, the program should transform the input[10]

```
Their^H^Hre was an Old Pear^H^Hrson of K^HCromer,
Who frequented the top of a tree@
Who stood on one leg to read homer^H^H^H^H^HHomer;
When he found he grew still^H^Hff, he jumped over
  the cliff,
Who was sadly annoyed by a flea@
Which concluded the person of c^HCromer.
```

to

---

10. This text was taken from *The Nonsense Books of Edward Lear* [Lear 1964].

```
There was an Old Person of Cromer,
Who stood on one leg to read Homer;
When he found he grew stiff, he jumped over
  the cliff,
Which concluded the person of Cromer.
```

8. Modify the `echo` program given in this chapter so that if the first argument is `-N`, then it prints its arguments on new lines. For example,

`echo a b c`

will print

`a b c`

while

`echo -N a b c`

will print

```
a
b
c
```

A command-line argument of the form *−letter* (such as `-N`) is called a command option or a flag in UNIX terminology.

Chapter 6

Independent Compilation and Data Abstraction

The text (source) of a complete C program can be kept in one file or, alternatively, it may be distributed over several files. Files containing components of a C program (functions, declarations and definitions) can be compiled independently. Independently compiled program components, along with precompiled library functions, can be joined (linked) together to produce a complete program.

Because C files can be compiled independently, it is often convenient and advantageous to partition C programs, especially large ones, into smaller and more manageable components. Each of the C files can be checked separately for syntactic and semantic errors and even tested for run-time errors. Moreover, when a program is modified, only the affected files need to be recompiled. If the whole program is kept in one file, then even a single small change will require recompilation of the whole program. This is undesirable, especially in case of large programs, because the recompilation may take a nontrivial amount of time and because it is wasteful of resources.

Files can also be used as an information hiding and data encapsulation mechanism. Only objects with the storage class `extern` can be referenced in other files; global objects with the storage class `static` cannot be referenced from other files. Files (along with the `extern` and `static` storage classes) can therefore be used to control the visibility of objects. Specifically, `extern` functions, but not `static` functions, can be referenced from other files. Implementation details of these functions, such as the data structures used and shared by them, can be made inaccessible from other files, thus preventing programs from becoming dependent on these details.

1. Independent Compilation

A complete C program can be partitioned into many files, say $file_1$.c, $file_2$.c, ..., $file_n$.c, which can be compiled into one executable program, say `final`, as follows:[1]

---

1. `cc` is the UNIX system C compiler. Note that it expects C source files to have the suffix `.c`. This convention is also followed by other tools used in conjunction with C programs such as `make` [Feldman 1979].

```
cc -o final file₁.c   file₂.c   ...   fileₙ.c
```

Alternatively, each file can be independently compiled; after all the files have been compiled, their translated versions can be combined to produce the final version of the complete program. For example, suppose each file *file$_i$*.c is independently compiled using the command

```
cc -c file_i.c
```

which results in the production of the *object* file *file$_i$*.o.[2] After all the component files have been compiled, the corresponding object files can be linked to produce an executable version of the program by using the command

```
cc -o final file₁.o   file₂.o   ...   fileₙ.o
```

2. Abstract Data Types and Information Hiding

Files can be used to implement *data abstraction* in much the same way that subprograms are used to implement control abstraction and information hiding. An *abstract data object* is an object that can be manipulated using *only* the operations specified in the definition of the object. The user cannot directly manipulate the underlying implementation of an abstract data object. Details of how such objects are implemented are hidden from the user. Hiding the details prevents the user from

1. making programs dependent on the representation. The representation of an abstract data type can be changed without affecting the rest of the program. For example, the abstract data type set may be initially implemented as an array, but this representation may be changed to an ordered list later on for storage efficiency.

2. accidentally or maliciously violating the integrity of an abstract data type object. Integrity of abstract data type objects is preserved by forcing the user to manipulate these objects using only the operations provided by the designer of the abstract data type.

Some examples of abstract data objects are queues, sets, databases and binary trees.

---

2. An *object file* is the machine language translation (i.e., a file produced by a compiler) of a program in a high-level language. By convention, object files produced by the UNIX C compiler have the suffix .o.

3. Examples

The following three examples illustrate the use of files to implement data abstraction.

3.1 Stacks

Consider a data object that is to be manipulated using only the following operations:

push(i)	Add the integer element i to the abstract data object.
pop()	Remove the top element from the abstract data object.
top()	Return the value of the top (most recently added) element of the abstract data object.
empty()	Return 1 if the abstract data object is empty; otherwise return 0.
full()	Return 1 if the abstract data object is full; otherwise return 0.
clear()	Empty the abstract data object.

A data object that can be manipulated in this manner is called a stack. It will be implemented by using an integer array s to store the values of the stack elements. Variable next will be used to point to the next free element in the array s. These implementation details will be hidden from the stack users by restricting the visibility of variables s and next to the file containing them by defining them as static variables.

File: `stack.c`

```
#include "stack.h"

static int s[MAX_SIZE];
static int next=0; /*first free slot on stack*/
void fatal(char *s);

void push(int i)    /*add "i" to the stack*/
{
    if (next == MAX_SIZE)
        fatal("push: Stack Full Error");
    s[next++] = i;
}
void pop(void)  /*remove the top stack element*/
{
    if (next == 0)
        fatal("pop: Stack Empty Error");
    next--;
}
int top(void)     /*return top stack element*/
{
    if (next == 0)
        fatal("top: Stack Empty Error");
    return s[next-1];
}
int empty(void)
{
    return next == 0;
}
int full(void)
{
    return next == MAX_SIZE;
}
void clear(void)     /*empty the stack*/
{
    next = 0;
}
```

Only the functions in file `stack.c` can be referenced from other files because they have the storage class `extern` (by default). Attempts to insert an element when the stack is full, or attempts to delete an element or determine the value of the top element when the stack is empty, will result in program termination.

3.1.1 Limitations of Files as a Data Abstraction Facility: A file is not a true data abstraction facility, because it only partially supports data abstraction. For example, it is not possible to define an array of files or to define a pointer to a file. Specifically, in the case of the stack example, it is not possible to define an array of stacks directly or to pass a stack as an argument. Files were not designed as a mechanism for information hiding and data abstraction! They were provided as a facility to support program partitioning and independent compilation. C++ [Stroustrup 1986] is a superset of C that provides full fledged data abstraction facilities. For details, see Appendix A.

3.2 Symbol Table Manipulation

The problem is to write a set of functions implementing a symbol table. A file containing a set of declarations for the benefit of symbol table users must also be provided. The symbol table functions perform the following actions:

1. Insert an item and associated information into the symbol table (the items are strings).
2. Retrieve the information associated with an item from the symbol table.
3. Determine whether or not the symbol table is full.
4. Check to see if an item is in the symbol table.
5. Reinitialize (reset) the symbol table.

Duplicate items should not be added to the symbol table. An item will be added to the symbol table only if the table is not full. The symbol table should be able to hold at least 200 items. The information associated with an item indicates whether the item is a variable identifier, a function or procedure name, a keyword, or a label name.

The type declarations used by the symbol table functions and their users are given in the file `symtab.h`:

File: symtab.h

```
   #define TRUE    1
   #define FALSE   0
   typedef enum {var, fun, proc, key_word,
                                label} item_type;
 5 typedef struct {
       char *id;
       item_type t;
   } item_info;
   void add(char *x, item_type it), clear(void);
10 int in_table(char *x), full(void);
   item_type get(char *x);
```

The various symbol table functions are now defined:

File: symtab.c

```
     #include <stdlib.h>
     #include <string.h>
     #include "symtab.h"
     #define N 200
5
     void fatal(char *s);
     static item_info st[N]; /* the symbol table */
     static int next = 0;
     void add(char *x, item_type it)
10   {
         if (next == N)
             fatal("add: symbol table overflow");
         if ((st[next].id=malloc(strlen(x)+1))==NULL)
             fatal("add: out of storage");
15       strcpy(st[next].id, x);
         st[next++].t = it;
     }
     int in_table(char *x)
     {
20       int i;
         for(i = 0; i < next; i++)
             if (strcmp(x, st[i].id) == 0) return TRUE;
         return FALSE;
     }
25   item_type get(char *x) /* *x must be in table*/
     {
         int i;
         for(i = 0; i < next;  i++)
             if (strcmp(x,st[i].id)==0) return st[i].t;
30       fatal("get: item not in symbol table");
     }
     int full(void)
     {
       return next == N;
35   }
     void clear(void)
     {
       next = 0;
     }
```

Note that the storage allocator `malloc` returns the null pointer when it runs out of memory.

The simple symbol table representation used in this example is not very efficient for performing a large number of searches. In such situations, a hashed table or an ordered binary tree representation, will be more appropriate.

3.3 List Manipulation Functions

The problem is to write a set of functions to manipulate lists. These functions may be informally described as

`add(head, i)`	Add the integer i to the list pointed to by `head`.
`delete(head, i)`	Delete the integer i from the list pointed to by `head`.
`in(head, i)`	Return 1 if the integer i is in the list pointed to by `head` and 0 otherwise.
`empty(head)`	Return 1 if the list pointed to by `head` is empty and 0 otherwise.

A List

Unlike the symbol table functions given earlier, which operate only with one symbol table, the list manipulation functions can operate on different lists, because the head of the list being manipulated is supplied explicitly as an argument. The list heads must be declared in the user program as pointers to list elements, which are of type `node`. Type `node` and other declarations necessary for using the list manipulation functions are given in the file `list.h`:

File: list.h

```
   #include <stddef.h>
   #define TRUE     1
   #define FALSE    0

 5 struct node {
     int value;
     struct node *next;
   };

10 void add(struct node **phead, int i);
   void delete(struct node **phead, int i);
   int in(struct node **phead, int i);
   int empty(struct node **phead);
```

Definitions of the list manipulation functions empty, in, add and delete
are shown below:

File: empty.c

```
   #include <stdlib.h>
   #include "list.h"

   int empty(struct node **phead);
 5 {
       return *phead == NULL;
   }
```

File: in.c

```
   #include <stdlib.h>
   #include "list.h"

   int in(struct node **phead, int i)
 5 {
       struct node *t;

       for (t = *phead; t != NULL; t = t->next)
           if (t->value == i)
10             return TRUE;
       return FALSE;
   }
```

File: add.c

```c
#include <stdlib.h>
#include "list.h"

void fatal(char *s);

void add(struct node **phead, int i)
        /*phead: address of list head*/
        /*i: element to be inserted*/
{
    struct node *t = *phead;

    /*search for i*/
        while (t != NULL && t->value != i)
            t = t->next;

    if (t == NULL) { /*insert "i" in the list*/
        if ((t=malloc(sizeof(struct node)))==NULL)
        fatal("add: out of storage");
        t->value = i;
        t->next = *phead;
        *phead = t;
    }
}
```

File: `delete.c`

```
#include <stdlib.h>
#include "list.h"

void delete(struct node **phead, int i)
{
   struct node *t, *temp;

   if (*phead != NULL) {
      if ((*phead)->value == i) {
         /*delete first list element*/
         temp = *phead;
         *phead = (*phead)->next;
         free(temp);
      }
      else {
         t = *phead;
         while (t->next!=NULL && t->next->value!=i)
         t = t->next;
         if (t->next != NULL) {
         temp = t->next;
         t->next = t->next->next;
         free(temp);
         }
      }
   }
}
```

4. Exercises

1. Modify the stack implementation so that the stack functions do not terminate the program when the user attempts to add an element to a full stack, delete an element from an empty stack and so on. Instead, the functions should return −1 in such situations and 0 under normal conditions.

2. In the implementation of the stack function push, instead of comparing the value of next with MAX_SIZE, I could have used the stack function full to determine whether or not the stack was full. Similarly, in the implementation of pop I could have used empty. What are the pros and cons of the two approaches?

3. Modify the symbol table routine add to incorporate a check for duplicate item insertion. How will you let the caller know that a

duplicate insertion was attempted?

4. Function `clear`, in the symbol table example, clears the symbol table by setting variable `next` to 0. The storage locations pointed to by elements of the symbol table array `st` will not be reused (that is, they are effectively lost) because the symbol table is not explicitly deallocated (e.g., by using the deallocation function `free`). Modify `clear` so that it deallocates the elements of `st` before setting `next` to 0.

5. Why was it necessary to impose a maximum limit on the number of items in the symbol table example? Is it possible to do away with the restriction of 200 items in the symbol table by using a list, instead of an array, to implement the symbol table? If yes, then implement the symbol table by using a list; make sure that this change is not visible to the users of these functions; i.e., syntactically and semantically, the functions have the same effect as far as the user is concerned.

6. What modifications are necessary so that the `stack` can be used to store both `int` and `float` values? *Hint*: Use unions.

Chapter 7
Exceptions

An *exception* is an event that occurs unexpectedly or infrequently, such as division by zero or the premature interruption of program execution. In languages that do not provide specific facilities for handling exceptions, the most common method for indicating exceptions is for functions to return *status codes* or "funny values" to indicate exceptional conditions [Lee 1983]. Appropriate action should be taken if the value returned by a function indicates that an exception occurred during the function call. The status code technique does not allow detection and handling of processor exceptions such as one raised by an attempt to divide by zero; nor can this technique help detect and handle exceptions raised from the program environment, e.g., an exception (interrupt) raised by a user to terminate a program prematurely.[1] Consequently, the status code technique must be supplemented by some other mechanism, such as signals, possibly provided by the operating system.

C does not provide specific facilities for handling exceptions. Exceptions in C programs are handled by using status codes and signals:

1. *Status Codes*: By convention, a −1 is often returned by functions to indicate that an exception occurred during function execution. For example, function get c returns a −1 if it encounters an end-of-file.

2. *Signals*: An exception handler is established by instructing the C run-time system to invoke a specific C function (the *exception handler*) upon the receipt of a signal. C programs set up signal handlers by calling a library function. Signals can be generated by the hardware or the software.

Signals in C are generally used to handle [Lee 1983]

1. exceptions raised from the environment that affect program execution; e.g., the *delete* character (assuming it is the "interrupt" character) is used to generate a signal indicating that the currently executing program

---

1. Typing the interrupt character causes the keyboard handler to send an interrupt signal to the currently executing program.

should terminate.

2. exceptions that are detected by the hardware, e.g., illegal memory reference.

3. exceptions that could have been handled by returning status codes.

Signals are generated either automatically as a result of program errors or explicitly from within the program or from the environment.

The use of status codes to indicate exceptions is straightforward and has been illustrated in many of the examples in earlier chapters. This chapter will focus on the use of signals to handle exceptions.

1. Signals

The signals that must be handled by all C implementations are defined in the header file `<signal.h>`:

name	comments
SIGABRT	Abnormal termination signal such as one generated by calling `abort`.
SIGFPE	Erroneous arithmetic operation, e.g., a floating-point overflow.
SIGILL	Illegal instruction.
SIGINT	Interrupt; an interactive attention signal.
SIGSEGV	Illegal memory reference.
SIGTERM	Software termination signal sent to the program typically by another program.

The signal names are constant identifiers denoting integers. C implementations may support additional signals.

2. Setting Up Signal/Exception Handlers

Signal (exception) handlers are set up by calling the library function `signal` which takes two arguments: the signal name (number) and a pointer to a `void` function that is be invoked upon the receipt of the signal, i.e., a pointer to the signal handler function. `signal` returns a pointer to the previous signal handler except in case of error when it returns the constant `SIG_ERR` (defined in the header file `signal.h`).

If `signal` is called with `SIG_DFL` as the signal handler, then default signal handling occurs. If `signal` is called with `SIG_IGN` as the signal handler, then the signal is ignored. The default signal handler for a signal will be either `SIG_DFL` or `SIG_IGN`; this is implementation dependent. (`SIG_DFL` and `SIG_IGN` are defined in `signal.h`).

The following program segment illustrates the association of the signal handler *handler* with the signal *signal_name*:

```
#include <signal.h>
...
{
    ...
    /*associate signal with its handler*/
        signal(signal_name, handler);
    ...
}
```

Another paradigm is one that associates a signal handler with a signal only if the signal is being ignored:

```
#include <signal.h>
...
{
    void (*old)(int);
    ...
    if ((old=signal(signal_name,SIG_IGN))!=SIG_IGN)
        signal(signal_name, handler);
    ...
}
```

A reference to the original signal handler is saved in the variable `old` for possible reassociation with signal *signal_name* later. If the original signal handler is not needed, then the above `if` statement can be written as

```
if (signal(signal_name, SIG_IGN) != SIG_IGN)
    signal(signal_name, handler);
```

The signal handler *handler* should be of the form

```
void handler(int i) /*Handle signal i*/
{
    ...
    /*Reassociate signal "i" with its*/
    /*handler*/
        signal(i, handler);
}
```

When a signal for which an exception handler has been specified is received, normal program execution is suspended and control is transferred to the exception handler. The signal number is passed as an argument to its exception handler. In the exception handler, the signal should be reassociated with the handler because most signals are automatically reset for default handling (i.e., the signal is associated with `SIG_DFL`). Upon normal completion of the exception handler, program execution is resumed at the point where it was interrupted. Program execution may not be resumed in some cases, e.g.,

- the exception handler may terminate the program by calling `exit` or
- the exception handler may resume program execution at a point other than the point of interruption by calling function `longjmp`.

3. Generating/Sending Signals

Signals can be generated implicitly or explicitly. Signals are generated implicitly in a program by the underlying software or hardware when some unusual condition occurs, e.g., a floating-point divide by zero, floating-point overflow or the user typing the interrupt character at the terminal.

Signals can also be generated explicitly by calling function `raise`. For example, the call

```
raise(sig)
```

will send the signal *sig* to the program executing this function call.

4. Examples

I will give two examples of exception handling: a relatively simple example that shows how to print an error message and terminate when an exception occurs, and a somewhat more complicated example that shows how to resume execution after handling an exception.

4.1 Roots of a Quadratic Equation

The problem is to write a program that computes the real roots of a quadratic equation. The program should print an appropriate error message if it is aborted as a result of a floating-point error such as a floating-point divide by zero or a floating-point overflow which generates the signal `SIGFPE`.

The two roots, r_1 and r_2, of a quadratic equation

$$a x^2 + b x + c = 0.0$$

are given by the equations

$$r_1 = \frac{-b - \sqrt{b^2 - 4.0 a c}}{2.0 a}$$

and

$$r_2 = \frac{-b + \sqrt{b^2 - 4.0 a c}}{2.0 a}$$

These roots will be real only if

$$b^2 - 4.0\,a\,c \geqslant 0.0$$

The program to compute the roots is

```
#include <stdio.h>
#include <stdlib.h>
#include <signal.h>
#include <math.h>
void float_error(int), fatal(char *s);

main(void)
{
    float a, b, c, r1, r2, temp;

    signal(SIGFPE, float_error);

    printf("Type the 3 coefficients:");
    if (scanf("%f%f%f", &a, &b, &c) != 3)
        fatal("Error: No or incomplete input");
    if (a == 0.0)
        fatal("First coeff is 0");
    if (b*b - 4.0*a*c < 0.0)
        fatal("Quadratic eqn has no real roots");

    temp = (float) sqrt(b*b - 4.0*a*c);
    r1 = (-b + temp)/(2.0*a);
    r2 = (-b - temp)/(2.0*a);

    printf("The roots are %g and %g\n", r1, r2);
    exit(EXIT_SUCCESS);
}

void float_error(int i)
{
    fatal("Floating point exception raised!\n");
}
void fatal(char *s)
{
    fprintf(stderr, "Error, %s\n", s);
    exit(EXIT_FAILURE);
}
```

The floating-point exception handler function `float_error` cannot print the values of the variables `a`, `b` and `c` because it cannot access them; these variables are local to function `main`. However, if they were made external variables, then they would become accessible from `float_error`, making it possible to print their values to provide the user with better information.

If an exception handler is not provided in this program, then it will abort with an error message upon the occurrence of a floating-point error.

The above program uses the function `sqrt` which is contained in the math library; consequently, the roots program (in file `roots.c`) must be linked and loaded with the math library, e.g., on the UNIX system this is done as

```
cc -o roots roots.c -lm
```

The final executable program is called `roots`.

4.2 Calculator with Exception Handling

The calculator example given in Chapter 1 will be modified so that it can handle exceptions resulting from both implicitly and explicitly generated signals. Three versions of the calculator example will be presented to illustrate exception handling semantics.

4.2.1 Calculator with Exception Handling (Version 1):

The problem is to modify the calculator example given in Chapter 1 so that it can handle floating-point exceptions and premature termination signals. A premature termination signal can be sent to the currently executing process by an interrupt character, such as the *delete* character, at the terminal. If the program receives a termination signal, a confirmation should be requested from the user. If the user answers affirmatively, then the program should terminate; otherwise, the program should continue execution.

The calculator program, modified to handle exceptions, is

```
#include <stdio.h>
#include <stdlib.h>
#include <signal.h>
#define PR putchar(':')
5
void float_error(int), keyboard_intr(int);

main(void)
{
10      float a, b, result; char opr;
        signal(SIGFPE, float_error);
        signal(SIGINT, keyboard_intr);
        while(PR,scanf("%f%c%f",&a,&opr,&b)!=EOF) {
            switch (opr) {
15              case '+': result = a + b; break;
                case '-': result = a - b; break;
                case '*': result = a * b; break;
                case '/': result = a / b; break;
                default:
20                  printf("ERROR, bad operator\n");
                    exit(EXIT_FAILURE);
            }
            printf("result is %g\n", result);
        }
25      exit(EXIT_SUCCESS);
}
void float_error(int i)
{
        signal(SIGFPE, float_error);
30      printf("Floating point error\n");
}
void keyboard_intr(int i)
{
        signal(SIGINT, keyboard_intr);
35      printf("Do you want to quit? Y or N:");
        switch (getchar()) {
            case 'Y': case 'y': exit(EXIT_SUCCESS);
            default: printf("continue\n");
        }
}
```

There are two problems with this solution:

1. A floating-point error may cause this version of the calculator program to go into an infinite loop because on some computers the instruction causing the error will be executed again upon return from the exception handler `float_error`.

2. The second problem arises due to the implementation of `scanf`. On some implementations, if an interrupt occurs in the middle of a call to an input function, `scanf` in this case, then this function will be retried on return from the interrupt handler; in other implementations, the input function will return a -1 (`EOF`). In the latter case, the program will terminate on return from the interrupt handler just as it will terminated upon encountering end-of-file.

4.2.2 Calculator with Exception Handling (Version 2): The infinite loop problem can be avoided by ensuring that the floating-point error does not occur again upon return from the exception handler. A simple way of doing this is to change the values of the operands of the operation that is causing the floating-point exception in the exception handler. In this example, the operation causing the exception can be one of +, -, * or /; changing the values of their operands, a and b, to `1.0` will ensure that the floating-point exception will not be raised upon return from the exception handler `float_error`. Variables a and b must be made global, i.e., external, to allow the exception handler `float_error` to change their values:[2]

---

2. This solution is implementation dependent because it relies on the fact that, upon return from the signal handler `float_error`, new values of variables a and b will be used upon resumption of normal program execution. Whether or not the new values are used depends upon the code generated by the C compiler. For example, if the compiler has stored the value of variable b in a register, then changing its value in the signal handler may not lead to the use of the new value upon resumption of normal program execution. A more robust solution can be implemented by using the `longjmp` strategy illustrated in the next version of the calculator; this strategy is better because it is not implementation dependent.

```
     #include <stdio.h>
     #include <stdlib.h>
     #include <signal.h>
     #define PR putchar(':')
  5  void float_error(int), keyboard_intr(int);
     float a, b, result; char opr;

     main(void)
     {
 10      signal(SIGFPE, float_error);
         signal(SIGINT, keyboard_intr);
         while(PR,scanf("%f%c%f",&a,&opr,&b)!=EOF) {
             switch (opr) {
                 case '+': result = a + b; break;
 15              case '-': result = a - b; break;
                 case '*': result = a * b; break;
                 case '/': result = a / b; break;
                 default:
                     printf("ERROR, bad operator\n");
 20                  exit(EXIT_FAILURE);
             }
             printf("result is %g\n", result);
         }
         exit(EXIT_SUCCESS);
 25  }
     void float_error(int i)
     {
         signal(SIGFPE, float_error);
         printf("Floating point error\n");
 30      a = b = 1.0;
     }
     void keyboard_intr(int i)
     {
         signal(SIGINT, keyboard_intr);
 35      printf("Do you want to quit? Y or N:");
         switch (getchar()) {
             case 'Y': case 'y': exit(EXIT_SUCCESS);
             default: printf("continue\n");
         }
     }
```

4.2.3 Calculator with Exception Handling (Version 3): I will now present a robust solution to avoid the problem resulting from the fact that scanf will, on some implementations, return EOF if its execution is interrupted by a signal. This will terminate the calculator program prematurely. Premature program termination can be prevented by invoking macro setjmp to save the environment at a safe point where execution can be resumed in case of an interrupt and then calling longjmp to restore the saved environment. Function longjmp does not return; instead, a return of the setjmp macro call which saved the environment takes place.

Here is the third version of the calculator program with exception handling:

File: `calcE3.c`

```
#include <stdio.h>
#include <stdlib.h>
#include <signal.h>
#include <setjmp.h>
#define PR putchar(':')

void float_error(int), keyboard_intr(int);
float a, b, result; char opr; jmp_buf env;
main(void)
{
    signal(SIGFPE, float_error);
    signal(SIGINT, keyboard_intr);
    setjmp(env);
    while(PR,scanf("%f%c%f",&a,&opr,&b)!=EOF) {
        switch (opr) {
            case '+': result = a + b; break;
            case '-': result = a - b; break;
            case '*': result = a * b; break;
            case '/': result = a / b; break;
            default:
                printf("ERROR, bad operator\n");
                exit(EXIT_FAILURE);
        }
        printf("result is %g\n", result);
    }
    exit(EXIT_SUCCESS);
}
void float_error(int i)
{
    signal(SIGFPE, float_error);
    printf("Floating point error\n");
    a = b = 1.0;
}
void keyboard_intr(int i)
{
    signal(SIGINT, keyboard_intr);
    printf("Do you want to quit? Y or N:");
    switch (getchar()) {
        case 'Y': case 'y': exit(EXIT_SUCCESS);
        default: printf("continue\n");
                 longjmp(env, 0);
    }
}
```

5. Exercises

1. In the calculator program, what happens when a user types the interrupt character instead of the typing Y or N in response to the question

        Do you really want to quit? Y or N:

printed by the exception handler `term_inter`? Try to verify your answer by executing the calculator program on your computer.

2. Modify the final version of the calculator program so that the exception handler `float_error` returns by executing `longjmp`.

3. Describe a situation where it is advantageous or necessary to ignore signals; i.e., a case in which the signal handler `SIG_IGN` must be associated with one or more signals.

Chapter 8

The C Preprocessor

A *preprocessor* is a tool for processing a program prior to its compilation. Preprocessors have been used to extend languages and to provide extra-language capabilities. Although innumerable preprocessors have been built to enhance the capabilities of programming languages, they are usually nonstandard and provide ad hoc facilities; few languages have provided a preprocessor as part of their standard environment. Two examples of major languages that provide preprocessors as part of their environment are C and PL/I.

The C preprocessor provides facilities for defining macros (constant definitions are a special case), file inclusion and conditional compilation. The C preprocessor is called automatically when the C compiler is invoked. On the UNIX system, a C program can be processed by just the preprocessor by using the -E option with the C compiler command cc; in this case, the program is not compiled:

cc -E *file-name*

The output of the preprocessor is placed on the standard output stream stdout. Running the preprocessor on a program without compiling it allows the programmer to examine the effect of preprocessor definitions, macro invocations, and conditional compilation.

Preprocessor instructions are usually different from the instructions of the associated language. For example, C preprocessor instructions begin with the character #; this character must be the first nonwhite space character on the line although it need not be the first character. C preprocessor instructions can appear anywhere in a program.

1. Macro Definition and Invocation

A *macro* definition associates an identifier with a string called the *replacement string*. All subsequent occurrences of this identifier are replaced by the string associated with it. C preprocessor macro definitions are of two forms, simple and parameterized:

```
#define macro-name replacement-string
#define macro-name( x_1 , x_2 , ... , x_n ) replacement-string
```

macro-name is an identifier; the body of a macro, i.e., the *replacement-string*, consists of preprocessing tokens such as identifiers, keywords, operators, separators such as a parenthesis or a square bracket, or a string of characters that does not contain any separators.

A macro name can be used in its definition; this does not cause infinite recursion because a macro cannot be invoked from within its own body. The macro body can be continued on the next line by appending a backslash at the end of the line to be continued. Future occurrences of the macro name in the file containing the macro definition cause the macro to be invoked (called).

1.1 Simple Macro Definitions

Some examples of simple macro definitions are

```
#define NULL 0
#define EOF (-1)
#define GET getc(stdin)
```

After the above macro definitions have been processed, every occurrence of NULL, EOF and GET will be replaced by the corresponding macro body. For example, every occurrence (invocation) of

```
GET
```

will be replaced by the string

```
getc(stdin)
```

Macros can be used to make limited changes in the syntax of a language. For example, the macro definitions

```
#define begin {
#define end }
```

can be used to make C programs take on a Pascal-like appearance. Using these definitions, a while statement can be written as

```
while (e)
begin
      ...
end
```

1.2 Parameterized Macro Definitions

Some examples of parameterized macro definitions are

```
#define getchar() getc(stdin)
#define putchar(x) putc(x, stdout)
#define MAX(x,y) ((x)>(y)?(x):(y))
#define MIN(x,y) ((x)>(y)?(y):(x))
#define UPPER(c) ((c)-'a'+'A')
                /*c must be lower case*/
#define LOWER(c) ((c)-'A'+'a')
                /*c must be upper case*/
```

Macros MAX and MIN return the values of their maximum and minimum arguments, respectively; macros UPPER and LOWER return the lower or upper case character corresponding to their arguments, respectively. (The reason for using so many parentheses in the definitions of the macros such as MAX, MIN, UPPER and LOWER is discussed later in this section.)

All occurrences of parameterized macro names, which must be followed by arguments enclosed within parentheses, are replaced by the corresponding macro bodies. Prior to the replacement of a macro name by its body, all occurrences of the parameters in the body are replaced by the corresponding arguments. Note that a parameterized macro invocation looks a function call.

Consider as an example, the following program fragment:

```
while ((c = getchar()) != EOF)
    putchar(UPPER(c));
```

The preprocessor transforms this program fragment to

```
while ((c = getc(stdin)) != (-1))
    putc(((c)-'a'+'A'), stdout);
```

1.3 Converting Macro Parameters into String Constants

The # preprocessor operator converts a macro parameter to a string constant after it has been replaced by the corresponding argument. For example, suppose we want to define a macro PRINTI with one parameter such that when it is called with one argument, say max, it expands to

```
printf("max = %d\n", max)
```

Defining it as

```
#define PRINTI(x) printf("x = %d\n", x)
```

means that the invocation PRINTI(max) will be expanded to

```
printf("x = %d\n", max)
```

and not to

```
printf("max = %d\", max)
```

which is what we want. Parameter names embedded within string constants are not recognized as parameters because string constants are not scanned for replacement.

Writing `PRINTI` as

```
printf(x "= %d\n", x)
```

will not solve the problem because the invocation `PRINTI(max)` will be expanded as

```
printf(max "= %d\n", max)
```

The problem is solved if the first occurrence of parameter `x`, after it has been replaced by the corresponding argument, can be made into a string constant. This is precisely what the `#` operator is used for. To make `PRINTI` have the desired semantics, it must be defined as

```
#define PRINTI(x) printf(#x " = %d\n", x)
```

Invocation `PRINTI(max)` will now expand to

```
printf(#max " = %d\n", max)
```

`#max` is equivalent to the string `"max"`; therefore the above expression is equivalent to

```
printf("max" " = %d\n", max)
```

which, after string concatenation, is equivalent to

```
printf("max = %d\n", max)
```

1.4 Pasting (Joining) Items in Macro Definitions

Items (tokens) in a macro definition can be pasted (joined) together with the `##` operator. As an example, consider the following definitions:

```
#define RedApple 3
#define GreenApple 5
#define Apple(x) x##Apple
```

Invocation `Apple(Red)` expands to `Red##Apple` which evaluates to the token `RedApple` which is replaced by the constant 3. Similarly, `Apple(Green)` is replaced by the constant 5.

1.5 Rescanning

After a macro invocation has been replaced by the corresponding body and arguments substituted for the corresponding parameters, the replacing body is rescanned to look for further macro invocations. Note that a macro cannot be invoked from within its own body. This rule allows one to write macros such as

```
#define sizeof (int) sizeof
```

which would otherwise result in infinite recursion.

1.6 Defining Constants

The C preprocessor is often used for defining constant identifiers in C programs; simple macro definitions are used for this purpose. Constant identifier definitions are usually of the form

```
#define constant-identifier constant-or-constant-identifier
#define constant-identifier (constant-expression)
```

Some examples of constant definitions are

```
#define NULL 0
#define EOF (-1)

#define TRUE 1
#define FALSE 0
```

If a constant is defined such that its value is a constant expression, then it is wise to surround the expression by parentheses. As an example, consider the constant definition

```
#define E 5+10
```

Using the constant E in expressions can produce strange results. For example, although the expression

```
E+10
```

evaluates correctly to 25, the expression

```
E*10
```

will not evaluate to 150 as expected. Instead, it evaluates to 105 because E is replaced by 5+10, which produces the expression

```
5+10*10
```

This problem arises because the C preprocessor does not understand constant definitions; actually, the C preprocessor does not know much about C at all. Constant definitions are just macro definitions. The above problem can be avoided by using parentheses to enclose the constant expression in the definition of E:

```
#define E (5+10)
```

1.7 In-line Code Generation

Function calls incur a run time overhead because registers must be saved and argument values must be copied, and because jumps must be made to the function body and back to the calling program. For small functions, especially those that are called repeatedly, this overhead can be significant. Consequently, a programmer may be tempted to avoid using functions in such cases and to manually replace each function call by the body of the function. This manual replacement has several disadvantages; for example, the code becomes difficult to read, understand and modify. Manual replacement can be discouraged by providing a facility using which a programmer can inform the compiler that calls to some functions should be replaced by the corresponding function body, i.e., a facility for *in-line code generation*. C preprocessor macros provide such a facility.

UPPER and LOWER were defined as the macros

```
#define UPPER(c)  ((c)-'a'+'A')
#define LOWER(c)  ((c)-'A'+'a')
```

rather than as functions so that code for them is generated in-line. This is appropriate because UPPER and LOWER perform very simple tasks. In this case, the in-line code generated for the expressions represented by UPPER and LOWER is less than that generated for a function call.

It is important to note that in-line code generation can, in some cases, lead to a significant increase in the storage required by the program itself.

1.8 Removing Macro Definitions

The preprocessor instruction

```
#undef  identifier
```

removes (erases) the definition of *identifier*.

Conditional compilation can be controlled by defining and undefining identifiers (discussed in Section 3). Note that an identifier defined as a macro must be undefined before it can be redefined. There is one exception to this rule: identical redefinitions are allowed.

1.9 Predefined Macros

The following predefined macros are provided:

macro	comments
_ _LINE_ _	Current line number in the source file.
_ _FILE_ _	Source file name.
_ _DATE_ _	Date of program compilation (translation).
_ _TIME_ _	Time of program compilation (translation).
_ _STDC_ _	Value one indicates that the implementation conforms to the ANSI standard.

These macro definitions cannot be removed with the #undef instruction.

2. File Inclusion

Arbitrary files can be textually included in a C program by using the #include instruction. The capability to include files textually in a program allows common constant, data, type and function declarations and definitions to be kept in separate files. These common declarations and definitions can then be used in many programs by one or more programmers. Keeping common declarations and definitions in separate files and then *including* them in C programs is a popular style used for writing C programs. A common example is the inclusion of the standard input/output declarations file stdio.h.

The #include instruction has three forms:

```
#include "fname"
#include <fname>
#include sequence-of-characters
```

Execution of the first form

```
#include "fname"
```

causes the instruction to be replaced by the contents of the file *fname* prior to the compilation of the program. The preprocessor looks for file *fname* in places associated with the source file containing it (e.g., in the directory containing the source file) and in some standard or prespecified places.

Execution of the second form

```
#include <fname>
```

has an effect similar to the first form except that the preprocessor looks for the file *fname* only in the standard or prespecified places. For example, on the UNIX system the standard place for finding many files is the directory /usr/include; the complete name of the specified file *fname* is /usr/include/*fname*.

Finally, execution of the third form

   #include *sequence-of-characters*

proceeds as follows. First, the specified character sequence is treated as normal text, e.g., macro invocations are recognized and replacement performed. After this, the resulting #include statement must match one of the first two forms and file inclusion is performed accordingly.

Instructions to include files can be nested. Finally, specification of the standard and prespecified places is not part of the language and is implementation dependent.

3. Conditional Compilation

Conditional compilation is the selective compilation of portions of programs. For example, only those portions of a program that are necessary for a desired version of a system may be compiled.

Some advantages of conditional compilation are listed below:

1. It provides a compile-time parameterization facility. For example, such a facility can be used to generate programs with different kinds of structures.

2. It leads to greater storage efficiency because extraneous code need not be kept around at run-time.

3. Decisions can be made at compile-time rather than at run-time. This is often more efficient (but less flexible).

The preprocessor #if instruction is used for conditional compilation. It has two forms—with or without the #else part:

   if-header
   lines$_{true}$
   #endif

and

   if-header
   lines$_{true}$
   #else
   lines$_{false}$
   #endif

where *if-header* is a preprocessor control line, and *lines*$_{true}$ *lines*$_{false}$ are lines of arbitrary text.

The preprocessor control line *if-header* contains a condition that evaluates to true or false causing the interpretation of *lines*$_{true}$ or *lines*$_{false}$, respectively.

The preprocessor control line *if-header* has three forms:

```
#if  constant-expression
#ifdef  identifier
#ifndef  identifier
```

In the first form, the condition is specified by the *constant-expression*, which is true or false depending upon whether it is nonzero or zero, respectively. In the second form, the condition is true if *identifier* has been defined previously (and not subsequently undefined) by means of a #define instruction; otherwise, it is false. In the third form, the condition is true if *identifier* has not been defined previously (or was defined, but then subsequently undefined); otherwise, it is false.

Constant expressions used in the preprocessor must be integral constant expressions that do not contain the sizeof operator, a cast or an enumeration constant. They can contain unary expressions of the form

```
defined  identifier
```

or

```
defined  (identifier)
```

The defined operator returns true if its operand is currently defined as a macro. It allows #if instructions to check for identifier definitions (this ANSI C addition to K&R C makes the #ifdef and #ifndef statements redundant).

One example of conditional compilation is the instruction

```
#ifndef MAX_STK_SIZE
#define MAX_STK_SIZE 128
#endif
```

This instruction defines the identifier MAX_STK_SIZE and gives it a default value provided the identifier has not been defined previously.

Another example of conditional compilation is the definition of the identifier BUFSIZ [AT&T UNIX 1983]:

```
if u370
#define BUFSIZ 4096
#endif
#if vax || u3b
#define BUFSIZ 1024
#endif
#if pdp11
#define BUFSIZ 512
#endif
```

The value of the constant BUFSIZ depends upon which one of the identifiers u370, vax u3b or pdp11 has been defined (assuming that only such one identifier will be defined).

The #elif instruction can be used to specify another branch of the #if conditional instruction; it reduces the number of the #endif instructions needed for the nested #if instructions to one. For example, the above set of preprocessor instructions can be written as

```
#if u370
#define BUFSIZ 4096
#elif vax || u3b
#define BUFSIZ 1024
#elif pdp11
#define BUFSIZ 512
#endif
```

As a final example, consider the declaration of the type FILE [AT&T UNIX 1983]:

```
typedef struct {
#if vax || u3b
    int _cnt;
    unsigned char *_ptr;
#else
    unsigned char *_ptr;
    int _cnt;
#endif
    unsigned char *_base;
    char _flag;
    char _file;
} FILE;
```

This conditionally compiled declaration is used for compatibility between different implementations of the UNIX system. If the identifier vax or u3b have been defined, then the resulting definition of type FILE will be

```
typedef struct {
    int _cnt;
    unsigned char *_ptr;
    unsigned char *_base;
    char _flag;
    char _file;
} FILE;
```

Otherwise, the definition of type FILE will be

```
typedef struct {
    unsigned char *_ptr;
    int _cnt;
    unsigned char *_base;
    char _flag;
    char _file;
} FILE;
```

4. Miscellaneous Instructions

4.1 Error Directive

The preprocessor #error instruction is used for printing diagnostic messages in the preprocessing phase (before the program is compiled). It has the form

#error *diagnostic-message*

4.2 Communicating with the Preprocessor

The #pragma instruction can be used to communicate with the preprocessor; the communication is implementation dependent. The #pragma instruction has the form

#pragma *message*

5. AnExample"

To illustrate the power of the C preprocessor, I will show you the definition of a *generic* function. A *generic* function is a template of an ordinary function. In addition to normal parameters, generic functions also take data types and operators as arguments. Ordinary functions are created from generic functions by instantiating them with appropriate arguments. Generic functions can be implemented in C by using the preprocessor.

Two advantages of having a generic facility in a programming language are [Gehani 1983b]

1. *Reduced Programming Effort*: It is less work to write and maintain one generic function instead of several ordinary functions.

2. *More Manageable Programs*: Program source becomes smaller and more manageable because only one generic function needs to be written for several ordinary functions.

The problem is to write a *generic* function (actually a macro) to exchange elements. This generic function can be instantiated to create ordinary functions. For example, suppose that the generic swap function is named `GENERIC_SWAP`. Then the ordinary swap functions `iswap` and `fswap` which exchange elements of type `int` and `float`, respectively, may be created by the macro invocations

```
GENERIC_SWAP(iswap, int)
GENERIC_SWAP(fswap, float)
```

Function `GENERIC_SWAP` is defined as

File: `gen-swap.c`

```
   #define GENERIC_SWAP(NAME, ELEM_TYPE)\
   void NAME(ELEM_TYPE *a, ELEM_TYPE *b)\
   {\
       ELEM_TYPE t;\
5      t = *a;\
       *a = *b;\
       *b = t; \
   }
```

The above instantiations will result in the creation of the ordinary functions `iswap` and `fswap`:

File: `iswap.c`

```
   void iswap (int *a, int *b)
   {
       int t;
       t = *a;
5      *a = *b;
       *b = t;
   }
```

```
                                                    File: fswap.c
    void fswap (float *a, float *b)
    {
        float t;
        t = *a;
5       *a = *b;
        *b = t;
    }
```

which can be called directly.

To illustrate the use of the pasting operator `##`, I will show you an alternative definition of the generic swap function, `GENERIC_SWAP2`, that automatically generates names for the instantiated functions:

```
                                                    File: gen-swap2.c
    #define GENERIC_SWAP2(ELEM_TYPE)\
    void ELEM_TYPE##s(ELEM_TYPE *a, ELEM_TYPE *b)\
    {\
        ELEM_TYPE t;\
5       t = *a;\
        *a = *b;\
        *b = t;  \
    }
```

The convention used for names of the generated swap functions is *element-types*. For example, the macro invocation

```
    GENERIC_SWAP2(long)
```

will generate a function named `longs` for swapping values of two variables of type `long`.

6. Exercises

1. What are the pros and cons of defining constant identifiers using the preprocessor rather than using the `const` type qualifier?

2. Why was it necessary to use so many parentheses in the definitions of `MAX` and `MIN`? Why are the following definitions not correct?

```
        #define MAX(x,y)  x>y?x:y
        #define MIN(x,y)  x>y?y:x
```

3. Write a macro `ADD` that generates a program segment to add the corresponding elements of two arrays and to put the result in the corresponding elements of a third array. For example,

```
ADD(x, y, z, n)
```

will generate instructions so that

```
x[i] = y[i] + z[i];
```

for values of i between 0 and n−1. *Hint*: A local loop variable must be defined.

4. Can you give a macro definition of the form

```
#define if if(
```

or will you have to use another keyword for *if*, e.g.,

```
#define IF if(
```

Explain your reasoning.

5. When would it be undesirable to use macros (for in-line code generation) instead of functions?

6. Write macro definitions that can be used to implement an ALGOL-like *if* statement of the form

```
if expression
then ...
else ...;
```

7. Write a generic sort function GENERIC_SORT that takes as parameters the sort function name, the array element type and the comparison operator. An example of an instantiation using GENERIC_SORT is

```
GENERIC_SORT(isort, int, <)
```

that produces an ordinary sort function isort to sorts int arrays in nondecreasing order.

What will be the result of the instantiation

```
GENERIC_SORT(isort, int, >)
```

8. Write a program that implements some of the capabilities of the C preprocessor, e.g., the #define statements.

Chapter 9

One Final Example

The example involves writing a set of functions interrogate the employee database of a small company (about 50 employees).[1] The employee information is kept in a file that is used by function `init` to initialize the database. This file contains lines of the form

name(19) room#(7) extension#(4) designation(11) companyid(5) signature(3) logid(3) maild(49)

The fields in the data lines are separated by a blank; numbers in parentheses indicate the length of the field (these numbers are not actually stored in the file). Here is a description of the fields:

field	description
name	name in the form *lastname, first_initial, middle_initial*
room#	office number
extension#	telephone number
designation	organizational rank
companyid	company identification number
signature	a three character password
logid	computer system identification
maild	name of mail directory

Some sample lines from the database file are

---

1. This problem is based on a database that was built as part of a prototype electronic form system [Gehani 1983a]; the system was designed as a test bed for an office environment where employees use electronic forms that can be mailed by one employee to another. The database was used to automatically fill in some information on the forms and to authenticate other information.

171

Limb,J.O.	3D479	2582	DeptHead	30479	LIM	jol	/a1/jol
Allen,R.B.	3D443	4755	MTS	30443	ALL	rba	/a1/rba
Gehani,N.H.	3D414	4461	MTS	30414	GEH	nhg	/a1/nhg
Maxemchuk,N.F.	3D402	6240	MTS	30402	MAX	nfm	/a1/nfm
Sharma,D.K.	3A402	2914	MTS	31402	SHA	dks	/a1/dks
Super,S.S.	3D400	2583	Supervisor	30400	SUP	sss	/a1/sss

The functions to be implemented are

function	comments
init(*db*)	Initialize the database using the file *db*.
print()	Print the database for debugging.
ext(*n*)	Return a pointer to a string containing the extension of person named *n*.
room(*n*)	Return a pointer to a string containing the room of the person named *n*.
desig(*n*)	Return a pointer to a string containing the designation of the person named *n*.
compid(*n*)	Return a pointer to a string containing the company id of the person named *n*.
sig(*n*)	Return a pointer to a string containing the signature of the person named *n*.
logid(*n*)	Return a pointer to a string containing the login id of the person named *n*.
get_desig(*id*)	Return a pointer to a string containing the designation of the person with logid *id*.
get_sig(*id*)	Return a pointer to a string containing the signature of the person with logid *id*.
get_maild(*id*)	Return a pointer to a string containing the mail directory of the person with logid *id*.

The functions with parameters expect strings as arguments. All functions return the value NULL if the specified argument is not in the database.

Based on anticipated use, it is expected that one employee query is followed by several other queries about the same employee. In other words, the database query sequence can be partitioned into subsequences such that each subsequence consists of queries about the same person. This information may be used to optimize retrieval of information from the database.

0.1 Database Design Strategy

Because the database is small, it will be kept in main memory; the file containing the employee information will be read into objects of type `emp`. Elements of array `db` will point to these objects. Variable `size` will be used to represent the current size of the database. Both variables `db` and `size` will be global to all the database functions. They are declared in the header file `db.h`

```
extern emp *db[];
extern int size;
```

and defined and initialized in file `init.c`:

```
emp *db[MAX_DB];
int cur = 0, size = 0;
```

Storage for the `emp` objects will be allocated as needed.

Function `search` is called by most of the other functions to search the database. Function `search` uses the employee name as the key to search the database; it sets the global variable `cur` to the index of the appropriate element, if any, of the database array `db`. Consequently, in most cases,[2] element `db[cur]` points to the employee involved in the last successful query. To take advantage of the clustering of queries, `search` first examines the employee information pointed to by `db[cur]` to determine if this employee is the one being sought. If `db[cur]` points to information about the employee in question, then `search` returns 1; otherwise, `search` examines the database sequentially. If the employee is in the database, then `search` sets `cur` to the index of the element of `db` that points to information about the employee and returns 1; otherwise it returns −1.

Variable `cur` is declared in the header file `db.h` as

```
extern int cur;
```

and defined and initialized in the file `init.c`.

0.2 The Database Functions

The database functions include the header file `db.h`:

---

2. Some functions such as `get_desig` do not call `search` to search the database because they do not use the employee name as the key.

File: db.h

```
    #include <stdio.h>
    #include <stdlib.h>
    #include <string.h>

5           /* LAYOUT of the database file */
    #define LN 20    /*length(name)+1*/
    #define LR 8     /*length(room)+1*/
    #define LE 5     /*length(extension)+1*/
    #define LD 12    /*length(designation)+1*/
10  #define LC 6     /*length(company id)+1*/
    #define LS 4     /*length(signature)+1*/
    #define LL 4     /*length(login id)+1*/
    #define LM 50    /*length(mail directory)+1*/

15  #define MAX_DB   100    /*max size of database*/

    typedef struct {
        char name[LN], room[LR], ext[LE],
             desig[LD], compid[LC], sig[LS],
20           logid[LL], maild[LM];
    } emp;

    extern emp *db[];/*pointer to database records*/
    extern int cur;
25          /*points to the last employee queried*/
            /*Typically, an employee query is     */
            /*followed by several other queries   */
            /*about the same employee.            */
    extern int size; /*number of records*/
30
    void init(char *db_file);
    int search(char name[]);
    char *strsave(char s[]);
    void fatal(char *s);
35  char *ext(char name[]), *room(char name[]),
         *desig(char name[]), *compid(char name[]),
         *sig(char name[]), *logid(char name[]),
         *get_desig(char log_id[]),
         *get_sig(char log_id[]),
         *get_maild(char log_id[]);
```

The database functions are straightforward and self-explanatory:

```
                                                    File: init.c
   #include "db.h"

   emp *db[MAX_DB];
   int cur = 0, size = 0;
 5
   void init(char *db_file)
   {
       FILE *fp;
       int i;
10
       if ((fp = fopen(db_file,"r")) == NULL)
           fatal("init: cannot open database");

       for (i = 0; ; i++) {
15         if (i == MAX_DB) {
               printf("init: Warning!");
               printf(" database full!\n");
               break;
           }
20         if ((db[i] = malloc(sizeof(emp)))==NULL)
               fatal("init: out of storage");

           if (fscanf(fp,"%s%s%s%s%s%s%s%s",
               db[i]->name, db[i]->room,
25             db[i]->ext, db[i]->desig,
               db[i]->compid, db[i]->sig,
               db[i]->logid, db[i]->maild) != 8)
               break;
       }
30     size = i;
       fclose(fp);
   }
```

```
#include "db.h"

int search(char name[])
     /*set cur to the index of db element that*/
5    /*contains name; return 1 if successful  */
     /*and 0 otherwise*/
{
     if (size == 0) return 0;
                    /*nothing in the database*/
10   if (strcmp(name, db[cur]->name) == 0)
          return 1;
     for(cur = 0; cur < size; cur++)
          if (strcmp(name, db[cur]->name) == 0)
               return 1;
15   cur = 0;
     return 0;
}

char *strsave(char s[])
20   /*allocate storage for s, copy s to it & */
     /*return a pointer to the copy*/
{
     char *p;

25   if ((p = malloc(strlen(s) + 1)) == NULL)
          fatal("strsave: out of storage\n");
     else
          strcpy(p, s);
     return p;
}
```

```
#include "db.h"

char *ext(char name[])
{
5    return search(name)?
               strsave(db[cur]->ext) : NULL;
}
```

File: `get_desig.c`

```
#include "db.h"

char *get_desig(char log_id[])
{
5       int i;

        for(i = 0; i < size; i++)
            if (strcmp(db[i]->logid, log_id) == 0)
                return strsave(db[i]->desig);
10      return NULL;
}
```

Function `fatal`, which is used by the above functions to print an error message and stop the program, is the same as the one used in earlier examples; it is reproduced here for your convenience:

File: `fatal.c`

```
#include <stdio.h>
#include <stdlib.h>

void fatal(char *s)
5 {
        fprintf(stderr, "Error, %s\n", s);
        exit(EXIT_FAILURE);
}
```

Functions `room`, `desig`, `compid`, `sig` and `logid` are all similar to function `ext`. Likewise, functions `get_sig` and `get_maild` are similar to function `get_desig`.

1. Exercises

1. Function `strsave` is used to make a copy of the query answer and it is the address of this copy that is returned to the program making the query. What is the harm in returning the address (in the database `db`) of the query answer? Suggest another strategy.

2. Suggest ways of increasing the efficiency of the database functions.

3. Extend the database example to allow changes to the database, e.g., the addition of new entries or the modification of the existing entries. Note that any modifications to the database must eventually be written to the file where the database information is stored permanently. Consequently, a function that writes the current contents of the database to a file must

also be provided.

4. Many of the database functions are similar, e.g., `ext`, `room`, `desig`, `compid`, `sig` and `logid`. Using the preprocessor facilities, write a generic function from which these functions can be instantiated.

5. The visibility of variables `db`, `cur` and `size` should be restricted to just the database functions. How can you modify the code shown to accomplish this? *Hint*: Your modification will require that all the database functions be kept in the same file.

6. Write a program to recognize strings generated by the following grammar written in extended BNF[3] (i.e., the program should determine whether or not the given input string is a valid expression):

> *statement* → *variable* = *expression*
> *variable* → *letter* { *letter-or-digit* }
> *expression* → *term* { + *term* }
> *term* → *factor* { * *factor* }
> *factor* → *variable* | (*expression*)

where *letter* stands for an upper-case letter and *letter-or-digit* stands for an upper-case letter or a digit.

Hint: Recursion will simplify the task of writing the syntax recognizer. Write one function for each term on the left hand side of the productions.

---

3. Extended BNF notation is used for defining the syntax of programming languages:

{a}	0 or more occurrences of item *a*.
a | b	Either item *a* or item *b*.
a → b	item *a* really stands for item *b* (a "production" or a "rewrite rule").

Appendix A
C++

The C++ language is a superset of C developed by Bjarne Stroustrup that provides facilities for data abstraction, inheritance, operator and function overloading, and in-line functions. The C++ data abstraction facility is called the *class*. As defined earlier, a type is a set of values plus a set of operations on these values. The class mechanism allows the declaration of full-fledged user-defined types. On the other hand, the `typedef` mechanism is not really a type definition facility because it provides facilities only for specifying a set of values; no facilities are provided for associating operations with these values.

In this appendix, I will give a brief overview of the C++ class facility. For a detailed explanation, see *The C++ Programming Language* [Stroustrup 1986].

1. Class Declarations

Class declarations consist of two parts: a specification and a body. The class specification represents the class "user interface". It contains all the information necessary for the user of a class. The class specification also contains information necessary for the compiler to allocate class objects. The class body consists of the bodies of functions that were declared in the class specification but whose bodies were not given there.

Class specifications have the form

```
                                        File: class.h
class class-name {
    private components
public:
    public components
};
```

The private components of a class are data items and functions that implement class objects. These represent internal details of the class and cannot be accessed directly by the user of a class. The internal details, i.e., the representation, of a class can be changed without affecting the user of the class provided that the changes do not affect the public components. Private components of a class can be accessed only by the four kinds of class functions:

179

constructors, destructors, members and friends.

The public class components can be data items, constructors, destructors, member functions (and operators), and friend functions (and operators). The public components (to be precise) represent the class user interface. These are the components that the user of a class can use or call.

Constructors are functions that are called automatically to construct a class value; they are typically used to initialize class objects when the latter are defined or allocated. Constructor definitions have the form

```
class-name :: class-name ( parameter declarations )
{
    ...
}
```

Destructors are the counterparts of constructors; these functions are called automatically at the end of the lifetime of a class object (after which the object will no longer be accessible). They are intended for performing "clean up" chores. For example, destructors may be used to explicitly deallocate dynamic objects so that the storage used by them can be reused. Destructor definitions have the form

```
class-name :: ~class-name ( parameter declarations )
{
    ...
}
```

Member and friend functions are used to manipulate class objects. Member function definitions have the form

```
result-type  class-name :: function-name ( parameter declarations )
{
    ...
}
```

Member functions are called using the selected component notation

```
class-object . member-function-name ( arguments )
ptr-to-class-object -> member-function-name ( arguments )
```

The class object specified in the call is passed as an implicit argument to the member function.

Typically, functions are specified as friends when they need to operate on more than one class object. Unlike member functions, friend function definitions are similar to the definitions of ordinary C++ functions.

Note that a class specification and the corresponding class functions are usually placed in different source files.

2. Other C + + Facilities

In this section, I will briefly summarize other C++ facilities.

2.1 Call-by-Reference

Arguments can also be passed by reference, i.e., parameters can be made synonyms for the corresponding arguments. This allows argument values to be changed by calling functions and avoids copying of the arguments themselves. Note that pointers are used frequently in C to pass addresses of arguments to simulate "call-by-reference".

2.2 Operator and Function Overloading

Operators and functions can be *overloaded*; i.e., the same operator symbol or function identifier can be associated with more than one operation or function. C++ automatically selects the right operator or function when an overloaded operator or function is called. This selection is based on the type and number of the arguments and the expected result type.

Overloading is particularly helpful when using classes to define new data types. For example, overloading can be used to extend the usual arithmetic operators for complex arithmetic (to be used in conjunction with a user-defined class type `complex`), thus providing a natural notation for complex arithmetic.

2.3 Inheritance

Suppose we have several geometrical objects that share common properties; for example, vehicles of different types such as cars, trucks, motorcycles and buses that share common properties like the manufacturer's name and the year of manufacture. However, each of these vehicles may have properties that are typically not associated with some or all of the other vehicles. For example, associated with trucks may be properties such as the number of axles and the weight and volume of goods they can carry. Similarly, associated with buses may be properties such as seating capacity and whether or not the bus is a school bus.

Instead of having to specify a different class for each of the different types of vehicles, C++ allows you to define a common base class, say `vehicle`, that contains the common properties. Then you can derive specialized classes from the base class. The advantage of using derived classes is that a pointer to the base class can be made to point to any of the derived class objects thus allowing the construction of data structures that can store different but similar objects. For more details, see *The C++ Programming Language* [Stroustrup

1986].

2.4 Virtual Functions

Member functions of a class can be declared as `virtual`. This allows a derived class to supply its own version of the function declared as virtual. For example, consider the class `geometric_figure`. The print function may be declared to be virtual and every class that is derived from it, for example `circle` and `square`, can supply its own print function.

3. Examples

In this section, I will give you three simple examples illustrating the use of classes to define new data types.

3.1 Complex Numbers

Consider the class *complex*:

File: `complex.h`

```
     class complex {
         double re, im;
     public:
         complex(double r, double i);
 5       complex(double r);
         complex();

         double real();
         double imag();
10
         friend complex operator+(complex, complex);
         friend complex operator-(complex, complex);
         friend complex operator-(complex);
         friend complex operator*(complex, complex);
15       friend complex operator/(complex, complex);
         friend int operator==(complex, complex);
         friend int operator!=(complex, complex);
     };
```

The first three lines (lines 4–6 of file `complex.h`) in the public part of the `complex` class shown above are declarations of constructors. An appropriate constructor, selected according to the initial values supplied, is called automatically when `complex` variables are defined. The next two lines, i.e., lines 8–9, are the declarations of member functions (`real` and `imag`) and the remaining declarations (lines 11–17) declare friend operators.

I will show you the definition of one constructor function, one member function and one friend operator.

File: `complex.c`

```
   #include "complex.h"
   complex::complex(double r, double i)
   {
       re = r; im = i;
 5 }

   double complex::real()
   {
       return re;
10 }

   complex operator+(complex a, complex b)
   {
       return complex(a.re+b.re, a.im+b.im);
   }
```

Here are some examples illustrating uses of class `complex`:

```
   complex p = complex(5.4,2.4), q = complex(3,3);
   complex r;
   double x;
       ...
 5 x = p.real();
   r = p + q;
```

Note that for illustration purposes, variables p and q have been initialized explicitly but not variable r. For variables p and q, the first constructor is automatically called to construct the initial values; the third constructor is called for variable r. The constructor called depends upon the initial arguments supplied (or not supplied) when defining a class variable.

3.2 Stacks

Consider the following class `stack` that is used for defining integer stacks:

```
                                                    File: stk.h
     class stack {
       int *s, next, max;
     public:
         stack(int size);
 5       ~stack();   /*destructor function*/
         void push(int i);
         void pop();
         int top();
         int empty()   { return next == 0; }
10       int full()    { return next == max; }
         void clear() { next = 0; }
     };
```

Class stack has three private components: s, which will point to a dynamically allocated array, next, which will point to the next free slot in the stack and max, whose value will be the maximum size of the stack. Class components cannot be initialized in their definitions; they must be initialized by the constructor functions.

The stack class has the destructor function ~stack which will be called at the end of the lifetime of a stack object. The bodies of several member functions have been given in-line, i.e., they have been given in the specification itself. Typically, in-line definitions are given for functions with small bodies.

The rest of the stack functions are defined as

File: s t k . c

```c
#include <stdio.h>
#include "stk.h"

void fatal(char *m)
{
    printf("%s\n", m); exit(1);
}
stack::stack(int size)
{
    s = new int[size];
    max = size; next = 0;
}
stack::~stack()
{
    delete(s);
}
void stack::push(int i)
{
    if (next == max)
        fatal("push: Stack Full Error");
    s[next++] = i;
}
void stack::pop()
{
    if (next == 0)
        fatal("pop: Stack Empty Error");
    next--;
}
int stack::top()
{
    if (next == 0)
        fatal("top: Stack Empty Error");
    return s[next - 1];
}
```

Notice the use of the new operator in the definition of the constructor stack to allocate an array dynamically (line 8) and the use of the delete operator (line 13) to free dynamically allocated storage.

Here are some examples illustrating the use of class stack to define stacks:

```c
stack sa(5), sb(10), *ps;
```

Variables `sa` and `sb` are individual stacks and `ps` is a pointer to a stack. These stacks must be manipulated by using the functions declared in class `stack`:

```
sa.push(i+14); /*add element i+14 to stack sa*/
```

Class objects can be explicitly allocated and deallocated using the predefined operators `new` and `delete`:

```
ps = new stack(5);
delete ps;
```

Note that the implementation of class `stack` can be changed to use a list instead of an array without affecting users of the class `stack` (the program will have to be recompiled).

3.3 Buffer

The problem is to specify a `buffer` class for defining circular character buffers (default size 128). The following `buffer` operations are to be provided:

`empty()`	Return 1 if the buffer is empty; otherwise, return 0.
`clear()`	Clear the buffer; this function must also be used to initialize the buffer.
`put(c)`	Add character c to the buffer if it is not full and return c to indicate success; otherwise, return −1 indicating failure.
`get()`	If the buffer is not empty, then return the next character in the buffer; otherwise return −1 indicating failure.

Here is the specification of class `buffer`:

File: `buffer.h`

```
class buffer {
    char *b;
    int max, in, out, count;
public:
5    buffer(int size = 128);
    int empty();
    void clear();
    int put(char);
    int get();
};
```

Notice that the `size` parameter in the declaration of the constructor `buffer` has been given a default initial value. This means that if an object of type `buffer` is defined or allocated without an initial value for the `size` parameter, then by default `size` will be assumed to be 128.

Here are the definitions of the `buffer` functions:

```
   #include "buffer.h"
   buffer::buffer(int size)
   {
        b = new char[size];
5       max = size; in = out = count = 0;
   }
   int buffer::empty()
   {
        return count == 0;
10 }
   void buffer::clear()
   {
        in = out = count = 0;
   }
15 int buffer::put(char c)
   {
        if (count == max) return -1;
        else {
            b[in] = c;
20          in = (in + 1) % max; /*wrap around*/
            count++;
            return c;
        }
   }
25 int buffer::get()
   {
        char result;
        if (count == 0) return -1;
        else {
30          result = b[out];
            out = (out + 1) % max; /*wrap around*/
            count--;
            return result;
        }
   }
```

4. Exercises

1. Define a class `string` for specifying strings of arbitrary length subject to the following specifications:

   a. The default string length should be 15.

   b. A destructor should be provided to deallocate the dynamic storage used for a string object at the end of its lifetime.

   c. Overload the assignment operator so that one string object can be copied to another.

   d. Overload operator + as the string concatenation operator.

2. Define a class `vector` with elements of type `int` for which the arithmetic operators are overloaded to support vector arithmetic.

Appendix B
Concurrent C

Concurrent C is a superset of C designed by Narain Gehani and Bill Roome that provides parallel programming facilities [Gehani & Roome 1986]. It has also been integrated with C++, which extends C to provide data-abstraction facilities [Stroustrup 1986; Gehani & Roome 1988]. Concurrent programming is desirable for many reasons [Hoare 1978; Gehani 1983b] including

- Notational convenience and conceptual elegance in writing operating systems, real-time systems, database systems and simulation programs, all of which may have many events occurring concurrently.

- Inherently concurrent algorithms are best expressed with the concurrency explicitly stated; otherwise, the structure of the algorithm may be lost.

- Program execution time can be reduced on genuine multiprocessing hardware because different parts of a program can execute in parallel.

- Program execution time can be reduced even on a single processor because lengthy input/output operations and program execution by the CPU (central processing unit) can proceed in parallel.

FORTRAN does not support recursion. Consequently, FORTRAN programmers rarely, if ever, develop recursive algorithms for solving problems. Similarly, if a programming language does not provide concurrent programming facilities, then programmers using that language will be unlikely to develop concurrent solutions for their applications.

In this appendix, I will give an overview of the Concurrent C model of parallelism, summarize Concurrent C facilities and explain them by means of examples.

1. Overview of the Concurrent C Model

A Concurrent C program consists of a set of sequential components, called *processes,* that execute in parallel and interact with each other to achieve a common goal. Concurrent C processes interact by means of transactions[1] that can be synchronous or asynchronous. Synchronous transactions implement the extended rendezvous concept (as in Ada): two processes interact by first synchronizing, then exchanging information (bidirectional information transfer) and, finally, by continuing their individual activities. A process calling a synchronous transaction is forced to wait (unless the transaction times out) until the called process accepts the transaction and performs the requested service. With asynchronous transactions, the caller does not wait for the called process to accept the transaction; instead the caller continues with other activities after issuing the transaction call. Information transfer in asynchronous transactions is unidirectional: from the calling process to the called process.

Concurrent C is based on the message passing model; the transactions are essentially message passing facilities. The synchronous transaction, which allows bidirectional information transfer, encapsulates sending of a message from one process to another and then getting an answering message back much like the bidirectional information transfer encapsulated in a function call. And an asynchronous transaction is simply an asynchronous message sending facility.

Concurrent C was designed primarily for writing distributed programs that run on a network of computers that interact with each other by sending messages and not by updating shared memory. However, this does not mean that Concurrent C does not run on shared-memory multiple processors. In fact, in such situations, Concurrent C exploits the presence of shared memory by passing pointers to messages between processes instead of copying messages between processes. However, Concurrent C does not provide any explicit facilities for controlling access to shared memory. Programmers can use shared memory (global variables and pointers) but they must synchronize access to the shared memory by using synchronous transactions.

2. Concurrent C Facilities: A Summary

Concurrent C extends C for parallel programming by providing facilities for

- process definitions, which consist of two parts, i.e., a specification (type) and a process body,
- creating processes (the `create` operator),
- specifying the processor on which a process is to run, (`processor` clause

---

1. To avoid confusion with "database transactions", please note that the term "transaction" is used to mean a Concurrent C process interaction. Transactions are like remote procedure calls with one important difference: the receiving process can schedule acceptance of the calls.

of the create operator),

- specifying, querying and changing process priorities (priority clause of the create operator and library functions),
- synchronous transactions, which allow bidirectional information transfer,
- returning a value to the caller of a synchronous transaction (treturn statement),
- asynchronous transactions, which allow unidirectional information transfer,
- delays and timeouts (the delay statement and the within operator), waiting for a set of events such as transactions (the select statement),
- accepting transactions (the accept statement) in a user-specified order (suchthat and by clauses of the accept statement and guards of the select statement),
- process abortion (the c_abort function),
- collective termination (terminate alternative of the select statement), and
- interrupt handling (the c_associate function),
-

Transactions are declared in a process specification (using the keyword trans); in case of asynchronous transactions, the keyword async is given instead of the transaction result type. Transactions are accepted by using the accept statement in the process body. For more details, see [Gehani & Roome 1986].

3. Examples

I will now give you a taste of Concurrent C by showing you three examples: the producer-consumer problem in which two processes interact with each other much like two programs connected by a UNIX pipe, the classic dining philosophers program [Dijkstra 1971] which is used as a bench mark for concurrent programming languages, and a lock manager process.

3.1 Producer-Consumer

The problem is to write a program which reads data, processes it, and then prints the results. Assume that the input data is a stream of characters and that processing it involves converting all the lower-case characters to upper-case characters.

The Concurrent C program implementing the producer-consumer problem will be structured as follows: one process, called the "producer", reads the data from the terminal and sends it to another process, called the "consumer". This data is converted to upper case by the consumer process after which it prints the data on the standard output (terminal):

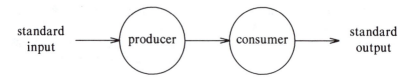

standard input → producer → consumer → standard output

The Concurrent C program implementing the producer-consumer problem:

File: pc.cc

```
   #include "concurrentc.h"
   #include <stdio.h>
   #include <ctype.h>

 5 process spec consumer()
   {
       trans void send(int);
   };
   process spec producer(process consumer);
10
   process body producer(cons)
   {
       int c;
       do {
15        cons.send(c = getchar());
       } while(c != EOF);
   }

   process body consumer()
20 {    int ch;
       for (;;) {
           accept send(c)
               ch = c;
           if (ch == EOF) break;
25        if (islower(ch)) putchar(toupper(ch));
           else putchar(ch);
       }
   }
   main()
30 {
       create producer(create consumer());
   }
```

Concurrent C source files are given the suffix .cc. Line 1 of the above program includes the header file concurrentc.h which should be included in every Concurrent C source file. Lines 5–9 are the specifications for two process types: consumer and producer. Associated with the consumer process is (the synchronous) transaction send, which is called by other processes to send a character to a consumer process. Note that no transactions are associated with the producer process, but that it has one parameter of type process consumer; a value for this parameter must be supplied when creating an instance of the producer process (line 31). The producer process may be thought of as a "client" process that calls services (transactions) associated with the "server" consumer process.

The producer process reads characters from the standard input stream and sends these characters, one at a time, to the consumer process by calling transaction send (line 15). The consumer process accepts send transaction calls. For each call accepted it records the character sent and then, after the completion of the transaction, it prints the upper-case version of the character on the standard output stream. The accept statement (lines 22–23) in the body of the consumer process (lines 19–28) is used to accept the send transaction call. This accept statement just records the character sent to it for subsequent processing.

The main process (lines 29–32) creates instances of the producer and consumer processes. The create operator returns the id of the process created by it. The id of the consumer process is supplied as an argument to the producer process (line 31).

Interaction between the producer and consumer processes is tightly coupled, i.e., they proceed in lock step. The producer process sends one character, the consumer process accepts it and these two steps are repeated until all the data are processed. The producer process cannot go ahead of the consumer process. Interaction between the two processes can be decoupled by interposing an intermediate buffer process or by using asynchronous transactions. Decoupling the process interactions by using asynchronous transactions is straightforward: transaction send of the consumer process is simply specified to be asynchronous:

```
process spec consumer( )
{
     trans async send(int);
};
```

Making send asynchronous will allow the producer process to send characters to the consumer process without waiting for the consumer process to accept them. Note that it is the programmer's responsibility to ensure that a process does not flood the system with asynchronous messages.

3.2 The Mortal Dining Philosophers

Five philosophers spend their lives thinking and eating spaghetti at a circular table in a dining room. The table has five chairs around it and philosopher i ($0 \leqslant i \leqslant 4$) is assigned chair number i. Five forks have also been laid out on the table so that there is precisely one fork between every adjacent two chairs. Consequently there is one fork to the left of each chair and one to its right; fork number i is to the left of chair number i. Before eating, a philosopher must enter the dining room and sit in the chair assigned to her. A philosopher must have two forks to eat (the forks placed to the left and right of every chair). If the philosopher cannot get two forks immediately, then she must wait until she can get them. The forks are picked up one at a time. When a philosopher has finished eating (after a finite amount of time), she puts the forks down and leaves the room.

Each of the five philosophers and five forks is implemented as a process. On activation, each philosopher is given an identification number (0–4) and the process ids of the forks she is supposed to use. Each philosopher is mortal and passes on to the next world soon after having eaten 100,000 times (three times a day for about 90 years).

The specifications of the `philosopher` and `fork` processes are

File: `phil.h`
```
process spec philosopher(int id,
                         process fork left,
                         process fork right);
```

File: `fork.h`
```
process spec fork()
{
    trans void pick_up(), put_down();
};
```

The `fork` process has two transactions: `pick_up` and `put_down`. Each `fork` process manages one fork. The ids of the `fork` processes managing the forks on either side of a philosopher are given as arguments to the corresponding `philosopher` process. The `philosophers` may be thought of as client processes, and the `forks` as server processes.

First the body of the `philosopher` process:

File: `phil.cc`

```
   #include "concurrentc.h"
   #include "fork.h"
   #include "phil.h"
   #define LIMIT 100000
 5 process body philosopher(id, left, right)
   {
       int n;

       for (n = 0; n < LIMIT; n++) {
10         /*think; then enter dining room */
           /*pick up forks*/
               right.pick_up();
               left.pick_up();
           /*eat*/
15             printf("Philosopher %d:*burp*\n",id);
           /*put down forks*/
               left.put_down();
               right.put_down();
               /*get up and leave dining room*/
20     }
       printf("Philosopher %d:Goodbye World\n",id);
   }
```

Each philosopher eats LIMIT times. Forks are picked up by calling transaction pick_up of the appropriate fork processes (lines 12–13) and put down by calling transaction put_down of the same fork processes (lines 17–18).

Here is the body of the fork process:

```
                                                    File: fork.cc
   #include "concurrentc.h"
   #include "fork.h"
   process body fork()
   {
5      for (;;)
           select {
               accept pick_up();
               accept put_down();
           or
10             terminate;
           }
   }
```

The body of a `fork` process consists of an infinite `for` loop whose body consists of just a `select` statement (lines 6–11). A `select` statement is used to wait for a set of events. When one of the alternatives becomes executable (i.e., the event associated with the alternative has happened), then the statements in the alternative are executed. If more than one alternative becomes executable, then one of the alternatives is selected nondeterministically (subject to the `select` statement semantics).

In this example, the `select` statement has two alternatives: an `accept` alternative (begins with line 7 and includes line 8) and a `terminate` alternative (line 10). Execution of this `select` statement occurs as follows: if a `pick_up` transaction call is pending, then it is accepted. A `put_down` transaction call must then be accepted to complete the execution of the `accept` alternative and the execution of the `select` statement.

If no `pick_up` transaction call is pending, then the `terminate` alternative is executed provided all other processes have either completed execution or are themselves waiting at a `terminate` alternative. Each process waiting at the `terminate` alternative then terminates causing the whole program to terminate. If execution of either alternative is not currently possible, the `select` statement makes the process executing it wait until one of the alternatives can be executed.

Finally, here is the body of the `main` process:

```
                                              File: dining.cc
   #include "concurrentc.h"
   #include "fork.h"
   #include "phil.h"

 5 main()
   {
      process fork f[5];
      int j;

10 /*first create forks, then the philosophers*/
      for (j = 0; j < 5; j++)
          f[j] = create fork();
      for (j = 0; j < 5; j++)
          create philosopher(j, f[j], f[(j+1) % 5]);
   }
```

The main process simply creates the fork processes (lines 11–12) and gives their ids to the philosopher process which it creates next (lines 13–14).

Once the philosophers have terminated, the forks have nothing else to do. Because each fork is then waiting at the terminate alternative of a select statement and their parent process (i.e., main) has completed, they all terminate. This allows the main process to terminate, which completes execution of the Concurrent C program.

Note that the output of the philosophers can get intermingled if two of them write to standard output at the same time. Output can be written to different portions of the screen by using a "window manager", which can be used to write to different portions of the same screen.

On a multiprocessor, the Concurrent C implementation will automatically place the different processes on different processors. If it is necessary to place specific processes on specific processors, then the program must be modified to use the processor clause with the create operator to indicate where the process being created should run. Note that the processor clause uses small integers to identify the processors. These integers are determined by using implementation facilities.

3.3 Lock Manager

The lock manager process manages locks for a large collection of items. Client processes can get and release locks on these items. If an item is already locked, a process requesting a lock on that item waits until that item is available. The specification of the lock manager process is (items are identified by a value of type `lockid`):

```
                                              File: lock.h
process spec lock_mngr()
{
    trans void lock(lockid id);
    trans void release(lockid id);
};
```

Clients call `get_lock` to lock an item, and `release_lock` to release an item they have previously locked.

Here is the body of the lock manager process:

```
                                              File: lock.cc
    #include "concurrentc.h"
    #include "lock.h"
    process body lock_mngr()
    {
5       lockid xid;

        for (;;)
            select {
                accept lock(id) suchthat(isfree(id))
10                  xid = id;
                    lock(xid);
            or
                accept release(id)
                    xid = id;
15                  unlock(xid);
            }
    }

    /*isfree(id) returns true if id is unlocked*/
20  /*lock(id) locks id*/
    /*unlock(id) unlocks id*/
```

Client processes call the lock manager process to request locks before accessing a shared resource. The process granted the lock is allowed exclusive access until it releases the lock. The `suchthat` clause is used to ensure that `get_lock` transaction calls are accepted if and only if the requested item is unlocked. Note that functions `isfree`, `lock`, and `unlock` manipulate a lock table.

4. Exercises

1. As suggested in the producer-consumer example, a simple way of decoupling the producer and consumer processes is by declaring transaction send to be asynchronous. Suppose that asynchronous transactions were not provided. Interaction between the producer and consumer processes could still be decoupled, but this would require interposing an intermediate buffer process:

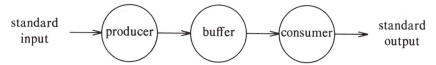

standard input → producer → buffer → consumer → standard output

Write the definition of the buffer process and modify the producer-consumer example to incorporate the buffer process.

2. Compare the asynchronous and buffered versions of the producer-consumer example.

3. The dining philosophers program given above will deadlock (i.e., the program will hang) if each philosopher picks up one fork. One way of avoiding deadlock is to allow at most four philosophers to sit at the table at any given time. This can be enforced by a "gatekeeper" process. Modify the dining philosopher program to incorporate a gatekeeper process.

4. Modify the lock manager process to grant two types of locks: read locks and write locks. Processes holding read locks can simultaneously read shared data, but a process holding a write lock is granted exclusive access to update shared data.

Appendix C

Library Routines

ANSI C requires each compiler to provide a set of standard library routines (i.e., macros and functions). These routines are part of the C environment. Moreover, each C compiler must provide the prototype declaration of each library function and the definition of each library macro in one of the standard header files (as specified in the ANSI C standard [ANSI 1988a]). These header files also contain the declarations of types and constants that are needed for using the library routines.

The standard header files that must be provided by every ANSI C compiler are

assert.h	locale.h	stddef.h
ctype.h	math.h	stdio.h
errno.h	setjmp.h	stdlib.h
float.h	signal.h	string.h
limits.h	stdarg.h	time.h

Standard header files may be included in any order. Multiple inclusions of these header files will not cause problems. Note that multiple inclusions of header files often occurs as a result of including files that include other files.

For some library routines, a compiler may provide both macro and function versions. To ensure that the macro version of a library routine is used, the library routine should not be declared explicitly. Instead, the appropriate header file should be included. Not including the appropriate header file rules out the use of the macro version of the library routine because header files contain the macro definitions. If the function version of a library routine is to be used, then the corresponding macro definition, if any, should first be explicitly removed by using the #undef instruction.

As an example, suppose that both function and macro versions of the library routine atoi are provided by the C compiler. The macro definition, if any, will be in the header file stdlib.h. The following paradigm ensures that macro version is used [ANSI 1988a]:

```
#include <stdlib.h>
...
i = atoi(str);
```

To use the function version of `atoi`, the following paradigm, which removes the definition of the macro `atoi`, can be used:

```
#include <stdlib.h>
#undef atoi
...
i = atoi( str );
```

Removing the macro definition, forces the linker to look for a function named `atoi` in the standard library which is then linked together with the rest of the program.

The description of each library routine consists of its syntactic specification and the description of its behavior or semantics. The syntactic specification of a C routine contains information that will allow the program to be compiled without error. By convention, the syntactic specification of a library routine consists of two parts:

1. One or more `#include` statements that include the header files containing the definition of the macro or the prototype declaration of the function implementing the routine, and declarations necessary to use the macro or function.

2. The function prototype declaration (an equivalent declaration is given in case of a macro).

When using a library routine, the `#include` statements specified in the specification of the routine should be given in the file containing references to the function (before the references).

For complete and detailed descriptions of these routines, please see the *American National Standard for Information Systems—Programming Language C* [ANSI C 1988a].

1. Diagnostic Routines

1.1 Macro `assert`

Include: `#include <assert.h>`
Prototype: `void assert(int expression);`

Behavior: `assert` is used to check whether or not the condition specified by `expression` is true. If `expression` is false, `assert` prints, on the standard error stream, diagnostic information such as the unsatisfied condition, and the name of the source file containing the `assert` call and its line number. It then terminates the program by calling `abort`.

2. Character Handling Routines

2.1 Function `isalnum`

Include: `#include <ctype.h>`
Prototype: `int isalnum(int c);`

Behavior: `isalnum` returns a nonzero value if `c` is a letter or a digit; otherwise, it returns zero.

2.2 Function `isalpha`

Include: `#include <ctype.h>`
Prototype: `int isalpha(int c);`

Behavior: `isalpha` returns a nonzero value if `c` is a letter; otherwise, it returns zero.

2.3 Function `iscntrl`

Include: `#include <ctype.h>`
Prototype: `int iscntrl(int c);`

Behavior: `iscntrl` returns a nonzero value if `c` is a control character; otherwise, it returns zero.

2.4 Function `isdigit`

Include: `#include <ctype.h>`
Prototype: `int isdigit(int c);`

Behavior: `isdigit` returns a nonzero value if `c` is a digit; otherwise, it returns zero.

2.5 Function `isgraph`

Include: `#include <ctype.h>`
Prototype: `int isgraph(int c);`

Behavior: `isgraph` returns a nonzero value if `c` is any printing character except the space (blank) character; otherwise, it returns zero.

2.6 Function `islower`

Include: `#include <ctype.h>`
Prototype: `int islower(int c);`

Behavior: `islower` returns a nonzero value if `c` is a lower-case letter; otherwise, it returns zero.

2.7 Function `isprint`

Include: `#include <ctype.h>`
Prototype: `int isprint(int c);`

Behavior: `isprint` returns a nonzero value if c is any printing character (including a space); otherwise, it returns zero.

2.8 Function `ispunct`

Include: `#include <ctype.h>`
Prototype: `int ispunct(int c);`

Behavior: `ispunct` returns a nonzero value if c is a punctuation character (but not a space); otherwise, it returns zero.

2.9 Function `isspace`

Include: `#include <ctype.h>`
Prototype: `int isspace(int c);`

Behavior: `isspace` returns a nonzero value if c is a white-space character (space, form-feed, new-line, carriage-return, horizontal-tab or vertical-tab); otherwise, it returns zero.

2.10 Function `isupper`

Include: `#include <ctype.h>`
Prototype: `int isupper(int c);`

Behavior: `isupper` returns a nonzero value if c is an upper-case character; otherwise, it returns zero.

2.11 Function `isxdigit`

Include: `#include <ctype.h>`
Prototype: `int isxdigit(int c);`

Behavior: `isxdigit` returns a nonzero value if c is a hexadecimal digit; otherwise, it returns zero.

2.12 Function `tolower`

Include: `#include <ctype.h>`
Prototype: `int tolower(int c);`

Behavior: If c is an upper-case character, then `tolower` returns the lower-case version of character c; otherwise, it returns c.

2.13 Function `toupper`

Include: `#include <ctype.h>`
Prototype: `int toupper(int c);`

Behavior: If `c` is a lower-case character, then `toupper` returns the upper-case version of `c`; otherwise, it returns `c`.

3. Mathematical Routines

3.1 Function `acos`

Include: `#include <math.h>`
Prototype: `double acos(double x);`

Behavior: `acos` returns the arc cosine of `x`, which must be in the range $[-1, +1]$.[1] The arc cosine computed will be in the range $[0, \pi]$ radians.

3.2 Function `asin`

Include: `#include <math.h>`
Prototype: `double asin(double x);`

Behavior: `asin` returns the arc sine of `x`, which must be in the range $[-1, +1]$. The arc sine computed is in the range $[-\pi/2, +\pi/2]$ radians.

3.3 Function `atan`

Include: `#include <math.h>`
Prototype: `double atan(double x);`

Behavior: `atan` returns the arc tangent of `x`, which must be in the range $[-1, +1]$. The arc tangent computed is in the range $[-\pi/2, +\pi/2]$ radians.

3.4 Function `atan2`

Include: `#include <math.h>`
Prototype: `double atan2(double y, double x);`

Behavior: `atan2` returns the arc tangent of `y/x`. The quadrant of the return value is determined by the signs of `x` and `y`. The arc tangent computed is in the range $[-\pi, +\pi]$ radians.

---

1. The notation $[a, b]$ specifies the interval from a to b, including the end values a and b. Using an opening (instead of [indicates that the end value a is not included in the interval. Similarly, using a closing) instead of] indicates that the end value b is not included in the interval.

3.5 Function `cos`

Include: `#include <math.h>`
Prototype: `double cos(double x);`
Behavior: `cos` returns the cosine of `x`, which must be in radians.

3.6 Function `sin`

Include: `#include <math.h>`
Prototype: `double sin(double x);`
Behavior: `sin` returns the sine of `x`, which must be in radians.

3.7 Function `tan`

Include: `#include <math.h>`
Prototype: `double tan(double x);`
Behavior: `tan` returns the tangent of `x`, which must be in radians.

3.8 Function `cosh`

Include: `#include <math.h>`
Prototype: `double cosh(double x);`
Behavior: `cosh` returns the hyperbolic cosine of `x`.

3.9 Function `sinh`

Include: `#include <math.h>`
Prototype: `double sinh(double x);`
Behavior: `sinh` returns the hyperbolic sine of `x`.

3.10 Function `tanh`

Include: `#include <math.h>`
Prototype: `double tanh(double x);`
Behavior: `tanh` returns the hyperbolic tangent of `x`.

3.11 Function `exp`

Include: `#include <math.h>`
Prototype: `double exp(double x);`
Behavior: `exp` returns e^x.

3.12 Function `frexp`

Include: `#include <math.h>`
Prototype: `double frexp(double value, int *exp);`

Behavior: `frexp` splits a floating-point number into a normalized fraction and an integral power of 2. It stores the integer power in `*exp` and returns a value x, such that x is in the interval [1/2, 1) or equal to zero, and `value` is equal to x multiplied by 2 to the power `*exp`.

3.13 Function `ldexp`

Include: `#include <math.h>`
Prototype: `double ldexp(double x, int exp);`

Behavior: `ldexp` returns x multiplied by 2^{exp}.

3.14 Function `log`

Include: `#include <math.h>`
Prototype: `double log(double x);`

Behavior: `log` returns the natural logarithm of x.

3.15 Function `log10`

Include: `#include <math.h>`
Prototype: `double log10(double x);`

Behavior: `log` returns the base-10 logarithm of x.

3.16 Function `modf`

Include: `#include <math.h>`
Prototype: `double modf(double value, double *iptr);`

Behavior: `modf` splits the argument `value` into integral and fractional parts (each has the same sign as `value`). It stores the integral part in `*iptr` and returns the fractional part.

3.17 Function `pow`

Include: `#include <math.h>`
Prototype: `double pow(double x, double y);`

Behavior: pow returns x^y.

3.18 Function `sqrt`

Include: `#include <math.h>`
Prototype: `double sqrt(double x);`

Behavior: `sqrt` returns the nonnegative square root of x.

3.19 Function `ceil`

Include: `#include <math.h>`
Prototype: `double ceil(double x);`
Behavior: `ceil` returns the smallest integer greater than or equal to x.

3.20 Function `fabs`

Include: `#include <math.h>`
Prototype: `double fabs(double x);`
Behavior: `fabs` returns the absolute value of x.

3.21 Function `floor`

Include: `#include <math.h>`
Prototype: `double floor(double x);`
Behavior: `floor` returns the largest integer less than or equal to x.

3.22 Function `fmod`

Include: `#include <math.h>`
Prototype: `double fmod(double x, double y);`
Behavior: `fmod` returns the floating-point remainder of x/y. i.e., it returns $x - iy$ for some integer i such that, if y is not zero, then the value returned is less than y and it has the same sign as x.

4. Nonlocal Jump Routines

Besides other items, header file `setjmp.h` contains the declaration of type `jmp_buf` which is used for saving and restoring environments in conjunction with the `setjmp` and `longjmp` routines.

4.1 Macro `setjmp`

Include: `#include <setjmp.h>`
Prototype: `int setjmp(jmp_buf env);`
Behavior: `setjmp` saves its calling environment in argument env for later use by `longjmp`. When returning from a direct invocation, `setjmp` returns zero. If it returns as a result of calling `longjmp`, then `setjmp` returns a nonzero value.

4.2 Function `longjmp`

Include: `#include <setjmp.h>`
Prototype: `void longjmp(jmp_buf env, int val);`
Behavior: `longjmp` restores the environment saved in `jmp_buf` by the last invocation of `setjmp`. If the function containing the `setjmp` invocation has

completed, then the behavior of longjmp is undefined. After executing a longjmp call, program execution continues as if the corresponding invocation of setjmp had just returned the value val. Note that longjmp cannot make setjmp return a zero. If val is equal to zero, setjmp will return one.

5. Signal Handling Routines

Besides other items, header file signal.h contains definitions of the macros SIG_DFL, SIG_ERR and SIG_IGN which are used for handling signals; these macros are discussed later. File signal.h also defines following constants identifying signals:

signal name	signal generated due to
SIGABRT	an abnormal termination, e.g., one caused by calling abort
SIGFPE	an erroneous arithmetic operation, e.g., zero divide or an overflow
SIGILL	an illegal instruction
SIGINT	an interrupt, e.g., from the keyboard
SIGSEGV	an invalid memory reference
SIGTERM	a termination request sent to the program

These signals are generated automatically; they can also be generated by calling function raise.

5.1 Function signal

Include: #include <signal.h>
Prototype: void (*signal(int sig,
                      void (*fun)(int)))(int);

Behavior: signal associates the function fun (signal handler) with the signal numbered sig. How the signal numbered sig is handled depends upon the value of fun:

value of fun	signal handling
SIG_DFL	default handling
SIG_IGN	signal is ignored
pointer to function f	function f (*signal handler*) is called.

At program startup, signals may be ignored or handled in the default manner; this treatment is implementation dependent.

If signal executes successfully, then it returns the value of the previous signal handler for sig. Otherwise, SIG_ERR is returned and a positive value is stored in `errno`.

5.2 Function `raise`

Include: `#include <signal.h>`
Prototype: `int raise(int sig);`

Behavior: `raise` generates signal `sig`. If successful, `raise` returns zero; otherwise, it returns a nonzero value.

6. Macros to Handle Variable Number of Arguments

Besides other items, header file `stdarg.h` contains the definitions of type `va_list` and the macros `va_start`, `va_arg` and `va_end`, which are used for accessing arguments of a function that can be called with a variable number of arguments. Information needed by the variable argument manipulation macros is stored in an object of type `va_list`.

The variable number of arguments, which do not have explicit names, is indicated by the ellipsis following the last parameter in the function header. The rightmost parameter of such a function is special (the one just before the ellipsis) and is designated as *parm$_n$* in the discussion below. Parameter *parm$_n$* must not be given the `register` storage class, or be a function or an array type or a type incompatible with the argument type (after the default argument promotions).

6.1 Macro `va_start`

Include: `#include <stdarg.h>`
Prototype: `void va_start(va_list ap, parm$_n$);`

Behavior: `va_start` must be invoked before invoking `va_arg` to access the unnamed arguments (represented by the ellipsis). `va_arg` initializes `ap`.

6.2 Macro `va_arg`

Include: `#include <stdarg.h>`
Prototype: *type* `va_arg(va_list ap, ` *type* `);`

Behavior: The ith invocation of `va_arg` (after invoking `va_start`) returns the value of argument *parm$_{n+i}$*. Parameter `ap` must be the one initialized by `va_start`. Parameter *type* specifies the type of the next argument.

6.3 Macro `va_end`

Include: `#include <stdarg.h>`
Prototype: `void va_end(va_list ap);`

Behavior: `va_end` must be called after accessing the variable arguments.

7. Input/Output Routines

Besides other items, header file `stdio.h` contains the definitions of the following types and macros:

types	macros	macros
size_t	NULL	SEEK_CUR
FILE	_IOFBF	_END
fpos_t	_IOLBF	SEEK_SET
	_IONBF	TMP_MAX
	BUFSIZ	tmpnam
	EOF	stderr
	FOPEN_MAX	stdin
	FILENAME_MAX	stdout
	L_tmpnam	

7.1 Function remove

Include: #include <stdio.h>
Prototype: int remove(const char *fname);
Behavior: remove deletes the file with the name pointed to by fname. If successful, remove returns zero; otherwise, it returns a nonzero value.

7.2 Function rename

Include: #include <stdio.h>
Prototype: int rename(const char *old,
                                  const char *new);
Behavior: rename changes the name of a file from that pointed to by old to that pointed to by new. If successful, rename returns zero; otherwise, it returns a nonzero value.

7.3 Function tmpfile

Include: #include <stdio.h>
Prototype: FILE *tmpfile(void);
Behavior: tmpfile creates a temporary file (opened for update). This file is automatically removed when it is closed, or upon program termination. If successful, tmpfile returns a pointer to the file created; otherwise, it returns the null pointer.

7.4 Function `tmpnam`

Include: `#include <stdio.h>`
Prototype: `char *tmpnam(char *s);`

Behavior: `tmpnam` generates a new unique file name (string) every time it is called. If `s` is the null pointer, then `tmpnam` stores the file name in an internal static object and returns a pointer to this object. Otherwise, `tmpnam` puts the file name in the array pointed to by `s` and returns `s`. Note that the array size must be greater than or equal to `L_tmpnam` (defined in `stdio.h`).

7.5 Function `fclose`

Include: `#include <stdio.h>`
Prototype: `int fclose(FILE *stream);`

Behavior: `fclose` flushes the stream pointed to by `stream` and closes the associated file. If successful, `fclose` returns zero; otherwise, it returns `EOF`.

7.6 Function `fflush`

Include: `#include <stdio.h>`
Prototype: `int fflush(FILE *stream);`

Behavior: `fflush` flushes `stream`, i.e., it starts writing unwritten buffered output to the file associated with `stream`. If `fflush` is called with a null pointer, then all output streams are flushed. If successful, `fflush` returns zero; otherwise, it returns `EOF`.

7.7 Function `fopen`

Include: `#include <stdio.h>`
Prototype: `FILE *fopen(const char *fname, const char *mode);`

Behavior: `fopen` opens the file with the name pointed to by `fname` and associates a stream with it. The values of argument `mode`, which specifies the file mode, are listed below:

mode	explanation
`"r"`	Open text file for reading.
`"w"`	Create text file for writing. Existing files are truncated to zero length.
`"a"`	Open or create text file for appending.
`"rb"`	Open binary file for reading.
`"wb"`	Create binary file for writing. Existing files are truncated to zero length.
`"ab"`	Open or create binary file for appending.
`"r+"`	Open text file for update (reading and writing).
`"w+"`	Create text file for update. Existing files are truncated to zero length.
`"a+"`	Open or create text file for update and appending.
`"r+b"`	Open binary file for update (reading and writing).
`"w+b"`	Create binary file for update. Existing files are truncated to zero length.
`"a+b"`	Open or create binary file for update and appending.

Both input and output may be performed on a stream if the associated file has been opened with the update mode. However, input may follow output only after an intervening call to `fflush`, or to one of the file positioning functions `fseek`, `fsetpos` or `rewind`. Output may follow input only after calling a file positioning function, except if the end-of-file has been encountered.

If successful, `fopen` returns a pointer to the stream; otherwise, it returns the null pointer.

7.8 Function `freopen`

Include: `#include <stdio.h>`
Prototype: `FILE *freopen(const char *fname,`
                        `const char *mode, FILE *stream);`

Behavior: `freopen` opens the file with the name pointed to by `fname` and associates with it the stream pointed to by `stream`. Before doing this, `freopen` closes the file, if any, associated with `stream`. Argument `mode` is used as in function `fopen`.

If successful, `freopen` returns the value of `stream`; otherwise, it returns the null pointer.

7.9 Function `setbuf`

Include: `#include <stdio.h>`
Prototype: `void setbuf(FILE *stream, char *buf);`
Behavior: Calling `setbuf` is equivalent to calling `setvbuf` with `mode` equal to `_IOFBF` (`_IONBF` if `buf` is the null pointer) and `size` equal to `BUFSIZ`. The only difference is that `setbuf`, unlike `setvbuf`, does not return a value.

7.10 Function `setvbuf`

Include: `#include <stdio.h>`
Prototype: `int setvbuf(FILE *stream, char *buf,`
                                `int mode, size_t size);`
Behavior: `setvbuf` is used to specify buffering of the stream pointed to by `stream` as indicated by parameter `mode`:

mode	effect
`_IOFBF`	fully buffered input/output
`_IOLBF`	line buffered output
`_IONBF`	unbuffered input/output

If `buf` is not the null pointer, the array it points to may be used to buffer the input/output (instead of an internally allocated buffer). `size` specifies the size of this array. `setvbuf` is used after associating an open file with a stream, but before performing input or output.

If successful, `setvbuf` returns zero; otherwise, it returns a nonzero value.

7.11 Function `fprintf`

Include: `#include <stdio.h>`
Prototype: `int fprintf(FILE *stream,`
                        `const char *fmt, ...);`
Behavior: `fprintf` writes output to the stream pointed to by `stream` as specified by the string pointed to by `fmt` which contains characters to be printed and conversion specifications (formats) specifying how the arguments (indicated by the ellipsis) are to be printed.

Each format begins with the `%` character which is followed by

1. Zero or more *flags* modifying the format.

2. An optional decimal integer specifying the minimum *field width*. If necessary, the value printed is left padded (right padded if the left adjustment flag is given) with blanks.

3. An optional *precision* (a period followed by a decimal integer) which specifies the

   a. minimum number of digits to be printed for d, i, o, u, x and X formats,
   b. number of digits to be printed after the decimal point for e, E and f formats,
   c. maximum number of significant digits for g and G formats, or
   d. maximum number of characters to be printed for the s format.

4. An optional h (l) specifying that the following d, i, o, u, x or X format applies to a short (long) int or unsigned short (long) int argument, or that the following n format applies to a short (long) int * argument; or an optional L specifying that the following e, E, f, g or G format applies to a long double argument.

5. A character specifying the format.

An asterisk * given for the field width (precision) indicates that an argument specifying the field width (precision) will be given before the argument to be printed.

The flags that can modify the format are listed below:

flag	meaning
–	Left-justify when output.
+	Print a leading plus or minus sign for signed values.
space	If the first character of a signed value is not a sign, then print a leading space.
#	o format: increase the precision to force the first digit of the output to be zero. x (X) format: print a leading 0x (0X) for nonzero results. e, E, f, g and G formats: print a decimal point. g and G formats: do not remove trailing zeros.
0	d, i, o, u, x, X, e, E, f, g and G formats: use leading zeros for padding.

The formats and their meanings are

format	meaning
d, i, o, u, x, X	Print an `int` argument as a signed decimal (d or i), an unsigned octal (o), an unsigned decimal (u) or as an unsigned hexadecimal (x or X).
f	Print the `double` argument (rounded appropriately) in the style [-]*ddd.ddd*. The number of digits printed after the decimal point is specified by the precision (default is 6).
e, E	Print the `double` argument (rounded appropriately) in the style [-]*d.e±dd*. One digit is printed before the decimal point and the number of digits printed after it is specified by the precision (default is 6). An e (E) is printed before the (at least two-digit) exponent.
g, G	The `double` argument is printed in the style specified by the f or e (E) formats. The e (E) format is used only for exponents less than −4 or greater than or equal to the precision.
c	Print the `int` argument as an `unsigned char`.
s	Print the string pointed to by the argument. Characters up to (but not including) the terminating null character are printed. If *n* is the precision, then only *n* characters will be printed.
p	Print the pointer argument, which must be of type `void *`.
n	The corresponding argument must point to an integer into which is written the number of characters printed up to now by this `fprintf` call. Nothing is printed.
%	Print the % character.

Notation [*a*] is used to specify the optional occurrence of item *a*.

If successful, `fprintf` returns the number of characters printed; otherwise, it returns a negative value.

7.12 Function `fscanf`

Include: `#include <stdio.h>`
Prototype: `int fscanf(FILE *stream, const char *fmt, ...);`

Behavior: `fscanf` reads input from the stream pointed to by stream, according to the formats specified in the string pointed to by fmt, and assigns the values read to the objects pointed to by the remaining arguments (indicated by the ellipsis), which must all be pointers.

Each format begins with the % character which is followed by

1. An optional * indicating that the input is to be read but not assigned to any object (no corresponding argument is given). This is equivalent to skipping over a data item.

2. An optional decimal integer specifying the maximum field width.

3. Formats d, i, n, o and x may be preceded by h (1) which indicates that the corresponding argument is a pointer to a short (long) int and not a pointer to int. Similarly, format u may be preceded by h (1) which indicates that the corresponding argument points to an unsigned short (long) int and not to an unsigned int. Finally, formats e, f and g may be preceded by a 1 (L) to indicate that the corresponding argument points to a (long) double and not a float.

4. A character specifying the format.

A white space in the format string indicates that input is to be read (but not assigned to any object) up to the first nonwhite-space character (which remains unread) or until no further characters can be read. An ordinary character in the format string indicates that the next input character is to be read only if it matches the specified character.

White-space characters are skipped in the input unless the next format specifier is a [, c or n. Input is read for each format except for the n format.

Unless an asterisk is given in the format to suppress assignment, the item read will be stored in the object pointed to by the corresponding argument.

The formats and their meanings are

format	meaning
d	Read a decimal integer; the corresponding argument must be an integer pointer.
i	Read an integer; the corresponding argument must be an integer pointer.
o	Read an optionally signed octal integer; the corresponding argument must be an integer pointer.
u	Read an unsigned decimal integer; the corresponding argument must be an unsigned integer pointer.
x	Read an optionally signed hexadecimal integer; the corresponding argument must be an integer pointer.
e, f, g	Read a floating-point integer; the corresponding argument must be a floating-point pointer.
s	Read a string, i.e., a sequence of nonwhite-space characters; the corresponding argument must be a pointer an array large enough to hold the string plus the automatically added terminating null character.
[	Read a string consisting of characters specified after the [and up to the terminating] (called the "matching set"); the corresponding argument must be a pointer an array large enough to hold the string plus the automatically added terminating null character. If the first character after the left bracket is a circumflex (^), then the characters read are those not in the matching set. As a special case, if the format begins with [ ] or [^], the right bracket is considered to be part of the matching set; the next] ends the matching set.
c	Reads *n* characters where *n* is the field width (default value is 1); the corresponding argument must be a pointer an array large enough to hold the string; a terminating null character is not added.
p	Read a pointer value (such as one printed with fprintf); the corresponding argument must be a void pointer.
n	No input is read; the corresponding argument must be a pointer to integer into which is written the number of characters read up to now by this fscanf call.
%	Matches a single %.

fscanf returns EOF if it fails before reading any data; otherwise, it returns the number of input items assigned (may not be the same as the number of items read).

7.13 Function `printf`

Include: `#include <stdio.h>`
Prototype: `int printf(const char *fmt, ...);`
Behavior: `printf` is similar to `fprintf` except that it writes to `stdout`.

7.14 Function `scanf`

Include: `#include <stdio.h>`
Prototype: `int scanf(const char *fmt, ...);`
Behavior: `scanf` is similar to `fscanf` except that it reads from `stdin`.

7.15 Function `sprintf`

Include: `#include <stdio.h>`
Prototype: `int sprintf(char *s, const char *fmt, ...);`
Behavior: `sprintf` similar to `fprintf`, except that it writes to an array (the first argument). A null character is written at the end of output; it is not included in the value returned by `sprintf`.

7.16 Function `sscanf`

Include: `#include <stdio.h>`
Prototype: `int sscanf(const char *s, const char *fmt,`
                                              `...);`
Behavior: `sscanf` is similar to `fscanf`, except that it reads from a string (the first argument). Reaching the end of the string is equivalent to encountering the end-of-file.

7.17 Function `vfprintf`

Include: `#include <stdarg.h>`
             `#include <stdio.h>`
Prototype: `int vfprintf(FILE *stream,`
                         `const char *fmt, va_list arg);`
Behavior: `vfprintf` is similar to `fprintf` except that the variable argument list is replaced by the argument `arg`, which contains information about variable arguments; `arg` must have been initialized by invoking `va_start` and it may have been used in subsequent `va_arg` invocations. Functions called with a variable number of arguments can pass a variable of type `va_list` holding information about the variable arguments to `vfprintf` for printing the variable arguments.

7.18 Function `vprintf`

Include: `#include <stdarg.h>`
`#include <stdio.h>`
Prototype: `int vprintf(const char *fmt, va_list arg);`

Behavior: `vprintf` is similar to `vfprintf` except that it writes to `stdout`.

7.19 Function `vsprintf`

Include: `#include <stdarg.h>`
`#include <stdio.h>`
Prototype: `int vsprintf(char *s, const char *fmt,`
`va_list arg);`

Behavior: `vsprintf` is similar to `vfprintf`, except that it writes its output to a character array (specified by parameter `s`).

7.20 Function `fgetc`

Include: `#include <stdio.h>`
Prototype: `int fgetc(FILE *stream);`

Behavior: `fgetc` returns the next character from the input stream pointed to by `stream`. On encountering the end-of-file, `fgetc` sets the end-of-file indicator associated with `stream` and returns `EOF`. If a read error occurs, `fgetc` sets the error indicator associated with `stream` and returns `EOF`.

7.21 Function `fgets`

Include: `#include <stdio.h>`
Prototype: `char *fgets(char *s, int n, FILE *stream);`

Behavior: `fgets` reads up to n—1 characters from the stream pointed to by `stream` into the array pointed to by `s`. After encountering a new-line character (which is stored in `s`) or the end-of-file, no further characters are read. A null character is written after the last character stored in `s`.

If successful, `fgets` returns `s`. Otherwise, if an end-of-file is encountered and no characters have been stored in `s`, or if a read error occurs, then `fgets` returns the null pointer.

7.22 Function `fputc`

Include: `#include <stdio.h>`
Prototype: `int fputc(int c, FILE *stream);`

Behavior: `fputc` writes character c to the output stream pointed to by `stream` and returns c. If a write error occurs, `fputc` sets the error indicator for `stream` and returns `EOF`.

7.23 Function `fputs`

Include: `#include <stdio.h>`
Prototype: `int fputs(const char *s, FILE *stream);`

Behavior: `fputs` writes the string pointed to by s (sans the terminating null character) to the stream pointed to by `stream`. If successful, `fputs` returns a nonnegative value; otherwise, it returns `EOF`.

7.24 Routine `getc`

Include: `#include <stdio.h>`
Prototype: `int getc(FILE *stream);`

Behavior: `getc` is similar to `fgetc` except that it may be implemented as a macro.

7.25 Function `getchar`

Include: `#include <stdio.h>`
Prototype: `int getchar(void);`

Behavior: `getchar` is similar to `getc` except that it reads from `stdin`.

7.26 Function `gets`

Include: `#include <stdio.h>`
Prototype: `char *gets(char *s);`

Behavior: `gets` reads characters from the input stream pointed to by `stdin` and stores them into the array pointed to by s. It reads characters until an end-of-file encountered or a new-line character is read. The new-line character is discarded; a null character is written after the last character stored in the array.

If successful, `gets` returns s; otherwise, if an end-of-file is encountered and no characters have been read into the array or if a read error occurs, then `gets` returns the null pointer.

7.27 Routine `putc`

Include: `#include <stdio.h>`
Prototype: `int putc(int c, FILE *stream);`

Behavior: `putc` is similar to `fputc` except that it may be implemented as a macro.

7.28 Function `putchar`

Include: `#include <stdio.h>`
Prototype: `int putchar(int c);`
Behavior: `putchar` is similar to `putc` except that it writes to `stdout`.

7.29 Function `puts`

Include: `#include <stdio.h>`
Prototype: `int puts(const char *s);`
Behavior: `puts` writes the string pointed to by `s` to `stdout` and prints a new-line character instead of the terminating null character. If successful, `puts` returns a nonnegative value; otherwise, it returns `EOF`.

7.30 Function `ungetc`

Include: `#include <stdio.h>`
Prototype: `int ungetc(int c, FILE *stream);`
Behavior: `ungetc` pushes argument `c` back into the input stream pointed to by `stream`. Character `c` will be returned by a subsequent read on `stream`. Only one character pushback is guaranteed. The pushed-back character will be discarded if a file positioning function is called with `stream` as an argument.

If successful, `ungetc` clears the end-of-file indicator associated with the stream and returns the pushed-back character `c`; otherwise, it returns `EOF`.

7.31 Function `fread`

Include: `#include <stdio.h>`
Prototype: `size_t fread(void *ptr, size_t size,`
`                 size_t nelem, FILE *stream);`
Behavior: `fread` reads, into the array pointed to by `ptr`, up to `nelem` elements of size `size` from the stream pointed to by `stream`. `fread` returns the number of elements read successfully.

7.32 Function `fwrite`

Include: `#include <stdio.h>`
Prototype: `size_t fwrite(const void *ptr,`
`                 size_t size, size_t nelem,`
`                 FILE *stream);`
Behavior: `fwrite` writes, from the array pointed to by `ptr`, up to `nelem` elements of size `size` to the stream pointed to by `stream`. `fwrite` returns the number of elements successfully written.

7.33 Function `fgetpos`

Include: #include <stdio.h>
Prototype: int fgetpos(FILE *stream, fpos_t *pos);

Behavior: `fgetpos` stores in *pos the current value of the file position indicator associated with the stream pointed to by `stream`. If successful, `fgetpos` returns zero; otherwise, it returns a nonzero value.

7.34 Function `fseek`

Include: #include <stdio.h>
Prototype: int fseek(FILE *stream, long int offset,
                                      int whence);

Behavior: `fseek` sets the file position indicator associated with the stream pointed to by `stream`. For a binary stream, the new position (measured in characters) is equal to `offset` plus the position specified by `whence`:

value of `whence`	specified position
SEEK_SET	beginning of the file
SEEK_CUR	the current position in the file
SEEK_END	end of the file

For a text stream, `offset` must be equal to zero or it must be a value returned by `ftell` and `whence` must be equal to SEEK_SET. After calling `fseek` either input or output can be performed on the stream.

If successful, `fseek` clears the end-of-file indicator, undoes the effects of `ungetc` and returns zero; otherwise, it returns a nonzero value.

7.35 Function `fsetpos`

Include: #include <stdio.h>
Prototype: int fsetpos(FILE *stream,
                           const fpos_t *pos);

Behavior: `fsetpos` sets the file position indicator for the stream pointed to by `stream` to *pos; the value of *pos must have been obtained by calling `fgetpos` on the same stream. After calling `fsetpos` either input or output can be performed on the stream.

If successful, `fsetpos` clears the end-of-file indicator, undoes the effects of `ungetc` and returns zero; otherwise, it returns a nonzero value.

7.36 Function `ftell`

Include: `#include <stdio.h>`
Prototype: `long int ftell(FILE *stream);`
Behavior: `ftell` returns the current value of the file position indicator associated with the stream pointed to by `stream`. If unsuccessful, `ftell` returns −1L.

7.37 Function `rewind`

Include: `#include <stdio.h>`
Prototype: `void rewind(FILE *stream);`
Behavior: `rewind` resets, to the beginning of the file, the file position indicator associated with the stream pointed to by `stream`.

7.38 Function `clearerr`

Include: `#include <stdio.h>`
Prototype: `void clearerr(FILE *stream);`
Behavior: `clearerr` clears the end-of-file and error indicators associated with the stream pointed to by `stream`.

7.39 Function `feof`

Include: `#include <stdio.h>`
Prototype: `int feof(FILE *stream);`
Behavior: `feof` returns a nonzero value if the end-of-file indicator is set for the stream pointed to by `stream`.

7.40 Function `ferror`

Include: `#include <stdio.h>`
Prototype: `int ferror(FILE *stream);`
Behavior: `ferror` returns a nonzero value if the error indicator is set for the stream pointed to by `stream`; otherwise, it returns zero.

7.41 Function `perror`

Include: `#include <stdio.h>`
Prototype: `void perror(const char *s);`
Behavior: `perror` prints, on `stderr`, an error message corresponding to the value of `errno`. This message is prefixed by the string pointed to by `s`.

8. General Utility Routines

Besides other items, header file `stdlib.h` contains definitions of the following types and macros:

types	macros
size_t	NULL
wchar_t	EXIT_FAILURE
div_t	EXIT_SUCCESS
ldiv_t	RAND_MAX
	MB_CUR_MAX
	MB_LEN_MAX

8.1 Function atof

Include: #include <stdlib.h>
Prototype: double atof(const char *nptr);
Behavior: atof converts the string pointed to by nptr to a double which it returns as its result.

8.2 Function atoi

Include: #include <stdlib.h>
Prototype: int atoi(const char *nptr);
Behavior: atoi converts the initial portion of the string pointed to by nptr to an int which it returns as its result.

8.3 Function atol

Include: #include <stdlib.h>
Prototype: long int atol(const char *nptr);
Behavior: atol converts the initial portion of the string pointed to by nptr to a long int which it returns as its result.

8.4 Function strtod

Include: #include <stdlib.h>
Prototype: double strtod(const char *nptr,
                              char **endptr);
Behavior: strtod converts the initial portion of the string pointed to by nptr to a double and returns this real as its result. A pointer to the remaining substring is stored in the object pointed to by endptr. In case no conversion is possible, nptr is stored in endptr. (endptr is assigned a value only if it is not the null pointer).

8.5 Function `strtol`

Include: `#include <stdlib.h>`
Prototype: `long int strtol(const char *nptr,`
                           `char **endptr, int base);`

Behavior: `strtol` converts the initial portion of the string pointed to by `nptr` to a `long int` which it returns as its result. A pointer to the remaining substring is stored in the object pointed to by `endptr`. In case no conversion is possible, `nptr` is stored in `endptr`. (`endptr` is assigned a value only if it is not the null pointer). If `base` is zero, then the string pointed to by `nptr` must be an optionally signed integer constant. For more details about values allowed for `base`, see the *ANSI C Reference Manual* [ANSI C 1988a].

8.6 Function `strtoul`

Include: `#include <stdlib.h>`
Prototype: `unsigned long int strtoul(const char *nptr,`
                             `char **endptr, int base);`

Behavior: `strtoul` converts the initial portion of the string pointed to by `nptr` to an `unsigned long int`; this integer is returned as the result. A pointer to the remaining substring is stored in the object pointed to by `endptr`. In case no conversion is possible, `nptr` is stored in `endptr`. (`endptr` is assigned a value only if it is not the null pointer). If `base` is zero, then the string pointed to by `nptr` must be an optionally signed integer constant. For more details about values allowed for `base`, see the *ANSI C Reference Manual* [ANSI C 1988a].

8.7 Function `rand`

Include: `#include <stdlib.h>`
Prototype: `int rand(void);`

Behavior: `rand` returns a pseudo-random integer between 0 and RAND_MAX.

8.8 Function `srand`

Include: `#include <stdlib.h>`
Prototype: `void srand(unsigned int seed);`

Behavior: `srand` uses the value of `seed` to initiate a new sequence of pseudo-random numbers to be generated by `rand`. Calling `srand` with the same seed value leads to the generation of the same pseudo-random number sequence. The default seed used is one.

8.9 Function `calloc`

Include: `#include <stdlib.h>`
Prototype: `void *calloc(size_t nelem, size_t size);`

Behavior: `calloc` allocates storage for an array of `nelem` elements, each of size `size`. All bits of the allocated storage are set to zero. If successful, `calloc` returns a pointer to the allocated storage; otherwise, it returns the null pointer.

8.10 Function `free`

Include: `#include <stdlib.h>`
Prototype: `void free(void *ptr);`

Behavior: `free` deallocates the storage pointed to by `ptr`. The storage pointed to by `ptr` must have been allocated previously by calling `calloc`, `malloc` or `realloc`.

8.11 Function `malloc`

Include: `#include <stdlib.h>`
Prototype: `void *malloc(size_t size);`

Behavior: `malloc` allocates `size` bytes of storage. If successful, `malloc` returns a pointer to the allocated storage; otherwise, it returns the null pointer.

8.12 Function `realloc`

Include: `#include <stdlib.h>`
Prototype: `void *realloc(void *ptr, size_t size);`

Behavior: `realloc` changes the size of the object pointed to by `ptr` to `size`. The contents of the object are unchanged (up to the smaller of the new and old sizes); if necessary, the contents of the old storage are copied to the new storage.

If successful, `realloc` returns a pointer to the possibly new allocated space; otherwise, it returns the null pointer (the contents of the old storage are not changed).

8.13 Function `abort`

Include: `#include <stdlib.h>`
Prototype: `void abort(void);`

Behavior: `abort` causes abnormal termination of the program executing it unless there is a handler for the signal `SIGABRT` (generated by `abort`) and this handler does not return.

8.14 Function `atexit`

Include: `#include <stdlib.h>`
Prototype: `int atexit(void (*func)(void));`

Behavior: `atexit` registers the function pointed to by `func`, for calling (without arguments) at normal program termination. If `atexit` is successful, then it returns zero; otherwise, it returns a nonzero value.

8.15 Function `exit`

Include: `#include <stdlib.h>`
Prototype: `void exit(int status);`

Behavior: `exit` causes normal program termination. Prior to program termination, functions registered by calling `atexit` are called, in the reverse order of their registration (a function registered n times will be called n times.) All open output streams are flushed, all open streams are closed and all temporary files (created by calling `tmpfile`) are removed.

Successful program termination is indicated to the host environment by calling `exit` with the value zero or `EXIT_SUCCESS`; failure is indicated by calling `exit` with the value `EXIT_FAILURE`.

8.16 Function `getenv`

Include: `#include <stdlib.h>`
Prototype: `char *getenv(const char *name);`

Behavior: `getenv` searches an environment list variable for a string that matches the string pointed to by `name`. If successful, `getenv` returns a pointer to a string associated with the matched string; otherwise, it returns the null pointer.

8.17 Function `system`

Include: `#include <stdlib.h>`
Prototype: `int system(const char *string);`

Behavior: `system` passes the string pointed to by `string` to the host environment for execution. The value returned by `system` is implementation dependent.

8.18 Function `bsearch`

Include: `#include <stdlib.h>`
Prototype: `void *bsearch(const void *key,`
              `const void *base, size_t nelem, size_t size,`
              `int (*cmp)(const void *, const void *));`

Behavior: `bsearch` searches an array of `nelem` elements, each of size `size`, for an element equal to `*key`; `base` points to the first element of this array which must be sorted in ascending order according to the comparison function cmp. This function takes two arguments and returns an integer less than, equal to or greater than zero depending upon whether its first argument is less than, equal to or greater than its second argument.

If successful, bsearch returns a pointer to the array element that matches *key; otherwise, it returns the null pointer.

8.19 Function qsort

Include: #include <stdlib.h>
Prototype: void qsort(void *base, size_t nelem,
            size_t size,
            int (*cmp)(const void *, const void *));

Behavior: qsort sorts an array of nelem elements, each of size size; base points to the first element of the array to be sorted. The array is sorted in increasing order using the comparison function pointed to by cmp, which is called with pointers to the two arguments to be compared. cmp returns an integer less than, equal to or greater than zero depending upon whether its first argument is less than, equal to or greater than its second argument.

8.20 Function abs

Include: #include <stdlib.h>
Prototype: int abs(int j);

Behavior: abs returns the absolute value of its argument.

8.21 Function div

Include: #include <stdlib.h>
Prototype: div_t div(int numer, int denom);

Behavior: div returns a structure of type div_t that contains the quotient and remainder resulting from dividing numer by denom:

```
typedef            struct div_t {
    int quot;   /*quotient*/
    int rem;    /*remainder*/
} div_t;
```

Note that quot*denom+rem is equal to numer.

8.22 Function labs

Include: #include <stdlib.h>
Prototype: long int labs(long int j);

Behavior: labs is similar to abs except it returns a long int value.

8.23 Function `ldiv`

Include: `#include <stdlib.h>`
Prototype:
`ldiv_t ldiv(long int numer, long int denom);`

Behavior: `ldiv` is similar to `div` except that the type of its arguments and that of the elements of the structure returned is `long int`.

9. String Handling Routines

Besides other items, header file `string.h` contains the declaration of the type `size_t` and the definition of the macro `NULL`.

9.1 Function `memcpy`

Include: `#include <string.h>`
Prototype: `void *memcpy(void *s1, const void *s2,`
`                                    size_t n);`

Behavior: `memcpy` copies n characters from the object pointed to by `s2` to the object pointed to by `s1`. Objects pointed to by `s1` and `s2` must not overlap. `memcpy` returns `s1`.

9.2 Function `memmove`

Include: `#include <string.h>`
Prototype: `void *memmove(void *s1, const void *s2,`
`                                    size_t n);`

Behavior: `memmove` copies n characters from the object pointed to by `s2` to the object pointed to by `s1`. Objects pointed to by `s1` and `s2` can overlap. `memmove` returns `s1`.

9.3 Function `strcpy`

Include: `#include <string.h>`
Prototype: `char *strcpy(char *s1, const char *s2);`

Behavior: `strcpy` copies the string pointed to by `s2` (including the terminating null character) to the array pointed to by `s1`. Objects pointed to by `s1` and `s2` must not overlap. `strcpy` returns `s1`.

9.4 Function `strncpy`

Include: `#include <string.h>`
Prototype: `char *strncpy(char *s1, const char *s2,`
`                                    size_t n);`

Behavior: `strncpy` copies up to n characters or up to the null character from the array pointed to by `s2` to the array pointed to by `s1`. These two arrays must not overlap. If the length of the string pointed to by `s2` is less than n, then s1 will be padded with null characters until n characters have been written. strncpy returns s1.

9.5 Function strcat

Include: #include <string.h>

Prototype: char *strcat(char *s1, const char *s2);

Behavior: strcat appends a copy of the string pointed to by s2 (including the terminating null character) to the end of the string pointed to by s1. The null character at the end of the string pointed to by s1 is overwritten. s1 and s2 must not overlap. strcat returns s1.

9.6 Function strncat

Include: #include <string.h>

Prototype: char *strncat(char *s1, const char *s2, size_t n);

Behavior: strncat appends up to n characters or up to the null character from the array pointed to by s2 to the end of the string pointed to by s1. The null character at the end of s1 is overwritten. A terminating null character is appended to the string pointed to by s1. s1 and s2 must not overlap. strncat returns s1.

9.7 Function memcmp

Include: #include <string.h>

Prototype: int memcmp(const void *s1, const void *s2, size_t n);

Behavior: memcmp compares the first n characters of the objects pointed to by s1 and s2 and returns an integer greater than, equal to or less than zero, depending upon whether the object pointed to by s1 is greater than, equal to or less than the object pointed to by s2.

9.8 Function strcmp

Include: #include <string.h>

Prototype: int strcmp(const char *s1, const char *s2);

Behavior: strcmp returns an integer greater than, equal to or less than zero, depending upon whether the string pointed to by s1 is greater than, equal to or less than the string pointed to by s2.

9.9 Function `strcoll`

Include: `#include <string.h>`

Prototype: `int strcoll(const char *s1, const char *s2);`

Behavior: `strcoll` is the same as `strcmp` but the comparison is based on interpreting the strings to be compared according to local conventions.

9.10 Function `strncmp`

Include: `#include <string.h>`

Prototype: `int strncmp(const char *s1, const char *s2,`
                                        `size_t n);`

Behavior: `strncmp` compares up to n characters or up to the null character from the arrays pointed to by s1 and s2.

`strncmp` returns an integer greater than, equal to or less than zero, depending upon whether the array pointed to by s1 is greater than, equal to or less than the array pointed to by s2.

9.11 Function `strxfrm`

Include: `#include <string.h>`

Prototype: `size_t strxfrm(char *s1, const char *s2,`
                                        `size_t n);`

Behavior: `strxfrm` transforms up to n characters (including the terminating null character) of the string pointed to by s2 (as described below) and places the resulting string in the array pointed to by s1. Objects pointed to by s1 and s2 must not overlap. The string pointed to by s2 is transformed so that the result of comparing two transformed strings with `strcmp` is equal to the result of comparing the two original strings with `strcoll`.

`strxfrm` returns the length of the transformed string.

9.12 Function `memchr`

Include: `#include <string.h>`

Prototype: `void *memchr(const void *s, int c,`
                                        `size_t n);`

Behavior: `memchr` returns a pointer to the first occurrence of c (converted to an `unsigned char`) in the first n characters of the string pointed to by s. If `memchr` does not find such a c, then it returns the null pointer.

9.13 Function `strchr`

Include: `#include <string.h>`
Prototype: `char *strchr(const char *s, int c);`

Behavior: `strchr` returns a pointer to the first occurrence of `c` (converted to `char`) in the string pointed to by `s` (the terminating null character is also considered to be part of the string). If `strchr` does not find such a `c`, then it returns the null pointer.

9.14 Function `strcspn`

Include: `#include <string.h>`
Prototype: `size_t strcspn(const char *s1`
                              `const char *s2);`

Behavior: `strcspn` returns the length of the maximum prefix of string pointed to by `s1`, which consists of characters *not* in the string pointed to by `s2`.

9.15 Function `strpbrk`

Include: `#include <string.h>`
Prototype: `char *strpbrk(const char *s1,`
                              `const char *s2);`

Behavior: `strpbrk` returns a pointer to the first occurrence of any character from the string pointed to by `s2` in the string pointed to by `s1`. If there is no such character, then `strpbrk` returns the null pointer.

9.16 Function `strrchr`

Include: `#include <string.h>`
Prototype: `char *strrchr(const char *s, int c);`

Behavior: `strrchr` returns a pointer to the last occurrence of `c` (converted to `char`) in the string pointed to by `s` (the terminating null character is also considered to be part of the string). If `c` does not occur in `s`, then `strrchr` returns the null pointer.

9.17 Function `strspn`

Include: `#include <string.h>`
Prototype: `size_t strspn(const char *s1,`
                              `const char *s2);`

Behavior: `strspn` returns the length of the maximum prefix of the string pointed to by `s1` which consists of just the characters in the string pointed to by `s2`.

9.18 Function `strstr`

Include: `#include <string.h>`
Prototype: `char *strstr(const char *s1,`
`const char *s2);`

Behavior: `strstr` returns a pointer to the first substring in the string pointed to by `s1` that matches the string pointed to by `s2`. If there is no such substring, `strstr` returns the null pointer. If `s2` points to a zero-length string, then `strstr` returns `s1`.

9.19 Function `strtok`

Include: `#include <string.h>`
Prototype: `char *strtok(char *s1, const char *s2);`

Behavior: A series of calls to `strtok` splits the string pointed to by `s1` into a series of tokens (items), each of which is delimited by a character from the separator string pointed to by `s2`. The first argument of the first call is the string to be split into tokens; this argument is replaced in subsequent calls by the null pointer. Leading occurrences of characters from the separator string pointed to by `s2` in the string pointed to by `s1` are ignored. The separator string can vary from call to call.

If a token is found, then `strtok` returns a pointer to the first character of the token; otherwise, it returns the null pointer.

9.20 Function `memset`

Include: `#include <string.h>`
Prototype: `void *memset(void *s, int c, size_t n);`

Behavior: `memset` sets each of the first n characters of the object pointed to by s to the character c. `memset` returns s.

9.21 Function `strlen`

Include: `#include <string.h>`
Prototype: `size_t strlen(const char *s);`

Behavior: `strlen` returns the length of the string pointed to by s (excluding the terminating null character).

10. Date and Time Functions

Besides other items, header file `time.h` contains the definition of the macros `NULL` and the `CLK_TCK`, the declarations of the types `size_t`, `clock_t`, `time_t` and `struct tm`.

`clock_t` and `time_t` are arithmetic types capable of representing times. Structure `tm` must have at least the following components:

```
int tm_sec;    /*seconds: 0 to 59*/
int tm_min;    /*minutes: 0 to 59*/
int tm_hour;   /*hours: 0 to 23*/
int tm_mday;   /*day: 1 to 31*/
int tm_mon;    /*month: 0 to 11*/
int tm_year;   /*years since 1900*/
int tm_wday;   /*days since Sunday: 0 to 6*/
int tm_yday;   /*days since January 1: 0 to 365*/
int tm_isdst;  /*Daylight Saving Time flag*/
```

`tm_isdst` is positive if Daylight Saving Time is in effect, zero if it is not in effect, and negative if information is unavailable.

10.1 Function `clock`

Include: `#include <time.h>`
Prototype: `clock_t clock(void);`

Behavior: `clock` returns the processor time in clock ticks used since the beginning of program execution. To determine the time in seconds, the value returned by `clock` is divided by `CLK_TCK`.

10.2 Function `difftime`

Include: `#include <time.h>`
Prototype: `double difftime(time_t t1, time_t t0);`

Behavior: `difftime` returns the value of the expression `t1-t0` (in seconds).

10.3 Function `mktime`

Include: `#include <time.h>`
Prototype: `time_t mktime(struct tm *timeptr);`

Behavior: `mktime` returns the calendar time (using the encoding used by `time`) corresponding to the time specified as components of the structure pointed to by `timeptr`.

10.4 Function `time`

Include: `#include <time.h>`
Prototype: `time_t time(time_t *timer);`

Behavior: `time` returns the current calendar time. If `timer` is not equal to the null pointer, then the value returned is stored in `*timer`.

10.5 Function `asctime`

Include: `#include <time.h>`
Prototype: `char *asctime(const struct tm *timeptr);`
Behavior: `asctime` converts the time specified as components in the structure `*timeptr` into a string of the form

`Wed May 18 22:43:56 1988\n\0`

and returns a pointer to this string.

10.6 Function `ctime`

Include: `#include <time.h>`
Prototype: `char *ctime(const time_t *timer);`
Behavior: `ctime` converts the calendar time pointed to by `timer` to local time and returns a pointer to the string containing the local time.

10.7 Function `gmtime`

Include: `#include <time.h>`
Prototype: `struct tm *gmtime(const time_t *timer);`
Behavior: `gmtime` splits the calendar time pointed to by `timer` into components in terms of the Coordinated Universal Time (UTC) and returns a pointer to the structure containing the components.

10.8 Function `localtime`

Include: `#include <time.h>`
Prototype: `struct tm *localtime(const time_t *timer);`
Behavior: `localtime` splits the calendar time pointed to by `timer` into components expressed as local time. It returns a pointer to a structure containing the components.

Appendix D

Differences between ANSI C and K & R C

I will now summarize the important differences between K&R C and ANSI C [Relph 1987; Kernighan & Ritchie 1978; ANSI C 1988a]. Unless qualified by K&R C or ANSI C, the discussion refers to the changes made to K&R C by the ANSI C standardization process, i.e., the discussion refers to ANSI C specific facilities. Note that many C compilers already implement some ANSI C extensions. This is because these compilers implement an extended form of K&R C that is described in *The C Programming Language — Reference Manual* [Ritchie 1980]. Extended K&R C includes features such as enumeration and `void` types, structure arguments in function calls, and structure assignment; these features have been incorporated into ANSI C.

1. General

1. A standard character set is specified whereas in K&R C the character set was implementation dependent.

2. The following trigraph sequences, denoting characters not found on all keyboards, are supported:

trigraph sequence	character denoted
??=	#
??(	[
??/	\
??)	]
??'	^
??<	{
??!	¦
??>	}
??-	~

3. Keywords `const`, `volatile`, `enum`, `signed` and `void` have been added.

4. Keywords `entry`, `fortran` and `asm` have been deleted.

237

5. Names beginning with an underscore are reserved for C implementations and they should not be used by application programmers.

6. All keywords, and function and macro names defined in the ANSI C standard are now reserved identifiers.

7. The first 31 characters of internal identifiers are considered significant.

8. The first 6 characters of external identifiers are considered significant.

2. Preprocessor

1. # must be the first nonwhite space character on a line with a preprocessor instruction (it need not be the first character).

2. The # operator converts a macro parameter into a string constant after the parameter has been replaced by the corresponding argument.

3. Items (tokens) in a macro definition can be pasted (joined) together using the ## operator.

4. Using a macro name in its own definition does not lead to infinite recursion because a macro cannot be invoked from within its own body.

5. The defined operator can be used to determine whether or not an identifier has been defined.

6. The #elif instruction can be used to specify another branch of the #if instruction. It reduces the number of the #endif instructions needed for nested #if instructions to one.

7. An identifier defined as a macro must be undefined before it can be redefined.

8. The #error instruction can be used to print error messages during the preprocessing phase.

9. The #pragma instruction can be used to communicate with the compiler.

10. The following predefined macros are provided:

    a. __LINE__,
    b. __FILE__,
    c. __DATE__,
    d. __TIME__ and
    e. __STDC__.

    Note that __STDC__ is the ANSI C standard conformance flag.

3. Constants

1. Unsigned integer constants are specified using the suffix U (or u).

2. Digits 8 and 9 cannot be used in octal constants to specify the octal values 10 and 11.

3. float constants can be specified with the suffix F (or f) and long double constants can be specified with the suffix L (or l); by default, floating-point constants are of type double.

4. String constants are automatically concatenated if they are separated just by white space.

5. "Wide" character and string constants (for specifying additional implementation-dependent characters such as those found in Asian languages) can now be specified by using an l or an L prefix, e.g., L'a\xfff' and L"a\xfff".

6. Four new escape sequences have been added: \a (alert character), \v (vertical tab), \" and \?. Printing the alert character produces an audible or visible signal. The double quotes and the question mark characters can also be specified directly as " and ?.

7. Characters can be specified using hexadecimal escape sequences.

4. Types

1. Several new types have been added:

   ```
   void
   void *
   signed char
   unsigned char
   unsigned short
   unsigned long
   long double
   ```

2. Incomplete types are partially defined types for which a complete definition will be given later.

3. Fundamental types are now known as basic types.

4. Enumeration types can be used to give symbolic names to integers.

5. void functions do not return values.

6. A parameterless function is specified by listing, in the function definition, the void type instead of the parameter types (or declarations).

7. `void` pointers are generic pointers; they can be assigned to any pointer type and vice versa. Many functions now return `void` pointers, e. g., `malloc`, which obviates the need for explicit casts.

8. There are now four integer types. In addition to `short`, `int` and `long`, the very small integer type `signed char` is now supported.

9. There are now three floating-point types. In addition to `float` and `double`, the extra precision type `long double` is now supported.

10. The type specifier combination `long float` (alternative way of specifying `double`) is no longer allowed.

11. File `limits.h` contains constants specifying minimum limits for integral types.

12. File `float.h` contains constants specifying minimum limits for floating-point numbers.

13. The implicit type conversion rules, the "usual arithmetic conversion" rules and argument-to-parameter conversion rules have been changed.

14. The `const` type qualifier is used to specify read-only variables.

15. The `volatile` type qualifier indicates that an object can be modified by the hardware and that accessing it may cause side effects. Compilers must not optimize the use of a `volatile` object and the object value stored in memory must accurately reflect its current value.

16. Each structure and union has a separate name space for its members; i.e., members of different structures and unions can have the same names.

5. Variable Declarations and Definitions

1. An external object can have only one definition.

2. If a union contains several structures with a common initial sequence, then members of this sequence are guaranteed to have the same values and they can be accessed via any of the structures after the union has been initialized via one of the structures.

6. Initialization

1. Automatic arrays and structures can be initialized.

2. The first member of a union can be initialized.

7. Operators and Expressions

1. The function call, subscript and selection (direct and indirect) operators along with the postfix increment and decrement operators, are now

collectively called the postfix operators.

2. The precedence level of the postfix increment and decrement operators has been changed to 1.

3. C now has a unary plus operator.

4. Header file `stddef.h` defines type `size_t` which is the type of the value returned by the `sizeof` operator; in K&R C, the `sizeof` operator returns an `unsigned` value.

5. The cast operator is now formally recognized as an operator.

6. Structure and union assignments are now allowed.

7. Parentheses can now be used to force the evaluation of an expression in a specific order.

8. `float` operands are not always automatically converted to `double`.

9. Pointer arithmetic is now defined more precisely.

8. Statements

1. The `switch` statement control and label expressions can now be integral types (instead of just `int`).

9. Functions

1. An extended form of a function declaration, called the function prototype, is introduced. A function prototype is like a function declaration except that parameter types or declarations are specified in the prototype.

2. Parameter declarations are now given in the function header. In K&R C only the parameter names were given in the function header; the parameter declarations followed the function header and preceded the function body. Note that the K&R C form of function declarations and headers is also allowed.

3. In functions calls, the default type promotions (conversions)

    *   `char` and `short` to `int` (or `unsigned`) and
    *   `float` to `double`

    are not performed automatically if the corresponding function prototype is in scope and if the corresponding parameter types are specified in the function prototype (trailing parameter types can be omitted by using ellipsis marks).

4. Standard (and portable) facilities are provided for writing functions that accept a variable number of arguments.

5. Structures and unions can now be passed as arguments to functions and returned as the function result.

6. A function call is specified using a pointer to a function; if the function name is used, then the name is automatically converted to a pointer to the function.

10. Libraries

The prototype of each library function must be contained in a header file. Every compiler must provide the following header files:

```
assert.h    locale.h    stdarg.h    string.h
ctype.h     math.h      stddef.h    time.h
float.h     setjmp.h    stdio.h
limits.h    signal.h    stdlib.h
```

The following libraries must be provided by every ANSI C compiler and they must contain the following functions:

library	functions included
assert	assert.
ctype	ialnum, isalpha, iscntrl, isdigit, isgraph, islower, isprint, ispunct, isspace, isupper, isxdigit, tolower and toupper.
locale	setlocale.
math	acos, asin, atan, atan2, cos, sin, tan, cosh, sinh, exp, frexp, ldexp, log, log10, modf, pow, sqrt, ceil, fabs, floor and fmod.
setjmp	setjmp and longjmp.
signal	signal and raise.
stdarg	va_start, va_arg and va_end.
stdio	remove, rename, tmpfile, tmpnam, fclose, fflush, fopen, freopen, setbuf, setvbuf, fprintf, fscanf, printf, scanf, sprintf, sscanf, vfprintf, vsprintf, fgetc, fputs, getc, getchar, putc, putchar, puts, ungetc, fread, fwrite, fgetpos, fseek, fsetpos, ftell, rewind, clearerr, feof, ferror and perror.
stdlib	atof, atoi, strod, strol, stroul, rand, srand, calloc, free, malloc, realloc, abort, atexit, exit, getenv, system, bsearch, qsort, compar, abs, div, labs and ldiv.
string	memcpy, memmove, strcpy, strncpy, strcat, strncat, memcmp, strcmp, strncmp, strcoll, memchr, strchr, strcspn, strpbrk, strrchr, strspn, strstr, strtok, memset, sterror and strlen.
time	clock, difftime, mktime, time, asctime, ctime, gmtime, localtime and strftime.

Annotated Bibliography

Ada 1983. *Reference Manual for the Ada Programming Language.* United States Department of Defense (January).

Anderson, B. 1980. Type Syntax in the Language C: An Object Lesson in Syntactic Innovation. *SIGPLAN Notices*, v15, no. 3 (March). Criticizes the C syntax for declaring types; argues that the syntax is cryptic and hard to read in contrast to the syntax for type declarations in languages like ALGOL 68 or Pascal.

ANSI C 1988a. *Draft Proposed American National Standard for Information Systems — Programming Language C* (May 13, 1988).

ANSI C 1988b. Rationale for *Draft Proposed American National Standard for Information Systems — Programming Language C* (May 13 1988).

AT&T UNIX 1983. *UNIX System V Release 2.0 Programmer Reference Manual.* AT&T Bell Laboratories.

Berkeley UNIX 1986. *UNIX Programmer's Manual (4.3 BSD).* Computer Science Division, Department of Electrical Engineering and Computer Science, University of California, Berkeley, CA 94720.

Berry, R. E., and B. A. E. Meekings 1985. A Style Analysis of C Programs. *CACM*, v28, no. 1 (January).

Bourne, S. R. 1982. *The UNIX System.* Addison-Wesley Publishing Co. A detailed and comprehensive guide to the UNIX operating system and the facilities available on it.

Bowles, K. L. 1977. *Problem Solving Using PASCAL.* Springer-Verlag.

Brinch Hansen, P. 1973. Concurrent Programming Concepts. *ACM Computing Surveys*, v6, no. 4 (December), pp. 223–245.

Brinch Hansen, P. 1975. The Programming Language Concurrent Pascal. *IEEE Transactions on Software Engineering*, vSE-1, no. 2 (June).

Byte Magazine 1983. Special Issue of *Byte* magazine on the C programming language, v8, no. 8 (August).

Christian, K. 1983. *The UNIX Operating System.* John Wiley. Chapter 15 discusses the relationship between C and the UNIX operating system.

Cmelik, R. F., N. H. Gehani and W. D. Roome 1987. Experience with Multiple Processor Versions of Concurrent C. To be published in *IEEE Transactions on Software Engineering*.

Collinson, R. P. A. 1981. Comments on Style in C. UKC Computing Lab-7, Computing Lab, Kent University, Canterbury, England.

Dahl, O. J., E. W. Dijkstra and C. A. R. Hoare 1972. *Structured Programming*. Academic Press. A classic book on the disciplined and methodological approach to programming that has come to be known as *structured programming*.

Darnell, P. A. and P. E. Margolis 1988. *Software Engineering in C*. Springer-Verlag.

Dijkstra, E. W. 1968. Goto Statement Considered Harmful. *CACM*, v11 (March), pp. 147–148. Dijkstra argues that the good programming constructs are those that allow the understanding of a program in time proportional to its length. In trying to understand a program containing *goto*s used in an undisciplined manner, the reader of the program is repeatedly forced to jump from one part of a program to another; the reader must follow the execution path of the program to understand the program. This slows program understanding. Dijkstra convincingly argues that constructs such as the *if-then-else* statement and the *while* loop do not cause such slowdowns.

Dijkstra, E. W. 1971. Hierarchical Ordering of Sequential Processes. *Acta Informatica*, v1, pp. 115–138.

Dijkstra, E. W. 1972. Notes on Structured Programming. In *Structured Programming* edited by O. J. Dahl, E. W. Dijkstra and C. A. R. Hoare, Academic Press.

Dijkstra, E. W. 1976. *A Discipline of Programming*. Prentice-Hall.

Evans Jr., A. 1984. A Comparison of Programming Languages: Ada, Pascal, C. In *Comparing and Assessing Programming Languages* edited by Alan Feuer and Narain Gehani, Prentice-Hall [Feuer & Gehani 1984]. The three programming languages are compared against a set of requirements for systems programming and with each other.

Feldman, S. I. 1979. Make—A Program for Maintaining Computer Programs. *Software—Practice and Experience*, v9, pp. 255–265. A tool for maintaining latest versions of programs that consist of many modules (actually files in C).

Feuer, A. 1982. *C Puzzle Book*. Prentice-Hall. A workbook containing convoluted problems, called puzzles, that aim to test and enhance the student's understanding of the operators in C.

Feuer, A. and N. Gehani 1982. A Comparison of the Programming Languages C and Pascal. *ACM Computing Surveys*, v14, no. 1 (March), pp. 73–92. The two languages are summarized and compared objectively. Topics covered include their design philosophies, their handling of data types, the programming facilities provide, the impact of these facilities on the quality of programs, and how useful are the facilities for programming in a variety of application domains.

Feuer, A. and N. Gehani (Editors) 1984. *Comparing and Assessing Programming Languages*. Prentice-Hall. Contains papers that compare and assess programming languages with a special focus on the languages Ada, C and Pascal.

Fitzhorn, P. A. and G. R. Johnson 1981. C: Toward a Concise Syntactic Description. *SIGPLAN Notices*, v16, no. 12 (December), pp. 14–21. The syntax of K&R C [Kernighan & Ritchie 1978; Ritchie 1980] is not complete and not defined rigorously; e.g., the syntax for

1. function definitions and declarations is incomplete;
2. statements is not clear, and
3. data and function types is not separated clearly.

A syntax of C that remedies these concerns is given. Unfortunately, because of printing problems, the syntax given in this paper is not readable. A more readable version, with some more comments, can be found in *SIGPLAN Notices*, v17, no. 8, pp. 84–95, August 1982. Note that ANSI C [1988a] defines the C syntax completely and rigorously.

Gannon, J. D. 1975. Language Design to Enhance Program Reliability. Technical Report CSRG-47, University of Toronto.

Gannon, J. D. 1977. An Experimental Evaluation of Data Type Conventions. *CACM*, v20, no. 8 (August).

Gehani, N. 1977. Units of Measure as a Data Attribute, *Computer Languages*, v2, pp. 93–111.

Gehani, N. H. 1981. Program Development by Stepwise Refinement and Related Topics. *Bell System Technical Journal*, v60, no. 3 (March), pp. 347–378. Takes another look at stepwise refinement in the context of recent developments in programming languages and programming methodology such as abstract data types, formal specifications and multiversion programs. Offers explicit suggestions for the refinement process.

Gehani, N. H. 1983a. An Electronic Form System: An Experience in Prototyping. *Software—Practice & Experience*, v13, pp. 479–486.

Gehani, Narain 1983b. *Ada: An Advanced Introduction Including Reference Manual for the Ada Language*. Prentice-Hall. The author first gives a quick introduction to the conventional aspects of the Ada language—features found in existing programming languages such as Pascal, C, PL/I, ALGOL 60 or FORTRAN, and then focuses on Ada's novel aspects: data encapsulation, concurrency, exception handling, generic facilities, program structure and representation clauses. Interesting differences between the Ada language and other languages are pointed out. The book contains many realistic examples, including some large ones, all of which have been tested on an Ada compiler.

Gehani, N. H. and W. D. Roome 1986. Concurrent C. *Software —Practice & Experience*, v16, no.9, pp. 821–844. Concurrent C is a parallel superset of C that provides facilities for declaring and creating processes, process synchronization and interaction, process termination and abortion, priority specification and waiting for multiple events, among other things.

Gehani, N. H. and W. D. Roome 1988. Concurrent C++: Concurrent Programming With Class(es). To be published in *Software —Practice and Experience*.

Gries, D. 1976. An Illustration of Current Ideas on the Derivation of Correctness Proofs and Correct Programs. *IEEE Transactions on Software Engineering*, v2, no. 4, pp. 238–243. Explains how to develop correct programs. A nontrivial example (a line justifier) is developed hand in hand with its correctness proof.

Gries, D. 1979. **cand** and **cor** before **and then or else** in Ada. Technical Report TR79–402, Department of Computer Science, Cornell University, Ithaca, NY 14853. This paper contains an argument for using the semicolon as a statement separator rather than as a terminator. The following quote says it all: "From the standpoint of tradition, grammar, theory, elegance and style, the semicolon deserves its place as a separator. To use the PL/I blunder of the semicolon as a terminator is, in my mind, intolerable. The grounds for this are very weak: a badly done experiment and the fact that it is supposed to help the compiler recover after errors."

Halfant, M. 1983. The UNIX C Compiler in a CP/M Environment. *Byte*, v8, no. 8 (August), pp. 243–267. A look at how compatible the standard C compiler is when it is used under CP/M.

Hamming, R. W. 1973. *Numerical Methods for Scientists and Engineers* (second edition). McGraw Hill.

Hancock, L. and M. Krieger 1982. *The C Primer*. McGraw-Hill.

Harbison, S. P. and G. L. Steele, Jr. 1983. *The C Language Reference Manual*. Tartan Labs. A detailed reference manual for the C language prepared for the ANSI standardization committee. The authors emphasize good programming conventions and describe the differences between various implementations of C.

Hoare, C. A. R. 1962. Quicksort. *Computer Journal*, v5, no. 1, pp. 10–15.

Hoare, C. A. R. 1973. Hints on Programming Language Design *ACM SIGACT/SIGPLAN Symposium on Principles of Programming Languages* (October). Boston, Mass.

Hoare, C. A. R. and N. Wirth 1973. An Axiomatic Definition of the Programming Language Pascal, *Acta Informatica*, v2, pp. 335–355.

Hoare, C. A. R. 1978. Towards a Theory of Parallel Programming. In *Programming Methodology, a Collection of Articles by Members of WG2.3* edited by D. Gries, Springer-Verlag. Proposes parallel programming constructs with objectives such as security from error, efficiency, simplicity and breadth of application. Introduces the idea of critical regions.

Horowitz, E. 1983. *Fundamentals of Programming Languages*. Computer Science Press.

Horning, J. J. 1979. Effects of Programming Languages on Reliability. In *Computing Systems Reliability* edited by T. Anderson and B. Randell, Cambridge University Press. The first part of the paper is a comprehensive survey of programming language features (e.g., types and the treatment of types) that aid in developing correct programs. Acknowledging the fact that faults and exceptional situations are inevitable in real programs, the author discusses language features (e.g., exception handling) for writing fault tolerant programs in the second part. The final part of the paper is a discussion of language features that encourage program correctness proofs.

Houston, J., J. Broderick and L. Kent 1983. Comparing C Compilers for CP/M-86. *Byte*, v8, no. 8 (August), pp. 82–106.

Pascal 1980. Second Draft Proposal of the ISO Pascal Standard (January 1981). *Pascal News*, no. 20.

Jensen, K. and N. Wirth 1974. *The Pascal User Manual and Report*. Springer-Verlag.

Johnson, S. C. and B. W. Kernighan 1973. The Programming Language B. Unpublished notes.

Johnson, S. C. 1978a. A Portable Compiler: Theory and Practice. *Fifth Annual ACM Symposium on Principles of Programming Languages* (January), Tucson, Arizona. Overview of the construction of a C compiler with goals such as easy compiler portability, production of reasonable quality object code and use of the latest results in code generation.

Johnson, S. C. and B. W. Kernighan 1983. The C Language and Models for Systems Programming. *Byte*, v8, no. 8 (August), pp. 48–60. A happy medium between low- and high-level languages. C provides a model for efficient programming.

Joyce, J. 1983a. A C Language Primer, Part 1: Constructs and Conventions. *Byte*, v8, no. 8 (August), pp. 64–78.

Joyce, J. 1983b. A C Language Primer, Part 2: Tool Building in C. *Byte*, v8, no. 9 (September), pp. 289–302.

Katzenelson, J. 1983a. Introduction to Enhanced C. *Software—Practice and Experience*, v13, no. 7 (July), pp. 551–576. A set-oriented extensible C-like language.

Katzenelson, J. 1983b. Higher Level Programming and Data Abstractions—A Case Study Using Enhanced C. *Software—Practice and Experience*, v13, no. 7 (July), pp. 577–595.

Kern, C. O. 1983. Five C Compilers for CP/M-80. *Byte*, v8, no. 8 (August), pp. 110–130. Evaluation of C compilers for the CP/M-80 operating system.

Kernighan, B. W. and P. J. Plauger 1974. *The Elements of Programming Style*. McGraw-Hill. Contains many simple and elegant suggestions on how to write good programs. Lots of examples.

Kernighan, B. W. and P. J. Plauger 1976. *Software Tools*. Addison-Wesley. Explains how to write programs that make good tools for constructing other programs. Contains real and nontrivial examples.

Kernighan, B. W. and P. J. Plauger 1981. *Software Tools in Pascal*. Addison-Wesley.

Kernighan, B. W. and D. M. Ritchie 1978. *The C Programming Language*. Prentice-Hall. Excellent introduction and the standard reference to C; contains *The C Reference Manual*.

Kernighan, B. W. and D. M. Ritchie 1988. *The C Programming Language* (Second Edition). Prentice-Hall. ANSI C version of [Kernighan & Ritchie 1978].

Kernighan, B. W. and M. D. McIlroy (Editors) 1979. *UNIX Programmer's Manual, Seventh Edition*. AT&T Bell Laboratories, Murray Hill, NJ 07974.

Kernighan, B. W. and R. Pike 1984. *The UNIX Programming Environment*. Prentice-Hall.

Lalonde, W. R. and J. R. Pugh 1983. A Simple Technique for Converting from a Pascal Shop to a C Shop. *Software—Practice and Experience*, v13, pp. 771–775. The C preprocessor #define statement is used to allow a programmer to write C programs that resemble Pascal programs. However, the programmer is still required to know a certain amount of C in order to use this

Pascal facility.

Lear, E. 1964. *The Nonsense Books of Edward Lear.* The New American Library.

Lee, P. A. 1983. Exception Handling in C Programs. *Software—Practice and Experience*, v13, no. 5 (May), pp. 389–405. Only limited exception handling facilities are provided in C. General exception handling facilities, based on the exception handling facilities in Ada, are provided in C by a software package that requires no modifications to the C compiler or the C preprocessor. The author describes this package and discusses practical experience in using it.

Linhart, J. 1983. Managing Software Development with C. *Byte*, v8, no. 8 (August), pp. 172–182. Choosing a good programming environment can affect programming ease and code quality more than one might imagine.

Liskov, B. and S. N. Zilles 1974. Programming with Abstract Data Types. *SIGPLAN Notices*, v9, no. 4 (April).

Liskov, B. 1976. Discussion in the *Design and Implementation of Programming Languages* edited by John H. Williams and D. A. Fisher, p. 25, Springer-Verlag.

Mateti, P. 1979. Pascal versus C: A Subjective Comparison. *Proceedings of the Symposium on Language Design and Programming Methodology* (September). Author expresses unhappiness over the presence of many potentially dangerous features in C that require programmers to use it with caution.

McGettrick, A. D. and P. D. Smith 1983. *Graded Problems in Computer Science.* Addison-Wesley.

McIlroy, M. D. 1960. Macro Instruction Extension of Compiler Languages. *CACM*, v3, no. 4, pp. 414–420. Classic paper in which the author discusses and advocates the use of macros in a high-level language as a language extension mechanism.

Morris, J. H., Jr. 1973. Types are not Sets. *Proceedings of the ACM Symposium on Principles of Programming Languages*, Boston, MA. Introduces the notion that a types is a set of values plus a set of operations on these values.

Naur, P. 1963. Revised Report on the Algorithmic Language ALGOL 60. *CACM*, v6, no. 1 (January), pp. 1–17.

Phraner, R. A. 1983. Nine C Compilers for the IBM PC. *Byte*, v8, no. 8 (August), pp. 134–168. A discriminating look at the C compilers available for this lucrative market.

Plum, T. 1983. *Learning to Program in C.* Plum Hall, Cardiff, N.J.

Pratt, T. W. 1975. *Programming Languages: Design and Implementation.* Prentice-Hall.

Pratt, V. 1983. Five Paradigm Shifts in Programming Language Design and Their Realization in Viron, a Dataflow Programming Environment. *Conference Record of the Tenth Annual ACM Symposium on Principles of Programming Languages* (January), Austin, TX.

Purdum, J. C. 1983. *C Programming Guide.* Que Corporation, Indianapolis, IN.

Relph, R. 1987. Preparing for ANSI C. *Dr. Dobbs Journal* (August), pp. 16–23.

Richards, M. 1969. BCPL: A Tool for Compiler Writing and Systems Programming. *Proc. AFIPS SICC*, v34, pp. 557–566.

Ritchie, D. M., S. C. Johnson, M. E. Lesk and B. W. Kernighan 1978. The C Programming Language. *Bell System Technical Journal*, Part 2, v57, no. 6 (July-August), pp. 1991–2019.

Ritchie, D. M. 1980. The C Programming Language—Reference Manual. AT&T Bell Laboratories, Murray Hill, NJ 07974. Revised version of the Reference Manual for the C Programming Language (as of September 1980).

Schwartz, J. T. 1975. On Programming—Interim Report of the SETL Project. Courant Institute of Mathematical Sciences, NY.

Sethi, R. 1980. A Case Study in Specifying the Semantics of a Programming Language. *Proceedings of the Seventh Annual ACM Symposium on Principles of Programming Languages* (January), Las Vegas, NV. Specification of the semantics of C.

Sethi, R. 1981. Uniform Syntax for Type Expressions and Declarators. *Software—Practice and Experience*, v11, no. 6 (June), pp. 623–628. Author explains that type declarations in C are hard to read primarily because the dereferencing operator is a prefix operator and not a postfix operator. The author concludes by saying that "in declarations, a little bit of syntactic sugar makes a big difference".

Stroustrup, B. 1986. *The C++ Programming Language.* Addison Wesley.

Stroustrup, B. 1982. A Set of C Classes for Coroutine-Style Programming. Computing Science Technical Report No. 90, AT&T Bell Laboratories, Murray Hill, NJ 07974. C++ is a superset of C that augments limited data structuring facilities of C by adding classes, a data abstraction facility.

Van Wyk, C. J., J. L. Bentley and P. J. Weinberger 1982. Efficiency Considerations for C Programs on a VAX 11/780. Technical Report CMU-CS-82-134, Dept. of Computer Science, Carnegie-Mellon University, Pittsburgh, PA 15213. Manual optimization of programs is a many step process. Here are some findings that may be used to optimize programs:

- It is always more expensive to operate on `char` or `short int` variables than on `int` variables. Use `char` or `short int` only where required semantically or where space is limited.
- It is always more expensive to operate on `float` than on `double` variables because of C's conversion rules. Use `float` only where required semantically or where space is limited.
- It is better to use increment operators (e.g., `+=`) than the assignment operator.
- Using arrays and array subscripts in loops can be more efficient than using pointers because it is possible to generate good code for arrays.

Ward, T. A. 1984. A Guide to Resources for the C Programmer. *Dr. Dobb's Journal* (November). Extensive list of C resources: books, periodicals with a focus on the UNIX system and C, C compilers, companies with C products and C articles (237 in number).

Welsh, J., M. J. Sneeringer and C. A. R. Hoare 1977. Ambiguities and Insecurities in Pascal. *Software—Practice and Experience*, v7, no. 6 (November), pp. 685–696.

Wirth, N. and C. A. R. Hoare 1966. A Contribution to the Development of ALGOL. *CACM*, v9, no. 6 (June), pp. 413–433.

Wirth, N. 1971a. The Design of a Pascal Compiler. *Software—Practice and Experience*, v1, pp. 309–333.

Wirth, N. 1971b. The Programming Language Pascal. *Acta Informatica*, v1, pp. 35–63.

Wirth, N. 1971c. Program Development by Stepwise Refinement. *CACM*, v14, no. 4, pp. 221–226. Classic paper on stepwise refinement.

Wirth, N. 1973. *Systematic Programming: An Introduction.* Prentice-Hall.

Wirth, N. 1975. An Assessment of the Programming Language Pascal. *Proceedings—1975 International Conference on Reliable Software* (April), Los Angeles, CA.

Wulf, W. and M. Shaw 1973. Global Variable Considered Harmful. *SIGPLAN Notices*, v8, n2, pp. 28–34.

Zahn, C. T. 1979. *C Notes: A Guide to the C Programming Language.* Yourdon Press, NY. Interesting comments that focus on many of C's implementation dependencies and semantic peculiarities.

Index

!, logical negation operator   65
!=, inequality operator   70
##, example of preprocessor pasting operator   169
    the preprocessor pasting operator   160
#, parameter-to-string conversion operator   159
#define instruction, example use of preprocessor   3
    preprocessor   157
#elif instruction   166
#error instruction   167
#if instruction, preprocessor   164
#include instruction, example   3
    preprocessor   163
#pragma instruction   167
%, remainder operator   66
&&, logical *and* operator   71
&, *address-of* operator   38, 65, 96
    bitwise *and* operator   71
( ), function call operator   64
*, dereferencing operator   65
    multiplication operator   66
    precedence of the dereferencing operator   49
++, postfix increment operator   64
    prefix increment operator   65
+, addition operator   67
^, bitwise *exclusive or* operator   71
~, bitwise complement operator   65
\, escape character   6, 11, 12
,, comma operator   74
-, negation operator   65
    subtraction operator   67
--, postfix decrement operator   64
    prefix decrement operator   65
->, right-arrow (selection) operator   40, 64
., selection operator   64
..., ellipsis notation   89
.c, C source file suffix   133
.o object file suffix   134
/, division operator   66
\0 string termination convention, null character   13
    null character constant   11
\n, new-line character constant   11
<, less than operator   69
<<, left-shift operator   68
<=, less than or equal to operator   69
=, simple assignment operator   73
==, equality operator   70
>, greater than operator   69
>=, greater than or equal to operator   69
>>, right-shift operator   68

?:, conditional operator   72
||, logical *or* operator   72
[ ], subscript operator   64
|, bitwise *inclusive or* operator   71

a

a.c, file   45
a.out executable file   7
abort function   227
abs function   229
absolute function   208
abstract data types and files   134
abstract data types, advantages of   134
abstract declarator   58
abstract statements   22
accept statement   191
acos function   205
active component of a union   31
actual parameters   94
add.c, file   141
addition operator +   67
additive operators   67
address-of operator &   38, 65, 96
aggregate types   18
alert character \f   11
aliases   37, 38
aliases, harmful effects of   38
allocator, storage   36
ANSI C   xi
ANSI C and K&R C, differences between   237
argc, count of command-line arguments   106
argument promotions, default   94
arguments   94
arguments by reference, passing   95, 181
arguments by value, passing   95
arguments passing in C   95
arguments, arrays as   94
    automatic conversion of   94
    command-line   105
    functions as   94
    passing array   95
    routines to handle variable number of   210
argv, array of command-line arguments   106
arithmetic conversions, usual   57
arithmetic types   18

255

arithmetic, pointer   67
array   24
array arguments, passing   95
array elements, numbering of   24
    referencing   25
array name to a pointer to function,   39
array names to pointers, conversion of   64
array parameter   92
array storage, row-major order   53
array type, incomplete   25
array, determining number of elements in an   66
array, sub-   25, 39
arrays and pointers, relationship between   39
arrays as arguments   94
arrays as parameters   92
arrays, and strings and pointers   39
    extern   45
    initial values for   52
    storage of   39
arrow (selection) operator `->`, right-   40
arrow operator `->`   64
`asctime` function   236
`asin` function   205
`assert`, macro   202
assignment operators   73
assignment operators, compound   78
    illustrative use of compound   128
assignment statement   78
    compound   73
assignment, multiple   78
associativity and precedence, operator   63
associativity summary, operator   75
associativity, operator   63
`atan` function   205
`atan2` function   205
`atexit` function   228
`atof` function   225
`atoi` function   225
`atol` function   225
`auto` storage class   44
automobile cruise controller example   122

b

`b.c`, file   45
backslash character `\`   11
backspace character `\b`   11
basic types   18
bibliography   245
bit-field   28
bit-field address   28
bit-field allocation order   29
bit-field structure   28
bit-field type   28
bit-field, accessing a   30
bit-fields   28
bit-fields, restrictions on   28

unnamed   29
bitwise *and* operator `&`   71
bitwise complement operator `~`   65
bitwise *exclusive or* operator `^`   71
bitwise *inclusive or* operator `|`   71
block   78
BNF notation   178
body of main program   3
Boolean type, lack of a   24
Boolean values   24
`break` statement   84
`break` statement, example use of   5
`bsearch` function   228
buffer example   186
`buffer.c`, file   187
`buffer.h`, file   186
buffered streams   101
by clause   191

c

C compiler, invoking the   7
C preprocessor, constant definitions using the   14
C programs, convention for files containing   133
C++   179
C, ANSI   xi
    K&R   xi
`calc.c`, file   2
`calcE1.c`, file   151
`calcE2.c`, file   153
calculator with exception handling (ver. 1) example   150
calculator with exception handling (ver. 2) example   152
calculator with exception handling (ver. 3) example   154
calculator example   1
`calloc` function   36, 227
carriage-return character `\r`   11
`case` labels of the `switch` statement   81
cast operator   66
casting   58
casting a `void` pointer   60
casts, allowed   58
`cc`, invoking the C compiler   7, 134
`ceil` function   208
`char` type   19, 48
character arrays and strings   13
character constant   10
character handling routines   203
character input/output functions   220
character set, basic execution   8
    basic source   8
    execution   8
    source   8
character types   19
character value, functions returning   20
characters and integers   10
characters and integers, the duality between   19
characters and string constants, nongraphic   13

characters using hexadecimal digits, specifying   11
characters using octal digits, specifying   11
characters, nongraphic   11
class declarations   179
class specifications   179
`class.h`, file   179
classes to declare objects, use of   183, 185
classes, C++   179
`clean.c`, file   109
`clearerr` function   224
`clock` function   235
comma operator ,   74
comma operator, example use of the   4
command-line arguments   105
comments   13
comparison functions   231
compilation, independent   133
compiler `cc`, invoking the C   134
compiler, invoking the C   7
compiling a file   134
complex numbers example   182
`complex.c`, file   183
`complex.h`, file   182
component of a union, active   31
component, accessing a structure   28
components packed into storage units, structure   28
compound assignment   73
compound assignment operators, use of   128
compound statement   78
concatenation functions   231
concurrency in programming languages   189
Concurrent C   189
Concurrent C on multiprocessors   197
concurrent programming facilities, the need for   189
concurrent programming, desirability of   189
conditional compilation using the preprocessor   164
conditional operator ? :   72
`const` type qualifier   46
constant definitions using the C preprocessor   14
constant expressions   75
constant expressions, restrictions on preprocessor   76
    use of   76
constant identifiers   14
constant identifiers, defining   14
constant, character   10
    enumeration   11
    floating-point   12
    integer   10
    long integer   10
    string   12
    unsigned integer   10
constants   10
constants, defining   161
constructors, class   180
`continue` statement   85
`continue` statement, example use of   6
control-D, character   7
conversion of arguments, automatic   94
conversion, explicit type   58
    implicit type   57

type   57
conversions, usual arithmetic   57
copying functions   230
`cos` function   206
`cosh` function   206
`cruise.c`, file   123
`ctime` function   236

d

dangling reference problem   38
"dangling else" problem & `if` statement   79
data abstraction and files   134
data abstraction facilities, C++   179
data abstraction, limitations of files for impl.   137
data encapsulation and files   133
data type, default   48
data, termination of   7
date routines   234
`db.h`, file   174
deallocation, storage   38
deallocator `free`, storage   38
declaration syntax, comments on the   53
declaration-definition, hybrid   50
declarations & definitions, syntactic diff. between   51
declarations versus definitions, object   18
declarations, equivalences between Pascal-like & C   54
    use of   18
    use of `typedef` to simplify   55
declarator with an initial value   49
declarator, abstract   58
declarators   48
declarators allowed, restrictions on the   49
declarators, examples   50
    list of   48
`default` alternative, `switch` statement   82
defined object   35
defined object, address of a   38
    pointing to a   38
`defined` operator   165
definition syntax, comments on the   53
definition, firm `extern`   45
    tentative `extern`   45
definition-declaration, hybrid   50
definitions & declarations, syntactic difference between   51
definitions versus declarations, object   18
definitions, equivalences between Pascal-like and C   54
    function   91
    identifier   43
    type   41
    use of `typedef` to simplify   55
`delay` statement   191
delays   191
`delete.c`, file   142
dereferencing operator *   65
dereferencing operator *, precedence of the   49
derived type   24

derived types 18
destructors, class 180
diagnostic routines 202
`difftime` function 235
dining philosophers example, *mortal* 194
`dining.cc`, file 197
`div` function 229
division operator / 66
do loop and Pascal *repeat* loop, C 82
do loop statement 82
double quote character " 12
`double` type 24, 48
dynamic object 35
dynamic object, lifetime of a 38
    referencing a 36

e

`echo`, command 106
`echo.c`, file 106
ellipsis notation . . . 89
`empty.c`, file 140
end of a string 13
end-of-file 7
enhancing displays on HP2621 terminals example 113
entity 17
`enum` type specifier 48
enumeration constant 11
enumeration tag 23
enumeration type 21
enumerators 22
environment functions, communication with the 227
`EOF`, definition of 4
equality operator == 70
equality/inequality operators 70
error file pointer `stderr`, standard 101
error-handling functions 224
escape character \ 6, 11, 12
example, *automobile cruise controller* 122
    buffer 186
    calculator with exception handling (ver. 1) 150
    calculator with exception handling (ver. 2) 152
    calculator with exception handling (ver. 3) 154
    calculator 1
    complex numbers 182
    enhancing displays on HP2621 terminals 113
    generic swap 168
    integration via the trapezoidal rule 124
    least-square's method of curve fitting 116
    list manipulation functions 139
    lock manager 197
    mortal dining philosophers 194
    pointer arithmetic 129
    producer-consumer 191
    producing form display from a table 110
    quicksort 119
    roots of a quadratic equation 148

searching an array 128
simple query database 171
sine function 116
stack 183
stack 135
stripping formatting characters 107
symbol table manipulation 137
exception handler, resuming program execution after 148
exception handlers, fun. `signal` for spec. 146
exception indication method, status code 145
exception, definition of 145
executable file 7
executable file, `a.out` 7
execution character set 8
`exit` function 148, 228
`exit` function, example use of the 6
`EXIT_FAILURE`, use of constant 6
`EXIT_SUCCESS`, use of constant 6
`exp` function 206
exponentiation functions 206
expression eval. with paren., changing order of 63
expression evaluation, order of 63
expression statements 77
expressions 75
expressions and statements 77
expressions to statements, conversion of 77
expressions, constant 75
    order of evaluation 75
    use of constant 76
`ext.c`, file 176
`extern` arrays 45
`extern` definition, firm 45
    tentative 45
`extern` identifier definition 45
`extern` identifiers for communication, use of 45
`extern` storage class 44
`extern` var. for function communication, use of 44
`extern`, storage class 133
external identifiers 9, 44
external ids. using `static`, restricting scope of 44
external, variables 44

f

`fabs` function 208
`FALSE`, constant 24
`fatal.c`, file 110, 177
`fclose`, file closing function 103, 212
`feof` function 224
`ferror` function 224
`fflush`, function 212
`fgetc` function 220
`fgetpos` function 223
`fgets` function 220
field address, bit- 28
field allocation order. bit- 29
field structure, bit- 28

field type, bit- 28
field width 29
field, accessing a bit- 30
field, bit- 28
fields, restrictions on bit- 28
fields, unnamed bit- 29
file 100
file access function 212
file inclusion using the preprocessor 163
file name, source 2
file closing function `fclose` 103
file opening function `fopen` 103
file operation routines 211
file position indicator 100, 102
file positioning functions 223
file, compiling a 134
    definition of 133
    end-of- 7
    object 134
`FILE`, predefined type 100
files 133
files and abstract data types 134
files and data abstraction 134
files and information hiding 133
files and program partitioning 133
files containing C programs, convention for 133
files for impl. data abstraction, limitations of 137
files to control visibility, use of 133
files, header 3
    independent compilation of 133
    source 3
`float` type 24, 48
`float.h`, header file 24
floating-point constant 12
floating-point limits 24
floating-point type 24
`floor` function 208
`fmod` function 208
`fopen`, file opening function 103
`fopen`, function 212
`for` loop statement 82
`for` loop, leaving out expressions in the 83
`for` loops in C, Pascal and Ada 83
`fork.cc`, file 196
`fork.h`, file 194
form-feed character \f 11
formal parameters 94
formatted input/output functions 214
formatted read 4
`fprintf` for writing to streams, function 103
`fprintf`, function 214
`fputc` function 220
`fputs` function 221
`fread` function 222
`free` function 227
free store 38
`free`, storage deallocator 38
`freopen`, function 213
`frexp` function 207
friend functions 180

`fscanf` for reading from streams, function 103
`fscanf`, function 216
`fseek` function 223
`fsetpos` function 223
`fswap.c`, file 169
`ftell` function 224
function call operator ( ) 64
function calls 94
function calls, value-returning 94
function definitions 91
function definitions, difference between two forms of 92
function name to a pointer to function, 58
function names to pointers, conversion of 64
function nesting 98
function prototype 89
function result type, restrictions on the 91
function specification 90
function type 41
function, generic 167
functions 89
functions and the storage class `static` 89, 91, 98
functions as arguments 94
functions as arguments, example of passing 124
functions as parameters 92, 96
functions before they are defined, referencing 93
functions declared within blocks, storage class of 45
functions returning character values 20
functions using the C preprocessor, defining generic 167
functions, controlling the visibility of 89, 91, 98
functions, friend 180
    member 180
    recursive 89
    virtual 182
`fwrite` function 222

g

garbage collector 38
`gen-swap.c`, file 168
`gen-swap2.c`, file 169
generic facilities, advantages of 167
generic function 167
generic functions using the C preprocessor, defining 167
generic swap example 168
`getc`, routine 221
`getchar` function 221
`getenv` function 228
`gets` function 221
`get_desig.c`, file 177
`gmtime` function 236
`goto` statement 84
`goto` statement, unrestricted use of 84
greater than operator > 69
greater than or equal to operator >= 69

h

header files   3
hexadecimal digits, specifying characters using   11
horizontal-tab character \t   11
hp2621.c, file   115
hyperbolic functions   206

i

identifier definition and declaration   43
identifier length   9
identifier, lifetime of an   43
    scope of an   43
    storage duration of an   43
identifiers   9
identifiers, external   9, 44
    reserved   9, 10
if statement   79
if statement & "dangling else" prob.   79
in.c, file   140
incomplete types   18
independent compilation   133
indirection operator *, precedence of   49
inequality operator != 70
information hiding   134
information hiding and files   133
inheritance   181
inheritance in C++   179
init.c, file   175
initial values of objects   51
initialization, default   52
initializers   51
input file pointer stdin, standard   101
input from stdin, reading   101
input functions and macros   101
input functions, direct   222
input routines   211
input, redirection of   103
int   20
integ.c, file   127
integer arithmetic functions   229
integer constant   10
integer constant, long   10
    unsigned   10
integer div. & remainder operation equivalence   66
integer functions, nearest   208
integer limits   21
integer types   20
integers and characters   10
integers and characters, the duality between   19
integral promotions   57
integral types   18
integration via trapezoidal rule example   124
interrupt handling   191
isalnum function   203

iscntrl function   203
isdigit function   203
isgraph function   203
islower function   203
isprint function   204
ispunct function   204
isspace function   204
isupper function   204
iswap.c, file   168
isxdigit function   204

j

jump routines, nonlocal   208
jump statements   84

k

K&R C   xi
K&R C and ANSI C, differences between   237
keywords   9

l

labels, statement   83
labs function   229
ldexp function   207
ldiv function   230
least-square's method of curve fitting example   116
left-shift operator << 68
less than operator < 69
less than or equal to operator <= 69
library routines   201
library routines, C   201
lifetime of an identifier   43
limits, floating-point   24
    integer   21
limits.h, header file   21
line numbers, source file   2
linking object files   134
list manipulation functions example   139
list.h, file   140
literal, string   12
localtime function   236
lock manager example   197
lock.cc, file   198
lock.h, file   198
log function   207
log10 function   207
logarithmic functions   206
logical and operator && 71

logical negation operator ! 65
logical *or* operator !! 72
logical values 24
long 20, 48
long double type 24, 48
long int type 20, 48
long integer constant 10
longjmp, function 148, 208
loops 82
lsq.c, file 118
lsq_fit.c, file 119

m

macro bodies after replacement, rescanning 160
macro bodies, string constants in 160
macro definitions 157
macro definitions, parameterized 158
   removing 162
   simple 158
macro invocation 158, 159
macro, redefining a preprocessor 162
main program 3, 105
main program body 3
main, result type of function 3
malloc function 36, 227
mask.c, file 113
mathematical routines 205
max.c, file 92
member functions 180
memchr function 232
memcmp function 231
memcpy function 230
memmove function 230
memory locations, referencing specific 38
memory-management functions 227
memset function 234
message passing 190
miscellaneous functions 234
mktime function 235
modf function 207
mortal dining philosophers example 194
multiplication operator * 66
multiplicative, operators 66
multiprocessors, Concurrent C on 197

n

name, object 43
negation operator - 65
new-line character \n 11
next.c, file 129
nongraphic characters 11
nongraphic characters and string constants 13

null character constant \0 11
null character \0 string termination convention 13
NULL constant identifier 36
null pointer value 36
null statement 77

o

object 17
object allocation 36
object definition examples 50
object file 134
object file suffix .o 134
object files, linking 134
object name 43
object, defined 35
   dynamic 35
   lifetime of a dynamic 38
   referencing a dynamic 36
objects, initial values of 51
octal digits, specifying characters using 11
operator &, *address-of* 38, 96
operator *, precedence of the dereferencing 49
operator ->, right-arrow (selection) 40
operator associativity 63
operator associativity summary 75
operator precedence 63
operator precedence and associativity 63
operator precedence summary 75
operator, cast 66
   sizeof 36
operators, additive 67
   assignment 73
   bitwise shift 68
   equality/inequality 70
   multiplicative 66
   prefix 65
   relational 69
   shift 68
   unary 65
opt subscript 29
output file pointer stdout. standard 101
output functions and macros 101
output functions, direct 222
output routines 211
output to a string, writing 102
output to stderr, writing 101
output to stdout, writing 101
output, redirection of 103
overloading 181
overloading in C++ 179

p

parameter declarations and storage classes   92
parameters   92, 94
parameters, actual   94
 arrays as   92
 formal   94
 function decl. with variable number of   89
 function defn. with variable number of   91
 functions as   92, 96
 scope of   100
 variable number   97
parentheses in preprocessor definitions, using   161
parentheses, changing order of expression eval. with   63
`partition.c`, file   121
pasting macro tokens (items)   160
pasting operator `##`, example of preprocessor   169
`pc.cc`, file   192
`perror` function   224
`phil.cc`, file   195
`phil.h`, file   194
pointer   35
pointer arithmetic   67
pointer arithmetic example   129
pointer type   35
pointer value, null   36
pointer, casting a `void`   60
 `void`   35
pointers and arrays, relationship between   39
pointers and structures   40
pointers and type qualifiers   46
pointers, arrays and strings   39
position indicator, file   102
postfix decrement operator `--`   64
postfix increment operator `++`   64
`pow` function   207
power functions   207
precedence and associativity, operator   63
precedence summary, operator   75
precedence, operator   63
prefix decrement operator `--`   65
prefix increment operator `++`   65
prefix operators   65
preprocessor constant expressions, restrictions on   76
preprocessor instruction format   157
preprocessor macro, redefining a   162
preprocessor to generate in-line code, use of   162
preprocessor `#define` instruction   157
preprocessor `#if` instruction   164
preprocessor `#include` instruction   163
preprocessor, conditional compilation using the   164
 defining generic functions using the C   167
 definition of a   157
 facilities provided by the C   157
 file inclusion using the   163
 invocation of the C   157
 invoking just the C   157
`printf`, example use of function   6
 function   219

priority specification   191
procedures   89
process abortion   191
process creation   190
process definition   190
process termination, collective   191
processes   189
processor specification   191
producer-consumer example   191
producing form display from a table example   110
program (status) exit value   6
program termination using the `exit` function   6
program, main   105
prototype, function   89
prototypes, function   36
pseudo-random sequence generation functions   226
`putc` function   221
`putchar` function   222
`puts` function   222

q

`qsort` function   229
qualifiers, type   46
quicksort example   119
`quicksort.c`, file   122
quote character `"`, double   12
quote character `\"`, double   11
quote character `\'`, single   11

r

`raise` function   210
`rand` function   226
read, formatted   4
read-only variable   17, 46
reading from a string, reading   102
`realloc` function   227
recursive function, `quicksort`   119
recursive functions   89
redirection of input and output   103
referencing specific memory locations   38
register declaration and program efficiency   44
`register` storage class   44
relational operators   69
remainder function   208
remainder operator `%`   66
`remove` function   211
`rename` function   211
`replace.c`, file   110
rescanning macro bodies after replacement   160
reserved identifiers   9, 10
`return` statement   86
`rewind` function   224

right-arrow (selection) operator `->` 40
right-shift operator `>>` 68
roots of a quadratic equation example 148
`roots.c`, file 149
routine 201
routine, semantic description of a 202
   syntactic specification of a 202
routines, library C 201
row major order 39

S

scalar types 18
`scanf`, function 219
scope of an identifier 43
scope of external ids. using `static`, restricting 44
`scope.c`, file 99
search functions, (string and memory) 232
searching function 228
searching an array example 128
`select` statement 191
selection operator `->` 64
selection operator `.` 64
semantic description of a routine 202
semicolon 77
semicolon, statement terminator character 13
`setbuf`, function 214
`setjmp`, macro 208
`setvbuf`, function 214
shift operators 68
shift operators, bitwise 68
`short` 20, 48
`short int` 20, 48
side effects 14
`signal` for setting up signal handlers, function 146
`signal` function 209
signal handlers, function `signal` for setting up 146
signal handling routines 209
signals 145
signals, different kinds of 146
   explicit generation of 148
   generating/sending 148
   implicit generation of 148
`signed` 20
`signed char` 19, 20, 48
`signed int` 20
`signed long int` 20, 48
`signed long` 20, 48
`signed short int` 20, 48
`signed short` 20, 48
simple assignment operator `=` 73
simple query database example 171
simple types 18
`sin` function 206
sine function example 116
`sine.c`, file 116
`sinh` function 206

`sizeof` operator 36, 65
sort, quick- 119
sorting function 228
source character set 8
source file line numbers 2
source file name 2
source files 3
space, white 8
specification of a routine, syntactic 202
specification, function 90
`sprintf`, function 219
`sqrt` function 207
`srand` function 226
`sscanf`, function 219
stack example 183
stack example 135
`stack.c`, file 136
standard streams 100
statement labels 83
statement terminator 13
statement, assignment 78
   `break` 84
   `continue` 85
   `do` loop 82
   `for` loop 82
   `goto` 84
   `if` 79
   `return` 86
   `switch` 80
   `while` loop 82
   compound 78
   null 77
statements and expressions 77
   abstract 22
   conversion of expressions to 77
   expression 77
`static` storage class 44
`static`, functions and storage class 89, 91, 98
   restricting scope of external identifiers using 44
   storage class 133
status code exception indication method 145
status codes 145
`stderr`, output to stream 104
   redirection of output to stream 104
   standard error file pointer 101
`stdin`, standard input file pointer 101
`stdio.h`, example use of 3
`stdout`, standard output file pointer 101
`stk.c`, file 185
`stk.h`, file 184
storage allocators 36
storage allocators, values returned by the 36
storage class 43
storage class example, `extern` and file `static` 45
storage class `extern` 133
storage class `static` 133
storage class, default 45
   `auto` 44
   `extern` 44
   `register` 44

`static` 44
storage classes and parameter declarations 92
storage deallocation 38
storage deallocator `free` 38
storage duration of an identifier 43
storage of arrays 39
storage-class specifiers 43
`strcat` function 231
`strchr` function 233
`strcmp` function 231
`strcoll` function 232
`strcpy` function 230
`strcspn` function 233
stream 100
stream pointer 100, 101
stream, binary 100
    text 100
streams, function `fprintf` for writing to 103
    function `fscanf` for writing to 103
    standard 100
    using streams other than the standard 103
string constant 12
string constant modification 12
string constants across line boundaries, continuing 12
string constants and nongraphic characters 13
string constants in macro bodies 160
string conversion functions 225
string copying functions 230
string handling routines 230
string literal 12
string termination convention, null char. \0 13
string type 39
string variables as character pointers, treatment of 39
strings 12, 39
strings and character arrays 13
strings as character pointers, adv. of treating 40
strings, dual treatment of 39
    pointers and arrays 39
stripping formatting characters example 107
`strlen` function 234
`strncat` function 231
`strncmp` function 232
`strncpy` function 230
`stroul` function 226
`strpbrk` function 233
`strrchr` function 233
`strspn` function 233
`strstr` function 234
`strtod` function 225
`strtok` function 234
`strtol` function 226
`struct` type specifier 48
structure component, accessing a 28
structure components packed into storage units 28
structure tag 27
structure tag & `typedef` used together 128
structure tag, necessity of 27
structure type 25
structure type, incomplete 30
    variant 33

structure, bit-field 28
    recursive 27
    variant 32
structures and pointers 40
structures, general format of variant 34
`strxfrm` function 232
subarray 25, 39
subroutines 89
subscript operator [ ] 64
subscript, *opt* 29
subtraction operator – 67
`suchthat` clause 191
suffix `.c`, C source file 133
`swap.c`, file 96
`switch` statement 80
`switch` statement `default` alt. 82
`switch` statement, example use of 5
    use of `break` statement in 81
symbol table manipulation example 137
`symtab.c`, file 139
`symtab.h`, file 137
syntactic specification of a routine 202
`system` function 228

t

tag, active component 33
    enumeration 23
    structure 27
    union 32
tags, scope of 43
`tan` function 206
`tanh` function 206
termination of a program 6
termination, collective process 191
time conversion functions 236
`time` function 235
time manipulation routines 235
time routines 234
`tmpfile` function 211
`tmpnam` function 212
token 158
`tolower` function 204
`toupper` function 205
transaction 189
transaction, asynchronous 190
    synchronous 190
trigonometric functions 205
trigraph sequences 8
`TRUE`, constant 24
type compatibility 57
type compatibility, name 57
    structural 57
type conversion 57
type conversion, explicit 58
    implicit 57
type definitions 41

type equivalence 57
type equivalence, name 57
    structural 57
type name 41, 58
type names, scope of 43
type of bit-fields 28
type qualifiers 46
type qualifiers and pointers 46
type specifiers 47
type, default 48
    definition of a 17
    derived 24
    enumeration 21
    floating-point 24
    function 17
    function 41
    incomplete 17
    object 17
    pointer 35
    simple 18
    string 39
    structure 25
    union 31
`typedef` and structure tag used together 128
`typedef` definition 42
`typedef` for decl. types, limitations of 179
`typedef` to simplify defn./decl., use of 55
typedef-name type specifier 48
types 17
types, aggregate 18
    arithmetic 18
    basic 18
    character 19
    derived 18
    incomplete 18
    integer 20
    integral 18
    limitations of `typedef` for declaring 179
    scalar 18
    simple 18

u

unary operators 65
underscore, names beginning with 10
`ungetc` function 222
union components, accessing 32, 33
    assigning values to 33
union object, processing a 33
union tag 32
union type 31
union type, incomplete 32
`union` type specifier 48
union, active component of a 31
unions, uses of 32
`unsigned` 21, 48
`unsigned char` 21, 48

`unsigned char` type 19
unsigned integer constant 10
`unsigned int` 21, 48
`unsigned long int` 21, 48
`unsigned long` 21, 48
`unsigned short int` 21
`unsigned short` 21
`util.c`, file 176
utilities, searching and sorting 228
utility routines, general 224

V

`var.c`, file 98
variable 17, 43
variable definitions example 4
variable number of arguments, routines to handle 210
variable, read-only 17, 46
variables external 44
variant structure 32
variant structure, form of a 34
variant structures, general format of 34
`va_arg`, macro 210
`va_end`, macro 210
`va_start`, macro 210
vertical-tab character \v 11
`vfprintf`, function 219
virtual functions 182
visibility, use of files to control 133
`void` pointer 35
`void` pointer, casting a 60
`void` type 19, 48
`vol.c`, file 47
`volatile` type qualifier 46
`vprintf`, function 220
`vsprintf`, function 220

w

`while` loop statement 82
`while` statement, example use of 4
white space 8
`within` operator 191
words, reserved 10